Connecting
Leadership
with
Learning

A Framework for
Reflection, Planning, and Action

Michael A. Copland and Michael S. Knapp

Association for Supervision and Curriculum Development
Alexandria, Virginia USA

Association for Supervision and Curriculum Development
1703 N. Beauregard St. • Alexandria, VA 22311-1714 USA
Phone: 800-933-2723 or 703-578-9600 • Fax: 703-575-5400
Web site: www.ascd.org • E-mail: member@ascd.org
Author guidelines: www.ascd.org/write

Gene R. Carter, *Executive Director;* Nancy Modrak, *Director of Publishing;* Julie Houtz, *Director of Book Editing & Production;* Leah Lakins, *Project Manager;* Judi Connelly, *Senior Graphic Designer;* Keith Demmons, *Typesetter;* Sarah Plumb, *Production Specialist*

All Web links in this book are correct as of the publication date below but may have become inactive or otherwise modified since that time. If you notice a deactivated or changed link, please e-mail books@ascd.org with the words "Link Update" in the subject line. In your message, please specify the Web link, the book title, and the page number on which the link appears.

PAPERBACK ISBN-13: 978-1-4166-0404-4 ASCD product #105003   s10/06
PAPERBACK ISBN-10: 1-4166-0404-9

e-books editions: retail PDF ISBN-13: 978-1-4166-0526-3; retail ISBN-10: 1-4166-0526-6
netLibrary ISBN-13: 978-1-4166-0527-0; netLibrary ISBN-10: 1-4166-0527-4
ebrary ISBN-13: 978-1-4166-0525-6; ebrary ISBN-10: 1-4166-0525-8

Quantity discounts for this book: 10–49 copies, 10%; 50+ copies, 15%; for 500 or more
    copies, call 800-933-2723, ext. 5634, or 703-575-5634.

Library of Congress Cataloging-in-Publication Data
Copland, Michael A.
  Connecting leadership with learning : a framework for reflection, planning, and ac-
    tion / Michael A. Copland and Michael S. Knapp.
      p. cm.
  Includes bibliographical references and index.
  ISBN-13: 978-1-4166-0404-4 (pbk. : alk. paper)
  ISBN-10: 1-4166-0404-9 (pbk. : alk. paper) 1. School management and organization–
    –United States. 2. Educational leadership–United States. 3. Learning. I. Knapp,
    Michael S. (Michael Sturgis), 1946–II. Title.

  LB2805.C6592 2006
  371.200973–dc22   2005034560

For Ken Sirotnik

Who constantly reminded us
what powerful, equitable practice means
for leaders and learners

Connecting Leadership with Learning

A Framework for Reflection, Planning, and Action

Acknowledgments vii

Preface: A Call for Leadership That Is Focused on Learning ix

**Part One: Leading for Learning: Establishing the
Foundational Ideas**
1   Hector's Challenge to Educational Leaders 3
2   Essential Ideas and Tasks for Learning-Focused Leaders 9

**Part Two: Exploring the Leading for Learning Framework
in Practice**
3   Establishing a Focus on Learning.. 29
4   Building Professional Communities That Value Learning 43
5   Engaging External Environments That Matter for Learning 56
6   Acting Strategically and Sharing Leadership 71
7   Creating Coherence... 87

Part Three: The Leading for Learning Framework in Action
8   Leading Learning in Schools 104
9   Leading Learning in School Districts 145
10   Using the Framework in Practice and
in Leadership Development 171

Epilogue: Hector and Mr. G. Revisited... 195

Appendix: Pathways to Learning
Content, Assessment, and Accountability Pathways............................. 205
Professionals and Professional Development Pathways 214
Learner and Learner Support Pathways... 230
Workplace and System Pathways 242

Methodological Notes 259
References 264
Index... 271
About the Authors 279

Acknowledgments

We wish to thank various individuals who made important contributions to our thinking at one or more stages during the development of this book. First of all, our collaborators in creating the Leading for Learning reports, which form the basis for this book, deserve special recognition: Brynnen Ford, Anneke Markholt, Michael Milliken, Milbrey McLaughlin, and Joan Talbert. Their ideas and hard work in assembling a literature and illustrative base were invaluable in developing the initial version of the framework, and are still an essential foundation for the work we present here.

Numerous others offered their ideas and experiences and they were each instrumental in shaping the framework, often in ways they probably don't even realize: Christopher Alejano, Anthony Alvarado, Anthony Amato, Vic Anderson, Nancy Arnold, Sandy Austin, Laura Bang-Knudsen, Peter Bang-Knudsen, Kathy Bartlett, Machelle Bielke, Denise Bill, Bruce Bivens, Craig Blum, Dina Blum, Elizabeth Boatright, Gene Bottoms, Richelle Bouse, Bill Boyd, Monte Bridges, Carl Bruner, Judy Buckmaster, Kathy Budge, Joe Burke, Tony Busch, Pete Bylsma, Anthony Byrd, Karen Carter, Sara Chace, Betty Cobbs, Sue Cohn, Eva Collins, Jane Creasy, Kevin Davis, Jessica DeBarros, Corrine DeRosa, Dan Domenech, Gordon Donaldson, Tara Dowd, Julie Drennon, Tom Duenwald, Donald Eismann, Sue Feldman, Luke Fennell, Steve Fink, Bill Firestone, Linda Fisher, Jennifer Fong, Cathy Fromme, Michael Fullan, Ben Gauyan, Terri Geaudreau, Steven Gering, Margery Ginsberg, Deborah Gonzalez, Steve

Grubb, Lauren Gundlach, Ron Heck, Ed Hamada, Betty Hannaford, Craig Harpel, James Harvey, Laurie Harvey, Flip Herndon, Linda Holloman, Jason Huff, Lisa Hyde, Tom Hiegler, Paul Hill, Amy Hightower, Paul Houston, Kathryn Hutchinson, Gwendolyn Kestrel, Kathy Kimball, Kyle Kinoshita, Monica Kinsey, David Jackson, Savanna Jamerson, Mark Johnson, Karen Jones, Karen Kearney, Paula Koehler, Diana Lam, Diane Lashinsky, Kenneth Leithwood, Richard Lentz, Ann Lieberman, Yih-Sheueh Lin, James Lytle, Julie Mack, Bernie Mahar, Matthew Manobianco, Julie Marsh, Claudia Mason, Tracy Maury, Gail McDonald, Doris McEwen, Gail Miller, Matt Miller, Terrance Mims, John Morefield, Christine Muldoon, Linda Murray, Brenda Naish, Peter Negroni, Bob Nelson, Eric Nelson, Dan Newell, Bill Nutting, Rodney Ogawa, Caleb Perkins, Liz Peterson, Kathleen Poole, Brad Portin, David Rector, Eddie Reed, Michelle Reid, Lauren Resnick, Leah Reuben-Werner, Melinda Reynvaan, Nancy Rikerson, Mike Riley, Andy Rogers, George Russell, Scott Sattler, Mike Schemmel, Derek Scheurell, Linda Skrla, Nikki Smith, Candace Simpson, Riley Sinder, Geoff Southworth, Lorna Spear, Tom Stritikus, Juli Swinnerton, Mary Kay Stein, Randy Stocker, Laura Stokes, Louise Stoll, Jung Tuanmu, Gary Tubbs, Mary Ann Unger, Tom Vander Ark, Bernardo Vidales, Spencer Welch, Mark Wenzel, Mel West, Pili Wolfe, Nicole Woodard, Norma Zavala, Jan Zuber, and Tricia Zurybida.

Finally, we owe a particular debt to staff of the Wallace Foundation, in particular, Kim Jinnett, Ed Pauly, and Paula Warford, who helped guide this process from beginning to end. Our ability to express the ideas in this book was also sharpened immeasurably by staff at the University of Washington, among them, Sally Brown, Michele Ferguson, Dean Driskell, and Linda Knapp, a freelance writer.

Michael A. Copland and Michael S. Knapp

Center for the Study of Teaching and Policy (CTP)

University of Washington

June 2005

Preface

A Call for Leadership
That Is Focused on Learning

Most of the current education workforce matriculated into a system of public schools that, over the past 100 years, became good at meeting the needs of some children. The system we inherited was designed to sort and select students through various mechanisms that produced high-quality learning for some students (maybe even most students in privileged communities) and weeded out the rest. Today, however, whether or not we agree with the politics that have shaped recent education policy, one thing is clear: the imperative to ensure that all children learn to high standards is inescapable. Merely meeting the needs of some students is no longer good enough for today's public schools.

For school and school system leaders, under ever increasing pressure and often diminishing support, simply hunkering down and doing more of the same isn't likely to bring about necessary change in student achievement. The tasks that educational leaders face, however, are often complex and unrelated to student achievement. Even with enough time to focus, many school and district administrators report that their time continues to be consumed by matters unconnected to learning improvement. How can school leaders make the shift from some kids to all kids? Where do they find the time and energy to focus on this central and difficult challenge?

Creating an agenda for equity and excellence in student achievement is of the utmost importance in the current education landscape. Despite the urgency embedded in this statement, such a shift in thinking presents new challenges that were previously unknown or perhaps not even considered for public education. Our schools need leaders who can systematically deliver on the promise of instructional expertise and high-quality learning for all children. To be successful, school leaders need new, more powerful tools to support their efforts to develop the most effective and sustainable leadership strategies.

Using the Leading for Learning Framework to Build a Learning Agenda

The ideas and examples presented in this book are meant to support leaders' efforts to improve learning in schools and school districts. Our aim is to help leaders create powerful, equitable learning for all students. To that end, this book introduces the Leading for Learning Framework. This framework highlights five areas of action for improvement including: (1) establishing a focus on learning, (2) building professional communities that value learning, (3) engaging external environments that matter for learning, (4) acting strategically and sharing leadership, and (5) creating coherence. Leaders take action along various pathways to advance student and professional learning while building a system that connects and sustains these efforts.

One can conceive the Leading for Learning Framework in three distinct ways. First, the ideas offer both a toolbox and a mental map for school and district leaders who are responsible for improving student learning and bringing influence and resources to support that goal. We recognize that leaders who lead for learning do so in different ways. These leaders include persons in typical traditional leadership roles such as principals and superintendents, but also those who lead in other spheres such as teacher leaders, teacher developers, union leaders, community leaders, professional developers, faculty members, and policymakers. We hope that individuals who have the potential to improve learning, in different ways and from various vantage points, will find these ideas useful in shaping their leadership actions.

Second, the Leading for Learning Framework can be used as a lens for examining existing leadership practices in schools and school districts. By using these ideas for analysis, leaders can examine how focused they are on learning. Clearly, while there is no easily identified best approach to leading for learning, common themes and methods are presented in this book from emerging and established leaders from across the country who are actively working to improve learning. Our hope is that the framework will guide leaders toward understanding, evaluating, and improving their leadership practice.

Finally, the Leading for Learning Framework is useful as a guide for planning leadership preparation and professional development. By applying the ideas in schools and school districts, as well as within organizations and institutions that provide leadership preparation and professional development, leaders can provide more effective learning opportunities for both prospective and experienced school leaders. As such, the ideas in the book offer a means for shaping preparation and professional development concerned with learning-focused leadership.

The ideas and suggestions presented here are based on published and ongoing research, combined with the craft knowledge of a wide range of practicing educators. We reviewed various bodies of literature from both inside and outside the field of education. These sources are detailed in the Methodological Notes as well as in *Leading for Learning: Reflective Tools for School and District Leaders* (Knapp, Copland, & Talbert, 2003), and its companion volume

Leading for Learning Sourcebook (Knapp et al., 2003). The review and revision process involved more than 300 educators, scholars, and other professionals whose suggestions were subsequently integrated into this book. By themselves, many of the ideas presented here are not new. Together, however, they provide a powerful synthesis of thoughts and ideas that can help leaders find direction in the face of complex challenges.

The book is not intended as a set of recipes or a specific change theory. In fact, we sought to avoid making such pronouncements because we find them typically of little use for guiding real change in particular schools and school districts. The book also doesn't outline explicit standards for leadership practice, such as those created by the Interstate School Leaders Licensure Consortium or by national administrators' associations. Although the ideas presented here are compatible with such standards, they are not prescriptions for how leaders should act in specific contexts or particular roles; rather, our aim is to offer leaders clarity in seeing, understanding, and defining problems and opportunities, and to suggest strategic actions that could work in their everyday classrooms and school systems.

Tools for Reflection, Teaching, and Planning

The ideas in the book are intended to promote reflection, guide teaching, and support more thoughtful planning for educational change. As reflective tools, the ideas can help leaders deepen their understanding of their current situation and imagine new possibilities for action. Reflection on action fosters self-assessment. Deep self-assessment provides opportunities for growth.

As teaching tools, the ideas presented here can engage leaders in discovering more powerful connections between leadership and learning. Preparing leaders who can lead for learning is important, yet the field lacks powerful strategies for developing this kind of leadership. This book offers a concise set of ideas that can help developing leaders see the possibilities in their schools and school districts, and it provides illustrations of how leadership can become more learning focused.

Finally, as a planning tool, the ideas may prove useful to leaders' efforts to devise new strategies for improvements in a specific school or district. Successful schools and school districts are in a state of continual improvement, always seeking ways to improve learning for students, teachers, and the organization as a whole. The ideas developed in this book will help leaders become more intentional in leading change efforts. Overall, our aim is to offer the Leading for Learning Framework to leaders and to those who are preparing and developing leaders. It is our hope that the framework will guide leaders toward building coherent, collaborative educational systems that deliver powerful, equitable learning to all students.

What to Expect from *Connecting Leadership with Learning*

This book presents a detailed picture of leading for learning that builds on the key ideas and elements found in *Leading for Learning* and the *Leading for Learning Sourcebook*. The book is organized into three primary parts and includes a preface and an epilogue. Part One (Chapters 1 and 2) use the story of one student, Hector, and his teacher, Mr. G., to illustrate central dilemmas that leaders face in attempting to improve learning for students, professionals, and systems. In response to these dilemmas, this opening section introduces the Leading for Learning Framework. The ideas and concepts from the framework can reconnect leaders' work with the basic challenges of teaching and learning that Hector's story dramatizes.

Part Two (Chapters 3–7) offers a distillation of what the Leading for Learning Framework means, both conceptually and in practice. Each of the five chapters introduces a critical domain of action that emerges from our research and dialogue with practitioners including: (1) focusing on learning, (2) developing a professional community, (3) engaging external environments, (4) acting strategically through shared leadership, and (5) creating coherence. Considered individually, each domain of activity is necessary for learning-focused leadership, yet one domain is insufficient unless it is considered with the others.

Part Three (Chapters 8–10) provides extended examples of the Leading for Learning Framework in action. The case examples of schools (Chapter 8) and districts (Chapter 9) trace how leaders evolve as they use a variety of leadership strategies. These case examples trace the evolution of leadership strategies aimed at learning improvement. We see the journeys from the beginning stages, when leadership is less closely linked to learning, to more advanced stages, which highlight many elements of the Leading for Learning Framework. Along the way, the case stories are annotated to show how the asserted connections between leading and learning play out in practice.

Chapter 10 presents images of the reflective tools currently in use within schools, districts, professional development settings, and leadership preparation programs. Here, we illustrate how practitioners, professional developers, and professors in leadership preparation programs can use the Leading for Learning Framework in context. We also include short examples drawn from our own experience at the University of Washington in a preparation program for aspiring systems-level leaders.

We close in an Epilogue by revisiting the story of Hector and Mr. G. and thinking about the implications of learning-focused leadership for improving schools and school districts.

How to Make the Most of This Book

Readers may decide to use the book in various ways. For example, it can be used as a prompt or guide for discussion within groups of leaders attempting to visualize what learning-focused leadership can be in particular educational settings. Individual readers may find the ideas helpful for focusing their own efforts on leadership actions that matter most. School or district leaders can also use it as a reference for planning while considering possibilities suggested by the framework. As a set of tools, the book offers practitioners a coherent analytic frame for examining leadership activity in existing settings. Finally, we envision these ideas being useful for university personnel who engage in developing and teaching leadership preparation or for other third-party support providers who seek to offer learning-focused professional development for K–12 leaders.

Part One

Leading for Learning: Establishing the Foundational Ideas

We begin in Chapter 1 with the story of one student, Hector, and his teacher, Mr. G. Hector and Mr. G. inhabit an all too familiar public school classroom. Their story illustrates a number of the dilemmas that leaders face when they attempt to improve learning for students, professionals, and systems.

We start with a single student and teacher for another reason—it is all too tempting, and often necessary, for leaders to think in terms of aggregates (e.g., the 750 students in this school, the student population served by this district, the average level of achievement in our four high schools, and so on). Aggregates too easily mask the individuals within them. We suggest it is a leader's mission to support the learning of individual students and the teaching of individual teachers. Leadership is ultimately all about learning and teaching and the ways these functions affect each learner, each teacher, and each educational system.

Chapter 2 introduces the Leading for Learning Framework and begins to explore potential responses by school and district leaders to various school dilemmas. These ideas constitute a useful and comprehensive foundation for understanding the connections between leadership and learning in schools and school systems. Chapters 3–7 further illustrate the Leading for Learning Framework and show how different areas of the framework can be applied to complex leadership challenges in a variety of school and district settings.

1

Hector's Challenge to
Educational Leaders

From the beginning, let's be clear about a fundamental assumption
on which this book rests: The primary work of educational leadership is to guide improvements in learning. As such, the leader's
work starts and ends with individual students and their learning. A glimpse of a young learner and his teacher, as described
in the *Leading for Learning* reports (Knapp, Copland, & Talbert,
2003), focuses on the challenges that school and district leaders
face as they seek to fulfill this responsibility.

Hector's Mathematics Lesson

It is Friday, and the Period 2 Mathematics class is about to
begin. Hector and his classmates, a mixture of white and Latino
children, crowd in from the busy hallway, find seats, and fum-
ble for their homework sheets. Some never find them; a few—
primarily a handful of boys located at seats around the edge of
the room—pay little attention to what is going on. The teacher,
Mr. G., appears not to notice. Today, Hector is feeling confident;
his older sister Marita, who excels at math, spent time at home
helping him complete the assignment, the first he has finished
this week.

The teacher uses the next 15 minutes to review the 35 assigned problems for solving simple equations with one unknown variable. Mr. G. stands in front of the class asking for the answer to each problem and providing it if no one volunteers promptly. Twice, Hector tentatively raises his hand, as if to offer an answer; the teacher does not recognize him. The students correct their sheets and report how many they got right. Mr. G. then shifts to a 15-minute presentation at the blackboard on the finer points of solving one-variable algebraic equations. Hector begins to fidget during the explanation; his nonparticipating classmates are becoming louder and more noticeable. "I'm not very good at math," he explains in our later conversation. "Maybe Marita will help me."

The class ends with a period of seatwork—more practice solving for x. Seated at his desk near the rear of the room, Mr. G. enters homework scores into his grade book. Hector works sporadically at the seatwork task, but appears distracted by the small contingent of nonparticipating boys who spend the time engaged in unrelated talk. Mr. G. pays little attention, except to broadcast a general "Shh" now and again. At one point, Hector quietly seeks assistance from a nearby classmate, questioning her in Spanish. "No talking, please," says the teacher. Shortly, Hector and his classmates are headed out the door for Period 3. (Knapp, Copland, & Talbert, 2003, p.7)

This snapshot of a lesson, typical of many classrooms, presents fundamental challenges to educational leaders who engage in the important work of improving learning and teaching. In this scene, the teacher is experienced and certificated, and many students are engaged in academic tasks. But students are not probing deeply into the content, and some are completely disengaged from any learning.

Further analysis into Hector's situation brings more dimensions to light. For example, even though the textbook used in Mr. G's class has been an accepted school district resource for teaching mathematics at this level for several years, there is little in the text material that aligns well with current state standards for student learning. Furthermore, although the school has an active ESL program that provides extra support for students who come to school speaking a language other than English, the services are provided mostly through classroom pullout sessions, and students are taught a separate curriculum by instructional assistants who are not certificated teachers. Meanwhile, Mr. G. has never had a conversation with the ELL specialist to discuss the particular needs of his second language learners in mathematics. Nor has he even taken notice of the fact that most of his struggling learners (easily a third of the class) are second language learners, whereas the successful ones are almost all from white families.

A cursory visit to Mr. G.'s classroom wouldn't raise alarms. Many students appear to be learning to solve math problems by following instructions from Mr. G. and their textbook. Influential PTA parents aren't raising any red flags about the nature of Mr. G.'s classroom instruction. He is regarded as a "pretty good" teacher in the community. In fact, Mr. G. is someone who colleagues say likes kids and earns their respect. Nearby classrooms reveal more obvious management concerns for school and district leaders to worry about. But for Hector and Mr. G., the deeper we look, the more it becomes clear that key aspects of the learning situation, both inside and outside the classroom, are lacking.

Mr. G.'s Reflection

After school, Mr. G. stands near the bus line, his typical Friday afternoon duty. He exchanges friendly barbs with some of the students waiting in line, and wishes each child a "good weekend" as they board. Walking back to the classroom, he reflects on the math lesson that transpired earlier. "Most of that class just doesn't seem to get it," he pines. A probe about instructional strategy indicates uncertainty on his part about his plan for teaching kids to solve for x. "Repeating the thing till they get it just doesn't seem to cut it," he reflects. When questioned about the progress of the nonparticipating group in the math class, Mr. G. intimates that he has tried hard to involve them and they "just don't respond; they don't seem to care about learning." But he

> feels an obligation to "plow ahead." The state test is only three
> months away. (Knapp, Copland, & Talbert, 2003, p. 8)

Although he is personable with most of his students, Mr. G.'s reliance on a drill-and-practice approach to instruction, coupled with a lack of skills needed to differentiate instruction in intentional and relevant ways, undermines his ability to teach math to all of his students at a high level. The content for his instruction is a far cry from what the district and state standards require. However, Mr. G. has had few opportunities to learn principles and approaches of standards-based mathematics education, nor has he sought any. He is reluctant to change a career-long teaching repertoire that seems to work pretty well for many students. Furthermore, Mr. G. has yet to focus on the instructional challenges posed by the school's growing population of second language learners who struggle to simultaneously master subject content, language, and school demands.

As in many schools, Mr. G. and his fellow teachers operate in relative isolation. Apart from brief collegial conversations that occur over the lunch table or in passing hallway conversations, Mr. G. has little interaction with colleagues at school. When opportunities for professional development occur, most often they are disconnected from the real work of Mr. G.'s classroom, and these opportunities rarely focus on the particular immediate needs of students in the school. Conversations about struggling students typically don't focus on helping teachers to improve instructional practices; rather, they reinforce the idea that students with particular learning needs must go elsewhere in the school to get needed services.

Administrators at Mr. G's school and district are too preoccupied with other things to notice what is taking place in his classroom. On the rare occasions when the principal or assistant principal sets foot in the classroom, it is typically to see Mr. G. about a managerial issue. For example, one week the school's administrators try to work out problems with the new schedule for a year-round school while at the same time attending to three new noncertificated teachers who are struggling with student discipline issues. The only conversation between Mr. G. and the principal that even remotely focused on learning occurred in early October during their 20-minute postconference following Mr. G.'s only formal evaluation of the year. Mr. G. recalls little about that conversation, except for the principal's complimentary comments about the bulletin board display that featured a photograph of each of his 146 students.

In addition, the district central office is trying to respond to pressure from a small, mostly upper-middle class segment of the white community who wants more advanced placement courses in the high school. At the same time, they are answering to account-ability pressures from the state and No Child Left Behind (NCLB) regulations to educate more second language learners. District administrators also are negotiating the next teachers' contract and they are at odds with the teacher's union over a number of issues. District administrators rarely engage in professional learning of their own, and when they do, the agenda is not typically focused on how to better support schools to improve learning. Instead, administrators spend this professional learning time focused on managerial concerns that are relatively unrelated to teaching and learning.

Given time to reflect, the vast majority of educators would want more for Hector and the other young learners in Mr. G.'s classroom. They would want more for Mr. G., and they would provide him with more support so that he can provide more powerful and equitable learning opportunities for all his students. Yet, to fulfill that responsibility, educational leaders must ask the following questions:

• How can leaders know enough about student learning and instructional methods in particular classrooms, subjects, and grades in order to focus improvement efforts?

• How can teachers learn to improve their practice, and what conditions can motivate and support their improvements?

• How do family and community conditions contribute to current school conditions, and how can they be a part of the solution?

• Once there is a focus on improvement, what specific actions will provide the greatest influence on changing what teachers and learners do? Who leads this work? How? What resistances stand in the way and what can leaders do about them?

• How can leaders' actions and resources have progressive and long-term effects on teaching and learning?

These questions are not simple ones to answer, and they may appear both overwhelming and paralyzing. However, doing nothing clearly is not an option. School and district leaders who can provide constructive answers to these questions do so based on their understanding of existing and potential connections between their leadership actions and the learning that occurs in their school or district. Our schools will open for business again tomorrow, but without a different type of leadership they will continue to operate as they have in the past. To spur change, leaders need clear goals to improving learning and the ability to visualize ways to move forward. With greater insight, school and district leaders can better understand when and how to take action that will leverage the greatest change.

2

Essential Ideas and Tasks for Learning-Focused Leaders

To imagine leading for learning, it is essential to grasp a set of foundational concepts about leadership, learning, and their potential connections. In this chapter, we offer definitions that clarify the constructs of the Leading for Learning Framework and the relationships among them. Then, we examine a strong learning community in action, explore the qualities of school and district leadership that focus on leadership, and analyze learning opportunities that optimize student achievement. This chapter also sets the stage for the latter part of the book, where we will explore leading for learning in school and district settings.

A Strong Learning Community in Action

Understanding the fundamentals of leading for learning begins with images of learning and teaching as it occurs in the classroom. To initiate this discussion, we turn once again to a practical example. Ms. M. is a fourth-year humanities teacher at an urban middle school. Let's look at what is going on in her classroom.

Ms. M.'s Humanities Class

Ms. M. and her colleagues devised a two-year humanities curriculum for their students, built around projects addressing broad topics that span U.S. history from the post-Civil War period to the present. Immigration is one of the topics for her 8th graders, who are African-American and Latino youngsters from predominantly low-income backgrounds. As part of this project, she divides them into three groups (e.g., Chinese, Mexican, and Eastern European immigrants). Students in each group do research and, with a partner, put together a debate, taking either a pro- or anti-immigrant position. To prepare for the debate, and to fulfill other requirements of this project, students are given a set of readings and other materials. Many of them are primary documents, such as the original form from the Homestead Act that people filled out to buy land; illustrations and photographs; advertisements announcing the great land rush and railroad routes; newspaper commentary about immigration; political cartoons, and much more.

Students respond enthusiastically to this curriculum, though few have encountered anything like it in their previous schooling. Ms. M. provides them a great deal of material and structure to help them work productively with this assignment and with each other. For example, the students receive a written outline of the project that includes objectives, checklists of what is needed before starting, the knowledge to be gained, writing plans, assignments, etc. Students hand in multiple drafts of written products and meet with the teacher regarding their progress. Rubrics with a four-point scale, roughly fashioned to correspond to state and district assessment scales, detail grading and assessment for both written products and oral presentations.

Ms. M. and her colleagues emphasize several skills they feel are critical for success in the project work (e. g., how to read text, mark it, and take bullet notes). In choosing which skills to teach, they are also responding to the requirements of the state exams. A fair amount of time is spent, especially at the beginning of the school year, directly teaching these skills. Time is also devoted to teaching the skills needed to engage in successful peer review and collaborative group work (adapted from Knapp, Copland, Ford, et al., 2003, p. 11).

This glimpse of instruction from Ms. M.'s class is a far cry from what takes place in Mr. G.'s classroom. All members of this classroom are a part of a learning community that is pushed to engage in forms of learning they have not experienced before, and they are rising to the challenge. Ms. M. sets high expectations for the written work that will be produced by all students while at the same time she recognizes the need to break down elements of the writing process for students who may need additional support. By using her knowledge of what motivates learning, Ms. M. provides choices in the context of the curriculum that allow students to bring their individual strengths and interests to the topic, and she uses pedagogical approaches that promote learning-focused student-to-student interaction in small, cooperative group settings. Moreover, Ms. M. demonstrates her own deep understanding of the content by developing new curriculum that links its development to specific state standards.

In Ms. M.'s classroom, there are no students left behind like Hector. Yet, there are more than a few students in the classroom with backgrounds similar to Hector's and with the same English skills. Ms. M. demands a lot of her charges, and in return she has their full engagement in the work at hand. Her immersion in the content that she teaches and her grasp of how to translate it into terms that all the young minds will find relevant is palpable.

What Does It Take to Get There?

Ms. M.'s urban middle school classroom exists in a school with a strong professional community that is guided by a principal who has a clear vision for powerful, equitable learning and who supports continuing opportunities to further that vision. Together with teacher leaders like Ms. M. and with the support of the district office, this principal has led her school staff to create curricula like the one shown in Ms. M.'s class for many areas in the school program.

This principal's efforts derive from a picture of what powerful instruction looks like. Through what others have noted as vital interactions between learners, this principal and other leaders like her have found various ways to be involved in instruction (Cohen, Raudenbush, & Ball, 2001; Hawkins, 1974). She is paying attention to the following dimensions in the classroom:

• **What teachers and learners bring to the classroom.** Teachers and learners bring prior knowledge, cultural backgrounds, and assumptions about schooling and each other. In this instance, Ms. M. came with experience in museum education, and she worked in a facility that focused on humanities. The students brought a mix of cultural, ethnic, and socioeconomic backgrounds that were different from the white middle-class experience of most teachers at the school. The backgrounds of participants in the classroom provide an important reference point for meaning and relevance in instruction.

• **How learners interact with each other and the teacher.** Teachers and students are assigned to work together (or choose to do so in high schools), and over time they develop perceptions of each other and their relationships. Ms. M. and her students developed a comfortable working relationship over a two-year period. Their school was small, and it made it easier for them to get to know each other well. The structure of classroom time and other time in the building gives Ms. M. many different ways to interact with her students (e.g., individual writing conferences, group guidance, direct whole group teaching, or small-group advisory sessions).

• **What teachers know about the content and how young people acquire the information.** State standards, district frameworks, and textbook choices define what is to be taught in the classroom, but ultimately teachers' own grasp of the subject matter largely determines what will be taught and learned. Studies show that teachers' knowledge of content and how young learners connect with it shapes the nature of academic tasks (Shulman, 1986). Ms. M. had a well-developed set of ideas about the humanities (history, literature, and social studies), and her expansive knowledge base complemented that of her colleagues. Together, they were able to bring a rich base of knowledge to their curriculum design and teaching strategies.

• **How learners engage with academic tasks and content.** Teachers who effectively guide and support their students in demanding academic tasks increase their students' opportunities for learning and give their students a greater degree of ownership over their learning experience. When Ms. M.'s students were given demanding and motivating academic tasks, they stayed engaged with a combination of teacher and peer support. The expectations were high for these students, but by their third year in this school they were comfortable and proficient completing challenging academic work.

• **What learning is and how it can be demonstrated.** What takes place in the classroom ultimately reflects the participants' notions about learning and how it is demonstrated. Ms. M. and her team devised various ways of representing learning in the humanities (project writing, oral presentations, and a portfolio of work that shows improvement), and they defined a standard for good student work. Their measures complemented existing state and district measures.

As shown in Figure 2.1, each aspect of teaching and learning may bear the stamp of leaders at various levels of the system. But before we explore how leaders can have an impact, it is helpful to clarify several things about leadership and the multiple levels of learning that optimize student achievement.

Leadership in Schools and Districts

Simply put, leadership has been characterized as an act of imparting purpose to an organization as well as motivating and sustaining those efforts (Burns, 1978; Gardner, 1990; Leithwood, 1992). In schools and districts, that can mean many things, such as

Figure 2.1

An Interactional View of Student Learning

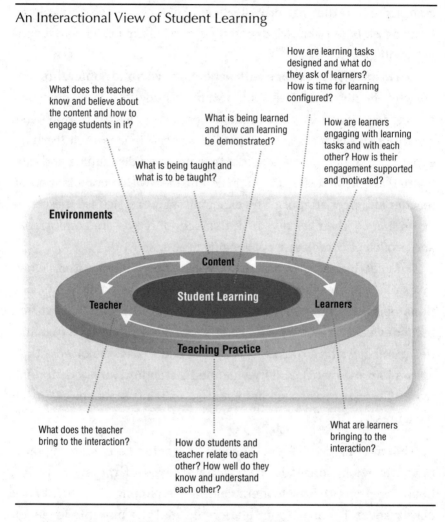

How are learning tasks designed and what do they ask of learners? How is time for learning configured?

What does the teacher know and believe about the content and how to engage students in it?

What is being learned and how can learning be demonstrated?

How are learners engaging with learning tasks and with each other? How is their engagement supported and motivated?

What is being taught and what is to be taught?

Environments

Content

Teacher   Student Learning   Learners

Teaching Practice

What does the teacher bring to the interaction?

How do students and teacher relate to each other? How well do they know and understand each other?

What are learners bringing to the interaction?

articulating broad visions for how the schools serve students and addressing the daily details of school operations.

Leadership theories and activities have long focused on the immediate support and supervision of instruction to improve student learning. We conceive of leadership more along the lines of what is generally referred to by various scholars as "instructional leadership" (Glickman, 2002; Leithwood & Duke, 1999; Murphy, 1988; Smith & Andrews, 1989). Traditionally, that concept has focused on the role of the principal (Hallinger & Heck, 1996; Hart, 1993; Leithwood & Duke, 1999), the superintendent (Hallinger & Murphy, 1982; Murphy & Hallinger, 1986; Peterson, 1999), and other school-level leaders such as staff developers, district coordinators, and mentor teachers who supervise, guide, and monitor instruction and instructional practice.

Although they are clearly relevant, typical definitions of instructional leadership miss what other scholars have painted as a more inclusive picture of leadership—embracing work that is carried out simultaneously by individuals at different levels of the system and with different purviews over instruction (Elmore, 2000; Lambert, 1998; Spillane, Halverson, & Diamond, 2001). At the school level, leading for learning includes the joint work of principals, assistant principals, department heads, school-based mentors and coaches, and teacher leaders. At the district level, the efforts of superintendents, school board members, directors, coordinators, district-supported staff, and community leaders all shape leadership.

Ogawa and Bossert (1995) assert that educational leadership is an attribute of the organization as a whole. They state that leadership is not only embedded in formal positions of authority (e.g., principals and superintendents), but also in functions that cut across positions (e.g., professional development, professional accountability, and curriculum development). In this perspective, leadership includes not only the leaders' actions, but also their thinking, feelings, and the meanings that they and others attach to events in the organization. Finally, a broader view of leadership highlights an array of leadership tools by noted scholars of organizations, sociology, and social psychology. Such tools include not only positional leaders (resources, requirements and sanctions, exhortations, and symbols), but also modeling, relationship building, systemic inquiry into organizational performance, and the creation of policies, structures, and incentives of many kinds.

(Argyris, 1991; Garvin, 1993; Pfeffer, 1998; Wenger, McDermott, & Snyder, 2002).

The concept of leadership employed here builds on several lines of thinking about the work of leaders in schools and districts. In addition to expanding ideas about instructional leadership, we assume that educational leaders must serve schools in two ways:

• **They act as moral agents.** The work of educational leadership is distinctly moral. It is different from leadership in other types of organizations because it is rooted in a set of common commitments to do right by children. School leadership practices should reflect a sense of common good and a promise that those moral values are required from everyone (Sergiovanni, 1999).

• **They act in transformative ways.** Transformational leadership assumes that the central focus of leadership ought to be the commitments and capacities of organizational members (Leithwood & Duke, 1999). Authority and influence are not necessarily allocated to those occupying formal administrative positions; rather, power is given by organization members to whoever can commit to the collective goals of the organization. Successful leadership in education rests on an organization's ability to collectively achieve a shared goal that transcends individual self-interests.

The Leadership Target: Student, Professional, and System Learning

In contemporary public education, the central goal of most educators, as noted in Ms. M.'s story, is to provide education that is powerful and equitable. Education scholars and researchers define powerful learning as gaining the means to master challenging content and skills in subject areas, developing habits for further learning, and preparing students for fulfilling occupational futures and citizenship in a democracy (e.g., Brandt, 1998; Bransford, Brown, & Cocking, 1999). Equitable learning, as discussed in the literature, affords all students, regardless of background, the same opportunities to acquire knowledge and gain mastery (Corbett, Wilson, & Williams, 2002; Ladson-Billings, 1994; Meier, 1995).

In seeking powerful and equitable education, leaders inevitably encounter three learning agendas—student learning, professional learning, and system learning. An essential step in leading for learning is to visualize how all three learning agendas and their opportunities and connections intersect to influence student achievement. Figure 2.2 displays these learning agendas and shows their relationships with the school or district, the community, and the larger policy environment.

Figure 2.2

Three Interrelated Learning Agendas in Schools and Districts

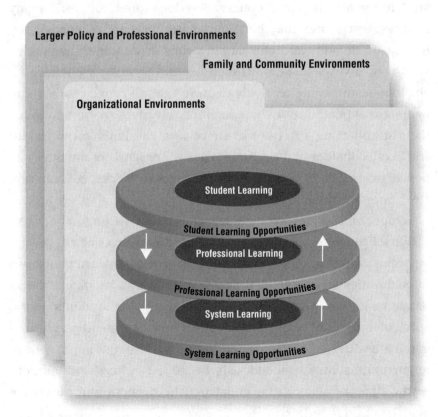

Student Learning

Powerful and equitable instruction, as illustrated in Ms. M.'s classroom, enables all students to develop what others have called deep subject-matter knowledge (i.e., the skills and habits of mind that will benefit them in new educational or working situations (Newmann, King, & Secada, 1996). Participating in this kind of learning builds a sense of empowerment and possibility in a world that is not always welcoming to young people from all walks of life.

Because learning can be thought of as both the act and result of acquiring knowledge, skills, habits of mind, and a sense of empowerment, schools need measures that show what and how much students have learned. Hence, measuring and interpreting student learning is also of concern to educational leaders. In many settings, test scores may be taken as the measure of learning, by decree or default, and the larger policy environment may give school or district leaders little choice in the matter. Because no single measure can effectively capture the full range of what students are expected to learn, educational leaders wishing to focus their attention on a richer picture of what students know and do will likely consider and promote using other kinds of measures as described in Ms. M.'s classroom (Newmann, Marks, & Gamoran, 1996; Shepard, 1995; Wiggins, 1989).

Opportunities for student learning occur through the interaction of teachers, learners, and subject-matter content. As the vignettes from Mr. G.'s and Ms. M.'s classrooms illustrate, those opportunities arise in numerous ways: teachers plan different academic tasks, teachers introduce ideas and guide students' work, curricular materials expose students to new ideas, and peers communicate with one another or are prohibited from doing so. These opportunities vary tremendously because teachers and learners with different backgrounds construct the process and outcomes of instruction together.

Professional Learning

For obvious and subtle reasons, students' learning depends on what the professionals who work with them know and do. Leaders, therefore, need an equally rich picture of what and how they and their colleagues learn (see Nelson, 1998; Spillane, 2002, for discussion of administrators' learning in action). Teachers' and administrators' learning includes acquiring knowledge, skills, and perspectives that inform their practice.

Learning for professionals like Mr. G. and Ms. M. occurs in many venues. Some of them are formal and intentionally designed to teach particular pedagogical strategies (e.g., cooperative learning or the Socratic method) or they deepen subject-matter knowledge in specific content areas (e.g., science, reading, or mathematics). Others are more informal or unplanned, yet communicate strong messages about what to do as a classroom teacher and how to live in that role in the context of the school (e.g., through interactions with grade-level or departmental colleagues). In essence, forms and venues for professional learning can be understood in terms that parallel what goes on in classrooms full of young learners. As learners, professionals encounter ideas about practice or instructional strategies with other peers in the field under the guidance of more experienced professionals who facilitate the learning. This type of learning is multifaceted and difficult to assess—and thus it is often left unassessed.

Figure 2.3 further illustrates how much professional learning takes place on the job, as teachers and administrators gradually develop the "wisdom of practice" (Bransford, Brown, & Cocking, 1999). Nonetheless, even there, it is instructive to reflect on the curriculum and the process of that learning in interactional terms.

Opportunities for continuous professional learning can take various forms. Those most valuable for improving professional practice include interactions with other professionals. Colleagues can offer ideas and evidence of effective practice, provide feedback and suggestions for improvement, and give moral support.

Such professional interactions to improve teaching and learning can occur in teacher communities within a school, in districtwide teacher or administrator communities, between coaches/mentors and teachers or administrators, and in institutes and networks within and beyond the local school systems (see, for example, Carpenter, Fennema, Peterson, Chiang, & Loef, 1989; Cohen & Hill, 2001; Darling-Hammond, 1996; Kruse, Louis, & Bryk, 1995; Lieberman & Grolnik, 1999; Little, 1999; Little & McLaughlin, 1993). Figure 2.3 shows how the interplay between the content, the facilitator or leader, and the professional community parallels the learning environment for students in the classroom. In this model, the main content of professional learning for teachers consists of ideas about any and all facets of instructional practice and how it can be improved. For administrators, ideas about instructional practice are also central, along with guidelines on improving instructional practice through professional or system learning.

Figure 2.3

An Interactional View of Professional Learning

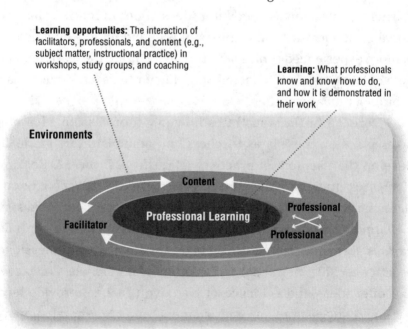

Learning opportunities: The interaction of facilitators, professionals, and content (e.g., subject matter, instructional practice) in workshops, study groups, and coaching

Learning: What professionals know and know how to do, and how it is demonstrated in their work

Environments

Content

Facilitator

Professional Learning

Professional

Professional

System Learning

Through inquiry into how a district or school functions and performs, leaders can support what we may call "system learning." This includes assembling and interpreting information about the system as a whole (note that either the school or district can be thought of as a "system") plus developing new policies, practices, and structures that alter and, hopefully, enhance its performance. The concept derives from scholarly notions of "organizational learning," which posit that the school or district as a whole accumulates information through institutional stories and routines, and over time, the organization alters its behavior in response to external stimuli and new understandings of the participants (Fullan, 1993; Leithwood & Louis, 2002; Resnick & Hall, 1998; Senge, 1990; Sproull & Cohen, 1996). In essence, system learning assumes an organizational whole is greater than the sum of individual professionals' thinking and efforts. The notion of system learning must not be taken too literally, however. Organizations do not "think" or "perceive," individuals do (Simon, 1999). Still, organizations act in ways that transcend individuals' efforts and can be guided by individuals, especially those who exercise leadership.

As suggested by Figure 2.4, opportunities for system learning arise through the interaction of professional staff and facilitators as the teachers guide the learners toward examining and shaping system performance. System learning also happens in initiating systemwide planning endeavors; evaluating policies, programs, and resource use, including self-studies and various assessments; implementing action research focused on systemwide issues; and identifying indicators to measure progress toward defined goals.

How the Learning Agendas Are Related

The three learning agendas—student, professional, and system— are shaped by each other and by their respective environments. Navigating these multiple contexts forms one of the more difficult

Figure 2.4

An Interactional View of System Learning

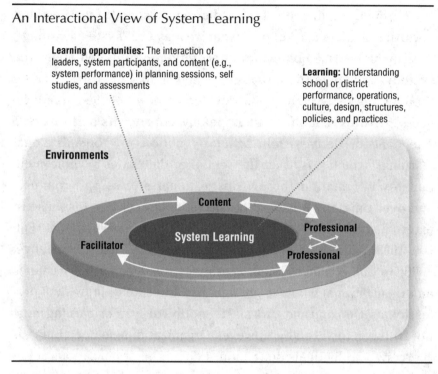

challenges for educational leaders: to see the points of connection and mutual influence. Leaders who make the connections learn several lessons:

• **How learning and teaching can be used to guide improvement.** Structured opportunities for teachers to work together to observe, learn, and practice various teaching strategies will enrich their own professional knowledge and skills. New knowledge and skills exercised in the classroom with guidance and support will create opportunities for students to learn in more intentional and powerful ways.

• **How classroom activities and professional development activities can be used to influence systemic learning.** Typically, district policy and expectations determine what teachers do in the classroom; however, when teachers learn and practice various strategies that help students learn in more powerful ways, they can shape district curriculum policy and expectations for student learning.

   • **How learning agendas are constrained and enriched by their environments.** Recognizing environmental factors can help to shape the policies and practices districts employ to develop teacher learning. For example, when there are high concentrations of second language learners present in a school or district community, teachers must know and be able to deliver instruction that meets students' particular needs.

Figure 2.2 shows the connection between these three learning agendas. The arrows in Figure 2.2 have several meanings. In one sense, they represent the flow of information from one set of learning transactions to another. At the same time, they signal the potential for mutual influence: learning at one level affects learning at others, and vice versa. Finally, the figure highlights potential disconnections as seen vividly in Hector's story, where the lack of attention to him and his experience in Mr. G.'s classroom limits the possibility for learning at other levels.

The Essence of Leading for Learning

Essentially, leading for learning means creating powerful, equitable learning opportunities for students, professionals, and systems, and motivating or compelling participants to take advantage of those opportunities. Research, theory, and craft knowledge culled from numerous scholarly sources suggest that leaders can accomplish this by committing themselves to five areas of action (Blase & Blase, 1999; Dana Center, 1999; Hallinger & Heck, 1998; Haycock, 1999; Learning First Alliance, 2003; Levine & Lezotte, 1990; Snipes, Doolittle, & Herlihy, 2002). The following activities have shown particular promise for effecting change in learning:

1. Establishing a focus on learning. Leaders can create a focus on learning by persistently and publicly focusing their attention and that of others on learning and teaching.

2. Building professional communities that value learning. Leaders build strong professional communities by nurturing work cultures that value and support their members' learning.

3. Engaging external environments that matter for learning. Schools and districts become stronger by building relationships with and securing resources from outside groups that can foster students' or teachers' learning.

4. Acting strategically and sharing leadership. Leaders maximize their actions by mobilizing effort along multiple pathways that lead to student, professional, or system learning, and by distributing leadership among individuals in different positions.

5. Creating coherence. Effective school leaders create coherence by connecting student, professional, and system learning with one another and their learning goals.

Central to these assertions about leading for learning is the notion that leaders take concrete steps along identifiable pathways that lead to student, professional, and system learning. In this sense, leaders can exert a direct and identifiable influence on learning results.

As represented by Figure 2.5, the Leading for Learning Framework is not a linear sequence of steps for improving learning and teaching. Rather, each action area supports the others, and leaders operating from different positions can pursue activities in each area simultaneously. Leaders may find it more natural to start with the first action area—establishing a focus on learning—which forms a foundation for the other four. But from there on, leaders could productively begin in many places, depending on the opportunities and constraints within the school or district, to build on the full set of conditions that support learning.

Figure 2.5

The Leading for Learning Framework

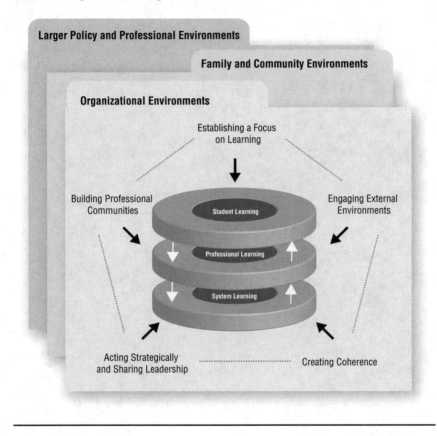

Leaders pursuing a few of these areas while ignoring others may achieve some positive learning results. Applied together, however, they constitute a more powerful array of conditions for supporting student, professional, and system learning.

Part Two

Exploring the Leading for Learning Framework in Practice

Leaders at different levels of public education can work to improve students' learning by pursuing the five areas of action in the Leading for Learning Framework introduced in Part One—*establishing a focus on learning, building professional communities that value learning, engaging external environments, acting strategically and sharing leadership*, and *creating coherence*. Each area of the Leading for Learning Framework is based on

- Underlying ideas that are derived from research and theory;
- Presumptions that leaders will undertake several essential tasks;
- Predictable challenges in the process of moving learning-focused leadership to action.

The chapters that comprise this part of the book discuss these matters and introduce a variety of practical examples drawn from research and practice. The examples illustrate what learning-focused leadership looks like in schools and districts. They also explore the issues and opportunities leaders might encounter as they work within particular school, community, and system contexts.

To keep the presentation concise, the examples are brief, simple vignettes of actions actual leaders have taken that bring to life the conceptual abstractions that comprise the Leading for Learning Framework. Annotated, longitudinal case studies that use the Leading for Learning Framework in action appear in Chapters 8 and 9.

3

Establishing a Focus on Learning

Administrators in Hector's district pay minimal attention to the nature and quality of learning for all students, even though they worry about test scores and the state's pressure on low-performing schools. In contrast, administrators and teacher leaders in some other districts have managed to make learning and teaching a visible and important priority in their daily affairs. In this chapter, we will examine the first part of the Leading for Learning Framework, which describes how leaders in improving schools or districts *establish and consistently communicate a public focus on learning and teaching*. School and district leaders can focus their own and others' attention on learning in a variety of ways, ranging from small details of their daily practice to large gestures and strategic actions. Consider one example from a district leader's weekly routine:

> The superintendent of an urban district serving 13,000 students devotes every Monday morning from 7:30 to 8:30 to meet with students at their respective schools to talk about what they are learning. Each week, she selects a different school and several students at random. She doesn't allow anything to interfere with this standing commitment (D. McEwen, personal communication, October 2002).

A principal of an elementary school with a large ESL population shares how he analyzes his school's data to focus on learning.

> In one school, which has a large ESL population, the principal has made a point of focusing his staff's attention on student learning by developing his and the school's ability to analyze student data and by basing plans for improving student learning on evidence of that learning. Because the state's analyses of disaggregated student test data is released too late to be useful for school planning, he found district staff who could do this analysis much earlier in the year and make it available to assess learning progress for his school as a whole, for each grade level, and for individual classrooms. He also collected district, school, and student data to identify areas where improvement is needed. By disaggregating the data in several ways, he is able to focus attention on the full range of students in the building, from the ESL magnet population to the gifted and talented program population, and others in between (Center for the Study of Teaching & Policy, 2003).

Through strategies like the examples shown above, school and district leaders make learning central to their own work. By consistently communicating that student learning is the shared mission of everyone in the school community, these leaders articulate core values that support a focus on powerful, equitable learning, and demonstrate that learning and teaching are public concerns and open to scrutiny. These leaders are simultaneously informing themselves about what students are learning in their respective institutions and sending strong messages to others about it. They are focusing attention on learning and on particular aspects of learning, and they are communicating these messages through actions as well as words (see, for example, Barkley, Bottoms, Feagin, & Clark, 1999).

Defining the Underlying Ideas
and Values for Focused Learning

Given that schools and districts in the United States are generally decentralized and that they are mandated to serve the public at large, a clear, shared focus on anything, let alone student learning, is not the natural state of affairs. Teachers can emphasize different things once the classroom doors are closed, and school and district administrators' energies can be consumed by a thousand distractions. In their preoccupation with the daily work of managing a district, a school, or even a classroom, teachers and educational leaders can easily lose sight of learning. Understandably, it is natural for these leaders to use crude proxies like aggregated test scores to suggest what and how much learning is taking place.

Leaders are in a position to alter this skewed vision by orchestrating a process that invites their colleagues and other stakeholders to jointly develop a focus on learning. Furthermore, their focus is not just on learning as some sort of global, general goal, but on learning that is powerful, equitable, and visible. Good leaders can make their focus even more specific by zeroing in on students' learning of particular subjects in specific grades.

Leaders are able to establish and sustain a stronger focus on learning when they share a set of fundamental values and norms about learning with other educators. As scholars have noted, leaders' beliefs and commitments to particular core values appear to play a central role in student achievement, especially in settings where students have been historically underserved (Lomotey, 1989; Scheurich, 1998; Sizemore, 1990). Authors who have discussed the transformational character of educational leadership and its moral, cultural, and symbolic dimensions, underscore the crucial role the leader's beliefs can play (Deal & Peterson, 1994; Leithwood & Jantzi, 1990; Sergiovanni, 1992). The following values form an especially strong foundation for learning improvement:

• **Ambitious standards for student learning.** Educators need a high level of understanding and skills in critical subject areas (Knapp & Associates, 1995).

• **Belief in human capacity.** Students are able to meet ambitious learning standards if they have effective instruction and support from their teachers. This belief rests on effort-based views of intelligence, which suggest that all students are able to learn with effort (Brophy & Good, 1986; Resnick, 1995).

• **Commitment to equity.** Educators must be dedicated to narrowing and ultimately eliminating the achievement gaps that exist among students who differ by class, race, ethnicity, and language (Darling-Hammond, 1997).

• **Belief in professional support and responsibility.** Strong teachers and administrators share responsibility, provide support, and hold one another accountable for improving educational quality and equity (Resnick & Glennan, 2002).

• **Commitment to inquiry.** Focused leaders use evidence to evaluate and change practice that is essential to continuous improvement in teaching and learning (see, for example, Hord, 1997; Leithwood & Louis, 2002; McLaughlin & Talbert, 2001; Szabo, 1996).

Essential Tasks for Focused Learning

Once leaders at both the school and district level are guided by common values, they can focus their attention on powerful, equitable learning by

1. **Making learning central to their own work.** Leaders find ways to focus on both learning in general and on particular aspects of student learning (e.g., how well certain kinds of students are learning and what is being learned in particular subjects or grade levels).

2. **Consistently communicating the importance of student learning.** Leaders who repeatedly tell and show others that

student learning is part of a shared mission that is supported by students, teachers, administrators, and the community are likely to succeed at creating more powerful, equitable learning.

3. Discussing and viewing other methods of student learning. Good leaders take time to observe teaching and other forms of learner support and to interact with teachers and other professionals about their practice.

Leaders who put these actions into effect and do so while minimizing potential distractions seem especially likely to bring about systemwide improvement.

What Focused Learning Looks Like in Schools

To establish a persistent, public focus on learning at the school level, principals, teacher leaders, and coaches can take the following actions.

Allow teachers to regularly visit classrooms and participate in professional learning activities with staff. In one urban district, leaders began classroom learning walk-throughs. During these walk-throughs teachers were able to visit different classrooms that focused on particular instructional content and pedagogy. Through focused initiatives like these, teachers are able to observe different areas of learning on an ongoing basis and talk about what they observe to enhance their own practice (Alvarado, 2003).

Encourage teachers to stay current on promising practices and research from the field and share learning with others. Teachers need regular opportunities to expand their learning and to discuss it with their colleagues. For example, when three teacher leaders from one suburban elementary school returned from a literacy training workshop, they jointly developed a way to systematically share their new knowledge with colleagues over the course of an early release day (UWCEL, 2004).

Initiate and guide conversations about student learning. For another school, 14 teachers met weekly to examine student progress and to focus on developing strategies to assist students who are failing one or more classes. Teachers become more learning focused when they are able to ask one another about what works and what doesn't work to achieve successful results for their students (Small Schools Project, 2004).

Make student learning a focus for performance evaluation. In one suburban district, when school administrators visited classrooms for observation, they held postconference meetings with the teachers to talk about what students were learning in their classes. Administrators who focus their attention on evidence of learning and create conversations designed to promote teachers' self-reflection on student learning can support a learning focused environment (M. Riley, personal communication, March 22, 2004).

Structure schoolwide faculty meetings for teaching and learning. For one rural elementary school, meeting times were formerly devoted to managerial concerns and "administrivia." Now each meeting is solely focused on instructional issues, joint examination of student work, and conversations about teaching practices. Administrative issues are now handled either via written communication or e-mail (UWCEL, 2004).

Examine student learning data and use it for school planning. One middle school used information from a literacy examination to identify Hispanic students who were significantly underperforming in relation to their white counterparts. This data led teachers to design instructional strategies targeted to improve literacy learning for all students, but in particular for those students identified as having the greatest learning needs (UWCEL, 2004).

Work with others to set learning improvement goals and review progress. A K–8 staff at a school on the West coast uses an inquiry process that establishes two overarching questions that guide their learning improvement work for an entire school year. Each staff member selects one student whom they identify as having specific learning needs related to the inquiry questions. Then, two teachers collaborate to design two-week individual inquiry goals to try to help the students learn in those specific areas. Teachers and other staff members share their progress toward their goals in all-staff meetings and talk about how those strategies worked with students (Center for Research on the Context of Teaching, 2002).

What Focused Learning Looks Like in School Districts

In addition to performing or taking part in comparable activities in schools, district administrators and professional development staff can take part in the following actions.

Be present in the schools to see and influence learning in action. Members of the administrative team from one medium-sized, diverse school system make observing instruction the focus for their ongoing professional development work. They work with a local university center and utilize coaches who have instructional expertise in key content areas to guide classroom visitations and debrief observations (UWCEL, 2004).

Establish procedures for collecting data about student learning and regularly share the data with school staff. In a small rural district, leaders routinely track student achievement data that includes both overarching, standardized testing results at various grades and district-developed classroom-based assessments that teachers use to guide instructional decisions. This data is disaggregated in various ways and is used as the basis for designing ongoing professional development in the district (M. Johnson & S. Austin, personal communication, October 21, 2003).

Structure district-level administrative meetings to focus on teaching and learning. A superintendent in a small suburban district mandated that regular administrative team meetings no longer focus heavily on administrative and managerial issues. Every meeting now begins with a segment focused on a topic related to improving instruction. This topic is first on the agenda and often delivered by master teachers and professional development staff from the district. Key management issues get second billing or are handled via electronic communication (D. Eismann, personal communication, April 15, 2003).

Develop and implement curriculum and assessment strategies that are aligned with high standards for student learning. In one medium-sized suburban district, the district administrators operate from a curricular theory of action. This theory includes in-house development of curricula and corresponding assessments by teachers and systemwide utilization of the assessments. The district is now developing a curriculum Web site that will eventually include the entire district curriculum in an accessible online format (M. Riley, personal communication, March 22, 2004).

Frequently communicate student learning to parents, the community, and media. A large urban district in northern California developed a parent/teacher home visit pilot program that allowed teachers to visit students in their homes. The program proved so successful in spurring student achievement and parent participation that the district received a $1.02 million grant from the federal government to replicate the program statewide. Students who participated in the home visiting program its first year increased their scores on the Stanford Achievement Test and completed their homework more regularly. Parents who took part in the program worked more with their children at home (Posnick-Goodwin, 2002).

Make contributions to student learning a primary reference point for district decision making, resource allocation, and personnel evaluation. The director of elementary education in one suburban district brought forward an analysis of disaggregated student learning data that revealed poor students and students of color were significantly underperforming other students in the system. This data prompted those in top leadership positions in the district to rethink their strategies for resource allocation (UWCEL, 2004).

Processes and Challenges for Creating Learning-Focused Schools and School Districts

In seeking to establish a focus on learning through these various means, leaders encounter competing interests and difficult questions. Issues arise concerning what is most important to learn, who determines the learning focus, what counts as learning, and how much to focus on teaching behaviors. The essential work of leadership includes resolving the underlying issues in ways that are morally and politically defensible.

What Is Essential for Focused Learning?

In building consensus around improvement and specific goals for improvement, leaders inevitably are forced to address conflicts over competing interests, learning priorities, and beliefs about education. In a number of prominent cases, districts are making the learning of particular subjects—especially literacy, but also mathematics—the focus of attention. Many leaders reason that literacy and mathematics are foundational for other subjects, and that these areas are given greatest weight in state assessment and accountability systems (Elmore & Burney, 1999; Snipes, Doolittle, & Herlihy, 2002). The following example illustrates a school-level effort to keep the working life of the school focused.

The staff at one urban Midwestern elementary school has a clear sense of their school's goals. They perceive that all of the programs and systems in place at the school help move them toward those goals. The school's principal explains this focus by frequently saying, "We keep it simple." The school's highest priority is their literacy initiative. The principal made it clear that all instructional staff, regardless of their particular assignment (e.g., PE teacher, bilingual staff, etc.), will work to teach literacy within their adopted framework. All staff members have been trained to work together on literacy goals, to share common instructional practices, learning tasks, and activities, and to use common achievement measures. In consideration of new programs, this school has been careful to take on only those new things which would strengthen the school's improvement momentum. They are wary of anything which might fragment teachers' time and focus (Newmann, Smith, Allensworth, & Bryk, 2001).

A corresponding effort has been made at the district level in settings like this one that places a high priority on improvement in literacy or other subjects.

While it is defensible in various ways, a focus on learning literacy means that other subjects get less attention and often fewer resources. So it is for any learning focus—something gets left out. In one prominent case of a district following such a strategy, the laser-like focus on literacy put an urban systemic reform grant from the National Science Foundation in jeopardy, and ultimately caused the foundation to withdraw its funding. The district's leaders were unapologetic. The science grant made too many demands on the system that, in their view, would dilute the attempt to improve literacy teaching (Hightower, 2001). Needless to say, leaders in such instances face continual pressure to give equal time, resources, and attention to everyone's priorities. But some degree of focus, whether directed from a district's central office or developed in more decentralized ways, is critical for making headway in many settings, especially low-performing schools and districts (Murphy & Hallinger, 1988; Newmann et al., 2001; Snipes, Doolittle, & Herlihy, 2002).

Whose Focus Is Most Important?

A persistent, public focus on learning often springs from a strong leader's vision, but there are clear political costs, as in this district case.

> Upon entering a district that had maintained a strong commitment to school-based decision making over more than a decade, a new superintendent made no bones about his particular vision of "good teaching." He modeled active instructional leadership in all the district's schools and engaged principals in a substantial expansion of their instructional leadership roles. Six years into the superintendent's regime, teachers new to the district, who knew no other system, expressed considerable support for what they perceived as strongly supportive district leadership. Many veterans, however, chafed at the lack of flexibility; they perceived themselves as needlessly restricted and without the curricular autonomy that they once enjoyed. While the district continues to perform well on state assessments, unhappiness persists among some staff members (Center for the Study of Teaching and Policy, 2003).

A systemwide focus on learning and particular student learning improvement goals can also result from a process of research, discussion, debate, and negotiation among stakeholders. In such instances, the challenge for leaders is to establish a collective focus on learning without compromises that dilute the focus or that result in oscillation from one focus to the next (e.g., this year we'll do math, next year we'll do science). Inherent in committing to a particular vision of teaching and learning is a tension over whether others' visions are valued or acknowledged.

What Counts as Learning?

When confronting testing and accountability issues, leaders face fundamental questions concerning how to represent what students know and can do. Though they lack complete control of the measurement of learning, local leaders can still influence how the public perceives standardized test scores and other data that are used to inform instruction. In addition, they can promote other measures that offer a more balanced picture of student accomplishments, thereby countering potential inequities in standardized assessment systems, as in this high school.

> The school shifted its entire assessment program to focus on providing meaningful feedback to students and teachers. In addition to the annual standardized assessments, this school organized a schoolwide external examination system for student projects and portfolios. As a culminating project, students present project work or a portfolio that documents evidence of their learning to a panel of external examiners or community judges (e.g., experts in the field, members of the local school board, members of the local business, and cultural community) who then provide feedback about their work verbally and in writing. Examiners also give the student work a score, and the combination of these scores is used in determining whether students pass to the next grade or graduate. Standardized tests fall to the background of assessments driving student learning at this school (Center for Research on the Context of Teaching, 2002).

As in this example, leaders can play a critical role in guiding productive responses to testing and accountability pressures.

Should Leaders Focus on Learning or Teaching or Both?

Finally, leaders are in a good position to bring learning to the foreground, and keep it there, especially when they occupy highly visible, formal leadership roles. Leaders, like the one in the next example, can make sure that the ultimate concern is what students are taking away from instruction, even when they are focused on teaching.

The principal of an inner-city elementary school in the Midwest says relatively little to his teachers about the teaching he observes when he visits their classrooms. His focus, instead, is on evidence of student learning, and this becomes the main topic of conversation when he and the teachers debrief the visit. Otherwise, he finds that the staff tends to concentrate on certain teaching behaviors, without verifying that their actions produce learning. By shifting focus to what individuals and groups are learning, this approach helps these teachers probe students' different responses to teaching (S. Conoway, personal communication, November 3, 2001).

In cases like these, the focus on learning does not automatically preclude conversation about teaching practice or technique, but it gives these matters a context and reference point.

The Payoff of a Persistent Focus on Learning

Learning fundamentally requires leaders at both the school and district level to make improving learning a central part of their work. Leaders who demonstrate success in this area continually seek out and find ways to focus on specific aspects of student learning. These leaders model what they value by observing classrooms, engaging in professional dialogue with teachers, and critically examining student work. By recognizing the importance of professional learning to produce better outcomes for students, these leaders drive resources to support focused professional development. They maintain a stance as learners themselves and strive to make their learning public. These leaders craft visions for their organizations that put learning at the center, and continually serve to remind others that learning is the shared mission of students, teachers, administrators, and the community. Without this foundation, other nagging urgencies easily clutter the daily landscape of leadership work in education.

Carving out the time to make learning a priority, and sustaining the energy and focus over the long term are incredible challenges for leaders. Yet, in those instances where leaders have promoted a clear and present focus on learning, and are able to sustain that focus over time, evidence of positive change in learning for students, professionals, and organizations can be attained.

4

Building Professional Communities
That Value Learning

Leaders in Mr. G.'s school, like many others, have not dedicated themselves to creating a professional community that would support his improvement in mathematics teaching. Professional norms in schools like these do not promote collaboration, knowledge sharing, and collective responsibility for improving teaching and learning for students like Hector and his peers.

Instead of using this ineffective model, successful leaders build work cultures where learning opportunities and mutual accountability for improving instruction can thrive. In this chapter, we will discuss the second part of the Leading for Learning Framework, which explores how teachers and district leaders *build professional communities that value learning*. By working with teachers in various departments and interdisciplinary teams, collegial networks across schools, and other organizations in the school or district, leaders can establish professional communities that place a priority on improving teaching and learning and creating environments where teachers support each other. Consider how the principal in the next example shapes the professional community in his high school.

The principal of a high school serving a diverse and relatively low-performing student population adamantly resists watering down standards or curriculum for students. He asserts that what needs to be changed for this population is not the level of expectations, but the kind and extent of support students receive for academic performance. He consistently engages teachers in schoolwide conversations about their beliefs concerning their students' abilities, effective teaching practices, and shared responsibility for student achievement. This school has improved consistently both on the state's measures of performance and in meeting its goals for moving a significant percentage of the lowest quartile of students up to higher levels of performance (Center for Research on the Context of Teaching, 2002).

This central office in an urban district also exemplifies a work culture that focuses on instruction.

District leaders in this central office treat administrators and staff as part of the learning community in the same way that school-level teachers and leaders are encouraged to form and participate in professional communities. By using open communication and welcoming discussion, this central office perceives itself as contributing to an enterprise that is fundamentally about learning. To realize this goal, all curriculum directors, professional development staff, and other staff members involved in academic programs or student support meet on a regular basis. Every other week, this staff spends several hours together exploring the nature of good teaching practice and their own efforts to guide improvement in teaching practice. These conversations parallel the regular meeting of all school principals in the district. The participants approach these interactions as learners and try to be explicit about what they are discovering about teaching, learning, and learning improvement (Center for the Study of Teaching and Policy, 2003).

Leaders in sites such as these are engaging professional staff in the difficult job of reconsidering their work and its meaning for student learning. Although their conversations differ, the participants are taking part in a community that guides their work and supports it. As members of these communities, these leaders help to build professional communities that value learning.

Defining the Underlying Ideas and Values That Shape Professional Learning Communities

Although they work in the same buildings, educators are often remarkably alone in their efforts to educate young people. Norms of privacy, assignment policies, schools organized in age-defined grades, and a host of other forces encourage isolation rather than collaborative engagement in common work (Huberman, 1993; Little, 1990; Lortie, 1975). Counterforces, however, are increasingly encouraging joint effort as professional learning and leadership theories show the potential power of the professional community in educators' working lives (see Little, 1999; Lord, 1994; Louis & Kruse, 1995; Talbert & McLaughlin, 1994).

Professional learning communities of educators are built around the needs of students. Educators work together to create a climate that focuses on reflective practice, collegiality, and ongoing professional development. Effective professional learning communities embody a number of common characteristics including shared vision and decision making, reflective practice, ongoing planning, and conversations about curriculum and instructional improvement. Ongoing dialogue about student work, observation of others' teaching, and exploration and open practice of new pedagogical strategies are common practices in schools where learning communities thrive. Leaders play an important role in facilitating this kind of community development. Through inquiring about improving learning and regularly scheduling opportunities for reflection on practice, leaders at both the school and district level can help set the stage for effective learning communities.

Professional communities that both value and promote learning improvement are harder to develop than current rhetoric would imply (Stein, Silver, & Smith, 1998). Despite widespread calls for such "learning communities," they are not readily created through restructuring designs or mandates. Faculties can get beyond the "pseudo community" when they confront their hidden differences and work to understand and learn from each other (Grossman, Wineburg, & Woolworth, 2001).

Sustaining professional communities requires relationships that are sufficiently formed and stable over time. These types of relationships engender trust as well as shared values that grow through interaction within the learning community. Such communities also need a reason for coming together, such as a task or responsibility that requires collaboration. Leaders have many ways of nurturing these relationships, including encouraging members of the community to share values that support learning and structuring joint work for community members to tackle.

Essential Tasks for Building Professional Communities

As suggested by the examples above, the practical work of building professional community involves these essential tasks for leaders.

1. Building trusting relationships among professionals in the school or district. Leaders who value others, display empathy, and deal forthrightly with their colleagues help set a tone of mutual trust and respect in their institutions.

2. Creating structures and schedules that sustain interaction among professionals. Leaders set the stage for a professional learning community by grouping professionals in ways that encourage natural collaboration over time and by creating regular blocks of time for them to interact. Leaders are also responsible for recruiting group members who will work well and enhance the existing team.

3. Helping to frame joint work and shared responsibilities. By working with professional group members, leaders are in a good position to define tasks that imply or require joint effort within the community.

4. Modeling, guiding, and facilitating participation in professional communities that value learning. Good leaders show what it means to be part of a viable community through questioning, setting norms, sharing intellectual resources, and guiding collaborative work.

5. Promoting a focus on learning and associated core values. Leaders who actively demonstrate their own persistent, public focus on learning and show their commitment to the underlying values discussed above give direction to their professional communities. In this respect, leaders' efforts in the first area of the Learning for Leadership Framework, *establishing a focus on learning*, directly influence their actions in the second area, *building professional communities that value learning.*

What Building Professional Communities Looks Like in Schools

School leaders can build work cultures that value learning by participating in the following actions.

Creating structures for teachers to make schoolwide decisions about learning and teaching. In a good professional learning community, administrators are committed to providing opportunities for teachers to lead decision-making efforts that pertain to goal setting, staff development, curriculum and instructional materials, budgets, personnel, and implementing and monitoring improvement strategies (Quellmalz, Shields, & Knapp, 1995). For example, in one Midwestern middle school, the school reform committee, composed primarily of teachers from the school, implemented a system of professional development strands. Each specific strand incorporated instructional content or a methodology and focused on different themes such as creating classrooms that effectively use the latest brain research, differentiating the curriculum, and meeting the needs of at-risk students. Participants in each strand met with a teacher-facilitator throughout the school year or sometimes over several years to gain expertise and learn new practices (McREL, 2003).

Setting up cycles of schoolwide inquiry into learning and teaching performance and participating in professional inquiry as a colleague. In one southern California elementary school with a track record of improving student achievement, inquiry cycles took multiple forms, including

• *Whole school assessment of learning outcomes.* All teachers and the principal participated in developing performance benchmarks; creating, administering, and scoring assessments; and examining results.

• *Small group action research projects.* Grade-level teams developed focused research questions quasi-independently from other groups, took their own unique approaches to pursuing those questions through mini-experiments and reflective processes, then reported back to colleagues.

• *Individual reflection with small group support.* Teachers voluntarily met twice a month in support groups for critical reflection on their own practices, with an emphasis on exploring the values and beliefs that supported them (Stokes, 2001).

Encouraging engaging in and sustaining conversation among staff about their assumptions concerning norms, values, and beliefs about student learning. In a suburban school in the Northwest, a staff survey that focused on eliciting teachers' beliefs about student learning revealed that teachers believed that others outside the classroom were mostly responsible for helping students with special learning needs. The principal began leading conversations with staff about these beliefs. From these conversations, the principal and her staff started reframing the problem of "fixing" students with special needs and instead, they worked to deepen teachers' awareness and sense of urgency about the need to improve instructional practices in light of changing student needs. As a result, teachers developed a collective sense of how their assumptions may limit student learning, and they worked in new ways to hold each other accountable to help all students achieve high standards (UWCEL, 2004).

Recruiting teachers whose values are consistent with the culture that leaders seek to develop. In one example, a principal was in charge of a newly created preK–8 school located in an urban center. The school was designed to attract a diverse student body and establish a clear commitment to an equity agenda. The principal developed questions to use for interviewing prospective teachers that were designed to specifically elicit their values related to social justice and equity. The leader of this school recognized and seized an opportunity to influence the character and capacities of the school staff, and ultimately the kind of community that could form (G. Tubbs, personal communication, May 2004).

Creating opportunities for staff to engage in structured, joint reflection on issues related to teaching and learning. At one middle school, the leadership team, comprising administrators and teacher leaders, introduced structured reflective practices at faculty meetings. Team members introduced a dialogue tool used by teams of teachers to reflect on their practice. Then, they led conversations about student work and analyzed case studies written by teachers via their own action research. By recognizing the staff's need to assess what they were doing and discovering some of their own innovations, the team redefined the inquiry process as a legitimate path to full faculty participation (Lambert, 1998).

What Building Professional Communities Looks Like in School Districts

At the district level, administrators and staff can act in similar ways to build a professional community among staff within the central office, across schools, and in the broader community of educational stakeholders. Specifically, they can take the following actions.

Support assignments and scheduling that enable district staff to work together or allow individuals from different schools to interact. To illustrate, a growing number of school districts across the country have implemented "early release days" or "late arrival days" as a regular part of the school calendar. During these time frames, students are not present for part of the regular school day and the time is reserved for ongoing professional development focused on school-specific and districtwide learning goals. These scheduling changes, however, are not executed without controversy. In some cases, district leaders face scrutiny and criticism from parents who must make alternate arrangements for their children during professional development times.

Work with the teachers' union to establish provisions that support developing a professional community focused on improving learning. A strong partnership between the superintendent and the leadership of a teacher's union for a large, East Coast, urban district led to a systemwide professional development focus on literacy and research-based practice. This district, which was typically one of the state's poorest performing systems, significantly raised student achievement scores after only one year as a result of this partnership. In January 2000, that state announced that students in the district made double-digit gains in nearly every category on the state test. In fact, test scores improved more in the prior year than in the prior four years combined (American Federation of Teachers, 2000).

Focus district work to strengthen teacher development. Some district leadership initiatives begin the day a new teacher enters the system. For example, a primary expectation for new teachers in one medium-sized district was to become familiar with state and district curriculum frameworks. Much of the teachers' professional development time was devoted to understanding and using these frameworks. One new teacher in this district stated that her engagement in these efforts helped her develop a clear understanding of the district frameworks, and she incorporated this understanding into her joint work with her colleagues and in her classroom curriculum (Grossman, Thompson, & Valencia, 2002).

Reorganize and reconstruct the district as a set of nested learning communities. Districts involved with the University of Pittsburgh's Institute for Learning receive intensive support and assistance to reorganize their districts as nested learning communities (i.e., organizations where all individuals and units are expected to upgrade their capacities continuously in accord with a shared set of instructional principles and strategies). In this design, instructional leadership, coupled with reciprocal accountability between school leaders and district leaders, provides professional learning opportunities specifically geared to the district's vision of instruction (Resnick & Glennan, 2002).

Focus district administrator meetings on a learning agenda. In one mid-sized, urban California school district, districtwide administrator meetings are now held at school sites with a specific focus on enhancing administrators' professional growth and linking it to the district's learning agenda. Office business at these gatherings is limited and set aside for other district management team meetings. During the meeting, principals and district-level administrators visit classrooms together. As they visit the classrooms, the leaders use their prior training on teacher evaluation and conducting effective, quick observations of classroom teachers based on the California Standards for the Teaching Profession. After the observations, they share reflections on what they learned. Significant academic achievement gains have been made at both the district and individual school-site levels as reflected by state and local assessment measures (Lairon & Vidales, 2003).

Processes and Challenges for Building Professional Communities That Value Learning

Building a professional culture that values learning will not happen overnight or by decree, especially in settings with low morale or high stress. In the pursuit of creating a professional community, leaders confront a series of issues including unmet "basic" professional needs, resistance to forming professional communities, the presence of closed as well as open communities, and the challenge of responding appropriately to poor practice (Payne & Kaba, 2001).

How Well Are Basic Professional Needs Met?

Creating a collaborative and learning-focused work culture presumes that there is a basic level of physical safety and order and a modicum of mutual respect and interaction among staff. Leaders may need to start with these fundamentals en route to a more fully developed community. This entry from a new principal at an urban elementary school tells a familiar story.

> The new principal found a school that was chaotic and disorganized. A sense of constant turmoil pervaded the setting. Fights in the hallways were common. Teachers hoarded scarce supplies, projected a general sense of suspicion, and communicated very little with each other or with parents. The principal knew that nothing good would happen without establishing a sense of order and safety while, at the same time, acknowledging and valuing the hard work that many teachers were doing. She began with immediate and regular communication with staff about the school, their work, and her commitments. Early in this process, she overheard one teacher say, "This is a breath of fresh air that someone recognizes the work that we do." She established and enforced a discipline policy, showed a persistent presence in the hallways and in classrooms, initiated outreach to parents, and made personal contact with students (she knew all 300 students by name and many of their family members as well). Within a year, the stage was set for the staff to dig deeper into the quality of their teaching and student performance (Dana Center, 1999).

When building a community the work does not stop once basic needs are met. No matter how good staff members feel about their working situation, a professional community may contribute little to learning improvement if it is not connected to an agenda for student, professional, and system learning.

Where Is the Resistance Coming From?

Resistance among professional staff to community building efforts is likely to be strong in some settings. For example, prevailing norms may perpetuate teachers working in isolation from one another. The working environment may be fraught with high stress, low morale, high staff turnover, or general resistance to change. Internal power struggles, specialization of staff, and inflexible procedures may challenge efforts to build community. A general lack of understanding or experience with the concept of a learning community may also cause resistance. Leaders are put in the position of diagnosing the sources of resistance, opening lines of communication, motivating participation, and providing a workable vision of collaborative effort. To move from a "community" to a "learning community" takes hard work, trust, and often specific teaching and modeling.

Should Communities Be Open or Closed?

Although the goal is to create strong professional communities, everyone is not open to new ideas, beliefs, or even new members, as research on communities of practice has shown (see, Gallucci, 2002; McLaughlin & Talbert, 2001; Westheimer, 1998). The following community of practice in one urban elementary school helped to insulate this 1st grade teacher from new ideas about teaching young people from low-income families to read.

> The teacher's immediate community of practice was a group of 1st grade teachers who had worked together for a long time. They saw eye to eye on many things and reinforced each other's

thinking about their work. They were generally suspicious of "new educational terms and buzz words, or whatever you want to call them," and took a dim view of the state's and district's efforts to reform their teaching of literacy. Teachers in this community of practice believed that they knew what the children needed. As they saw it, these "South End kids" just weren't up to a demanding curriculum; they needed "the basics." The teachers' mutually reinforcing philosophy acted as a buffer to the district's attempts to advance the level of practice, and in effect limited their ability and willingness to reconsider the effectiveness of their literacy teaching (Gallucci, 2002).

This kind of professional community poses a leadership challenge. The ultimate goal is for teachers to work together to build new knowledge for themselves to improve practice. Reassigning staff to break apart tight, insular groupings may be a necessary step toward that goal. Leaders also need to establish a desirable vision of good practice and help their staff assemble evidence to reach their goals.

How Can Leaders Confront Poor Practice?

In order for professional communities to be a vehicle for improving learning, their members need to be able to scrutinize each others' practice and offer helpful critique. To accomplish this, leaders need solid relationships with their colleagues and an environment that supports honest, critical exchanges about practice. Strong relationships, when created in a viable professional community, can foster professional improvement, as in the case of this assistant superintendent in an urban district.

In order for the assistant superintendent to tell principals the "hard stuff" and for them to hear it, she felt it was important to develop a relationship with them. Through a series of interactions, the assistant superintendent communicated respect, care, willingness to listen, and conveyed the message that "it's all about the work." This permitted her to push individuals to higher levels of performance. During several visits to a particular school, the assistant superintendent continually heard the principal misla-bel the components of balanced literacy (e.g., calling round-robin reading a guided reading lesson). The assistant superintendent decided it was time to push. She knew the principal wanted to please her and was working hard, so the assistant superinten-dent combined her critique with positive support. One day over coffee, she said to the principal, "You're fooling yourself. You don't understand this stuff. Let's solve this together because we are not doing our jobs and the kids are being cheated." The prin-cipal was devastated, but she took the role of the learner and she changed her leadership practice (Center for the Study of Teach-ing and Policy, 2003).

When district leaders have healthy relationships with the members of their professional community, they not only help them confront poor practice, but these leaders also help their staff members visu-alize good practice and build the knowledge base that supports it. With solid professional relationships, leaders can find ways to provoke or stretch the thinking of the community by introducing promising ideas, assembling evidence of what works, and inspiring collaborative effort to solve problems of practice.

Breaking Isolation to Build Professional Communities

If schools and school systems seek to improve learning in systemic ways, this type of learning will not develop when teachers and leaders are isolated from one another. Clearly, isolation and lack of professional growth provide the breeding ground for cynicism and contempt for change. The key for leaders is to overcome the inherent challenges of gathering professionals to work together in an ongoing and meaningful way. As the examples in this chapter have shown, there is power in creating and developing a profes-sional community for educators that values learning for teachers, their students, and the organization as a whole.

5

Engaging External Environments
That Matter for Learning

Leaders in Mr. G.'s school and district share the same view that he and many of his colleagues hold—learning for Hector is constrained by his family and community. Although they would like to help him, few leaders or teachers have sought to understand or work with his community. The administrators focus more on responding to state and federal policies and they have yet to connect those policies with improving Hector's learning.

As leaders look inward to develop their professional communities, they also need to *interact with the local community and other external environments in ways that define and create opportunities for learning improvement.* In this chapter, we will consider the third area of the Leading for Learning Framework, which delves into how leaders build relationships and secure resources from groups outside the school or district to foster students' and teachers' learning. In addition to helping leaders improve these kinds of relationships, this chapter also shows leaders how to be on the lookout for challenges such as external pressures, demands, crises, or other events that may preempt or constrain attempts to advance a learning improvement agenda (Hess, 1999; Hill, Campbell, &

Harvey, 2000). Engagement can take subtle forms as educators come to understand the communities where they work. The next example, an urban elementary school that serves a linguistically diverse population, illustrates how schools can begin to engage their communities.

> Over three years, two principals and a cadre of teacher leaders worked intensively to develop support for having critical conversations about how race, class, and language influenced their teaching. While the teachers rallied for support, they also reached out aggressively to families in the community through home visits, educational activities for parents, and other efforts. Building consensus in the school was a considerable struggle as the school staff faced conflicts with each other and their preconceptions about the community they were serving. Initially, it was very difficult for participants to connect critical conversation with dialogue about their instructional practice. Ultimately, as the staff worked together to engage the community in school life, they began to understand how the children's origins from a disenfranchised, linguistically diverse community impacted their teaching practices (Markholt, 2002).

Engaging communities and external environments can also be more overt and wide ranging, as in the example from this district.

> One district's emphasis on narrowing the achievement gap resulted in marshalling resources from all sectors of the community for their learning acceleration program. Initially, the district's program offered additional instruction before and after school for students in grades 3 through 8. In its second year, the program expanded to 1st and 2nd grade students before finally moving into the high school. Volunteers were trained to be literacy coaches and to start tutorial programs. The program also had computer labs in churches and businesses and volunteers provided clothing for students in need. District leaders are now seeking support from the business and faith communities so that students can receive help in other areas (Center for the Study of Teaching and Policy, 2003).

The superintendent and other leaders in this district are proactively seeking connections with local communities. They recognize that the success of their learning improvement agenda may depend on how well they establish and manage these contacts.

Engaging external environments implies that teachers and leaders develop relationships in ways similar to how they would build a professional community. This work is simultaneously personal and political. The work becomes personal when leaders need to cultivate durable human connections with colleagues, potential allies, and others; and political when leaders need to mobilize allies in support of a learning agenda and create coalitions of diverse interests, often in the face of significant conflict.

Defining the Underlying Ideas and Values for Engaging External Environments

Teaching and learning happens in multiple contexts or environments that are embedded in one another (Talbert & McLaughlin, 1993). Because these contexts influence the interaction of learners, teachers, and content, they become a special concern for leaders, especially those in positions of authority within their respective schools and districts. Consequently, learning-focused leaders seek to understand and use these environments, and when necessary, protect or buffer teaching and learning from negative environmental influences. Three kinds of external environments play important roles in enabling or constraining effective teaching and learning:

• **Family and community environments.** This environment embraces the interests, demands, and resources of parents, advocacy groups, human service agencies, municipal bodies, media, corporate interests, and taxpayers. The district's school board can be a bridge to these interests and represent them within the school community.

• **Professional environments.** This environment includes the resources and constraints posed by unions, professional networks and associations, higher education institutions, and the local educator labor market.

• **Larger policy environments.** This environment embodies state reform policies and federal programs and its related regulations, policies, and requirements. (From the school's point of view, the district is part of the larger policy environment.)

These environments look very different when viewed from the vantage point of the school and district, as shown in Figure 5.1 and Figure 5.2.

External environments are a source of both constraints and resources (Fullan, 1993). The constraints are likely to preoccupy educators' attention in the form of unwelcome demands "from above," financial crises, political maneuvering, and other outside events that impact districts and schools. But, environments also offer many resources that include more than funding, including intellectual resources (e.g., university faculty or professional networks), human resources (e.g., volunteers), political resources (e.g., allies on the city council), and social or cultural resources (e.g., the cultural makeup of the community). Organizations like public schools are completely dependent on their environments for resources such as these and, indeed, for their identity and legitimacy as public institutions (Meyer, 1978). The ability to produce learning improvement agendas is intimately linked to the environments where learning takes place.

Essential Tasks for Engaging External Environments

To engage external environments that matter for learning, leaders must take the following actions.

1. **Make efforts to understand community, professional, and policy environments.** Through continual environmental scanning,

Figure 5.1

School's-Eye View of External Environments That Matter for Learning

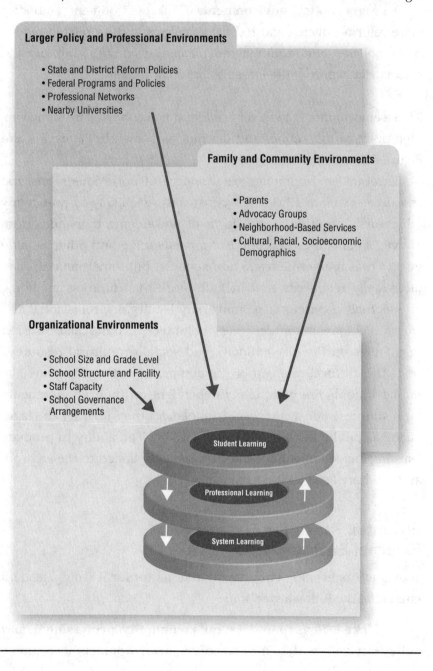

Figure 5.2

District-Eye View of External Environments That Matter for Learning

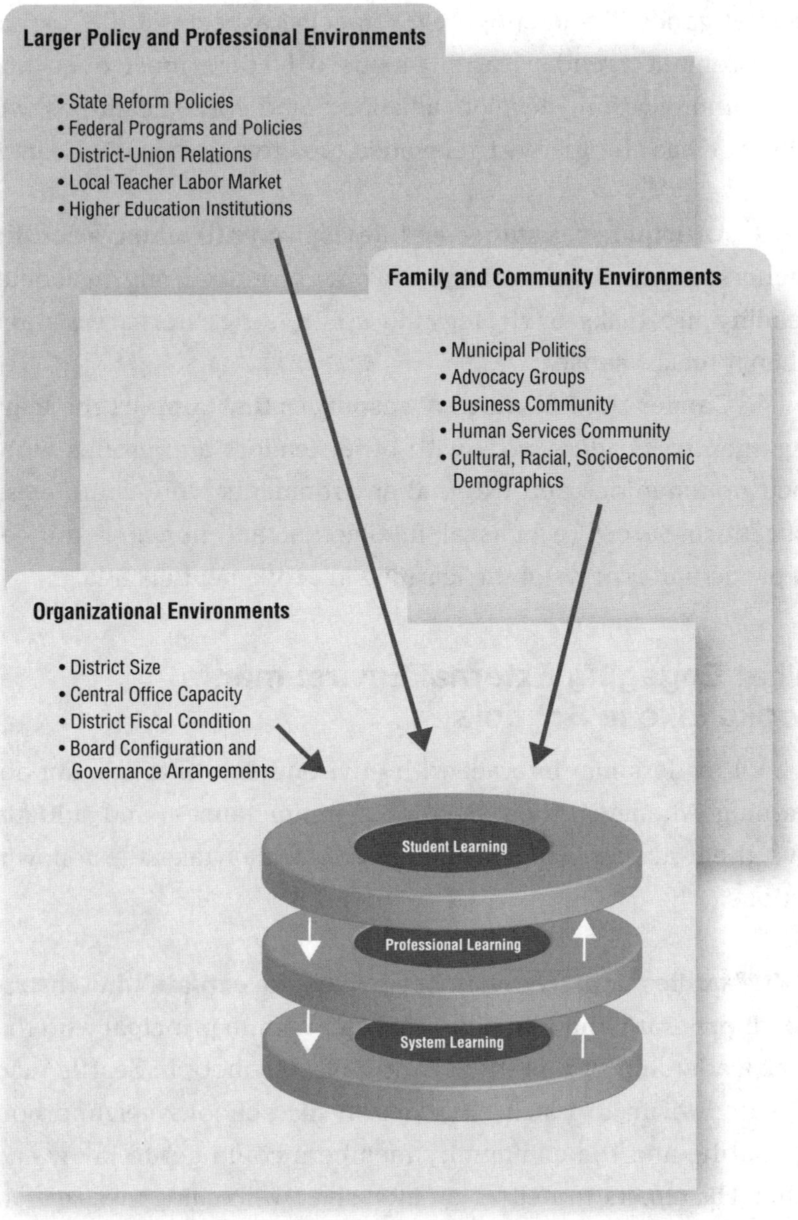

Larger Policy and Professional Environments

- State Reform Policies
- Federal Programs and Policies
- District-Union Relations
- Local Teacher Labor Market
- Higher Education Institutions

Family and Community Environments

- Municipal Politics
- Advocacy Groups
- Business Community
- Human Services Community
- Cultural, Racial, Socioeconomic Demographics

Organizational Environments

- District Size
- Central Office Capacity
- District Fiscal Condition
- Board Configuration and Governance Arrangements

Student Learning

Professional Learning

System Learning

leaders make it their business to figure out which elements of their environments matter the most for learning and teaching.

2. **Build relationships with individuals and groups.** To foster general goodwill and support for specific aspects of the learning improvement agenda, learning-focused leaders must open lines of communication, develop alliances, and form coalitions with whoever has the greatest relevance, positive or negative, for the initiative.

3. **Anticipate resistance and devise ways to manage conflict.** Leaders engage in the political work of neutralizing resistance, heading off attacks, or strategically confronting external resistance when it makes sense.

4. **Garner the full range of resources that support the learning agenda.** Leaders work with other leaders and groups within their communities and external environments who can offer significant resources (e.g., fiscal, intellectual, and human resources) to particular aspects of the learning improvement agenda.

What Engaging External Environments Looks Like in Schools

School leaders can interact with environments that can support learning whenever their position, circumstances, and initiative give them access. For example, leaders may take the following actions.

Visit families and community groups to explain the instructional program and learning agenda. A white principal who took over leadership of a predominantly black school in Seattle made repeated visits to black churches in his school's neighborhood so that he and the community members could get to know each other. His efforts to deliver an inclusive, welcoming message and to articulate his hopes for what the school could achieve were successful. Because of his outreach, there was a tremendous increase in parent and community involvement in the school and a sense of neighborhood ownership for the school and its children that had not been seen before (J. Morefield, personal communication, 2003).

Establish educational opportunities for parents and community members that complement the learning focus for students. The principal of a northern California charter school, located on the edge of a neighborhood populated mainly by Mexican immigrants, faced the challenge of educating many non-English speakers new to the country. The principal and her leadership team, who were frustrated with flat student achievement scores despite concerted efforts inside the school to improve teacher capacity, enlisted the help of a neighborhood community center. The center was affiliated with a local feeder high school and the staff agreed to offer adult literacy classes for the school's parents in the evenings. Through this strategy to build English literacy among parents in the community, the school added another dimension of support for students as they learned the English language (N. Woodard, personal communication, 2000).

Develop allies in the central office and proactively seek support for student and professional learning goals. The principal of an elementary school that served a diverse population of students in a western suburb of a large urban center successfully elicited the support of the school district for a series of early release days. These days enabled the school's staff to focus collectively on improving literacy instruction. District officials, including the superintendent and board, supported the principal's request publicly when a small element of the parent community came before the school board to challenge a series of early release days (A. Byrd, personal communication, 2000).

Form partnerships with traditionally underrepresented neighborhood groups to focus on improving learning. A principal in the Rio Grande Valley of Texas served a community who lived primarily in *colonias* (i.e., small parcels of land sold to new immigrants, often with no water, sewer, or electrical facilities). Many of the parents who lived in the colonias did not come to any school meetings. The principal's response, rather than to say that these parents didn't care, was to walk door to door in the colonias and meet and talk directly with the parents. He wanted the parents to see that he was someone who cared and respected them, and someone who wanted and needed their involvement with him in their children's education. Next, he established meetings for the parents in the colonias by getting some families to host the meetings in their yards. After he used this strategy for some time, the same parents began coming to meetings at the school and became strong advocates for him and his work to educate their children (Scheurich & Skrla, 2003).

What Engaging External Environments Looks Like in School Districts

Given their wide exposure to external environments, district administrators and staff may be in a good position to engage potential friends or critics. For example, they may take part in the following actions.

Educate school board members in building an improvement agenda and engage them as part of a district learning community. After approving a plan for a new curriculum adoption, board members in one small city district accepted an invitation from district leaders to join teachers and administrators in key professional development activities designed to aid in implementing new curriculum. As a result, board members felt they gained greater understanding of the curriculum and how it would improve student learning. The experience also increased the board members' confidence in their decision to adopt the agenda (Center for Educational Leadership, 2003).

Promote the learning agenda through direct, ongoing contact with parents and community members. One superintendent, new to a large, troubled urban district, entered the role with a clear theory of action for improving learning for students and teachers. Among the eight strategies she developed to address the learning agenda was a community outreach effort that included an ongoing series of living room chats. The meetings were held in the homes of parents in every one of the city's numerous neighborhoods. Rather than talk at those who attended, the superintendent used the chats primarily as an opportunity to listen to the hopes and concerns expressed by parents and community members about their children's schools. At the same time, the superintendent invited a group of high-profile CEOs from the city's business community to form a CEO Cabinet that met with her frequently to discuss progress in the district. Over time, the cabinet proved to be influential in securing resources and community support for the superintendent's agenda. The leader's high visibility in the community during her first few years in her role produced much positive public enthusiasm for the schools and substantial concrete support for the school district by parents and the business community. Student achievement trends in the district have shown steady gains over the past five years (Hall, 2003).

Form partnerships with civic, business, or professional bodies that focus on learning improvement agendas. One large, Northeastern, urban school district strategically attracted private sector investments that were focused on the superintendent's overall program for standards-based reform. Although the funds were less oriented toward narrow, special interest corporate projects than had previously been the norm, the superintendent's initiative resulted in 10 million dollars in additional private funding that anchored the school system's new teaching and learning programs (Usdan & Cuban, 2003).

Strategically use external requirements and resources to advance an instructional agenda. One study about reforming districts suggests that a strong instructional focus enables districts to maintain a coherent reform agenda in the face of numerous state initiatives and high-stakes accountability measures. For example, despite state-required standardized testing, leaders in one of the districts continued to rely heavily on locally developed assessments that they believed were essential for understanding and meeting student learning needs (McLaughlin & Talbert, 2002).

Processes and Challenges for Engaging External Environments

Building positive relationships with external groups and responding effectively to outside pressures and conditions compounds the work of school and district leaders. Given all that must be attended to inside their respective organizations, it is hard to know where and how much energy to invest externally. Developing these relationships, or even responding appropriately to outside pressures and conditions, requires understanding the surrounding cultural and political environments.

Should Leaders Be Reactive or Proactive?

A proactive approach to external environments, though initially time consuming, is the best way to avoid responding to external events reactively later on. The following district's case illustrates this point.

A new superintendent set out to build support for his troubled urban school district by assuming the role of "marketeer" (i.e., convincing the community that great things were happening in their public schools). Initially, he held community meetings to hear what the public perceived as good and what needed to be improved in the schools. Then, to appeal to the business community, he and his staff created a business plan focused on specific, achievable measures, which he talked through with anyone who would listen. He approached the media and marketed the schools through television, radio newspapers, and speeches. The free coverage continued in news articles, billboards, and daily faxes to local businesses. The superintendent noted, "I knew we were beginning to have the 'saturation' effect we wanted when taxi drivers, waitresses, parking attendants, and business executives began stopping me to say how excited they are about what our school system is doing for children." In due time, the public schools' nonprofit fundraising arm was able to generate large sums of money, help from volunteers, and goodwill to support the public school. Without this superintendent's efforts, these resources would have remained untapped (Stanford, 1999).

This superintendent's success in developing a commitment to public education is notable. Far too often, municipal politics, hostile unions, economic crises in the community, or organized opposition to reform can overwhelm leaders' best efforts. Had this superintendent not seized the initiative, he would likely have had to spend an equal or greater time reacting to external pressures.

Should Leaders Reach Out or Draw In?

Often characterized as outreach, engagement with external environments can be a two-way process that brings external participants, resources, and ideas into the schools, and also acknowledges and works within the current teaching and learning environment. Drawing in participants and resources can substantially alter the character of schools, as in this example.

An elementary principal garnered support from the ESL coordinator at the district office and from local social service agencies to develop a family learning center at the school. This learning support center, which is open daily, has several computers and is staffed by a home/school coordinator. Families use the facility for parent education, tutoring and homework assistance for their children, and accessing information about health and other issues. In response to a relatively large immigrant population, the center also conducts ESL classes for parents at night, plus there are bilingual tutors who help them address language-related learning issues (Center for the Study of Teaching and Policy, 2003).

Programmatic responses to community conditions like these has substantially changed the way this school relates to the community it serves. These changes rested on a clear understanding of the makeup and resources of the community, as well as a commitment to bringing these concerns into an expanded picture of the school community.

How Can Leaders Survive in Turbulent Environments?

In schools or districts that face turbulent environments, external relationships can be a matter of survival for school or district leaders. In districts where the school boards are elected, the tension between superintendents and the school board can be intense (Carter & Cunningham, 1997). District leaders who manage to work with boards productively are able to define their respective roles appropriately (e.g., minimizing the board's role in micromanaging the daily work of the district) and focus attention on a common learning improvement agenda. In one such instance, the urban district and board found common cause in addressing a pattern of unacceptably low performance.

> In one city district, data about low graduation rates and student performance prompted the board and other community groups to demand action. State and local testing revealed that less than half of all students had met the state standards. The chamber of commerce, in particular, was adamant that it could not endorse another tax levy if the district was performing this poorly. District leaders immediately began building a partnership with the chamber and a local community foundation. Initially, their collaboration resulted in a set of performance indicators that could be used to specifically define what students and schools should be accomplishing and to establish a clear basis for accountability. This step began a process of rebuilding trust

in the schools and a base of local support for levy proposals (Learning First Alliance, 2003).

This example shows one form of external pressure on districts and schools that provided the impetus for reform. Frequently, external groups oppose or resist leaders' attempts to advance a learning improvement agenda. Parents who believe the agendas ignore their children's needs or disagree with the improvement focus may balk. Teacher unions may see the improvement strategies as a threat to the teachers' contract or their power base. Community members may also resist if they believe that the attempts to improve learning undermine their interests or values. In the next example, district and school leaders needed to take strong action to head off a challenge to upgrading mathematics instruction in one of their high schools.

> The math department of a local high school sought to pilot a new curriculum. Although the pilot was more closely aligned to the demanding state standards, the new curriculum faced opposition from the community, especially from parents whose children had been through a difficult period in elementary school when their teachers had struggled with a newly adopted nontraditional math curriculum. The process was further compounded when teachers in the department struggled to master the new curriculum, which was a big departure from their familiar approach to math teaching. Both school and district leaders got into the act and extended the pilot to two years which was an unusual move in this district. Issues that were specifically individual concerns (e.g., between a teacher and a particular student) were contained at that level, rather than becoming the pretexts for a sweeping rejection of the new curriculum. In addition, leaders sought to repeatedly explain to parents the nature of the new program, the rationale for adopting it, and the relationship of the program to the district's goal of closing the achievement gap (Jones, 2002).

Leading for learning means searching for ways to make a learning agenda "good politics." Today's critics can become tomorrow's allies in furthering an improvement plan. School and district leaders' best hope for neutralizing resistance or turning it into support is to proactively engage relevant external groups.

Connecting Learning Agendas and School Environments

Schools and school districts are important elements of a larger social, political, and civic landscape. Engaging various constituencies and partners in external environments is key for those learning-focused leaders seeking to create positive change. Just as individual teachers must band together to accomplish significant change inside schools, those who lead schools and districts are more likely to make progress when they work in cooperation with various external support providers, community and parent groups, civic organizations, state governments, professional organizations, and members of the business community. Through these efforts, leaders stand to gain chances to harness resources, opportunities to influence policies, possibilities to expand the school's or school district's capacity, and general support for the learning agenda.

6

Acting Strategically and Sharing Leadership

In Mr. G.'s district, administrators manage district programs and functions without recognizing the relationships between them and without an overall learning agenda to guide them. School administrators are largely consumed with daily demands and the crisis of the moment. Consequently, administrators at both the school and district levels have been unable to develop a strategy for creating a learning-improvement plan.

The leadership actions discussed so far (*establishing a learning focus, building professional communities, and engaging external environments*) still beg the question of the fourth area of the Leading for Learning Framework: How can leaders act strategically and share leadership to exert specific influences on the interaction of teachers, learners, and content? The approach taken in this school offers an image of how this might be done.

> The faculty and principal at one school, aided by a small comprehensive school reform grant, created a comprehensive plan that combined multiple interventions to improve mathematics and literacy learning in the school. Each intervention was examined by a separate faculty task/study group and each group took on different facets of a collective task. The first group came up

with ways to reach out to the community while the second group reviewed the rigor and relevance of the curriculum and tried to correlate it to a set of best practices. A third group worked on homework issues and created a schoolwide homework policy, while the fourth group considered how to maximize planning time for teachers that emphasized classroom visitations and collaborative work on curriculum. Finally, the fifth group looked more specifically at how the math and language arts curriculum could be better aligned with state and district standards. These activities, facilitated by both the principal and teacher leaders, were used to develop a strategic plan (Center for the Study of Teaching & Policy, 2003).

Although this is only one effort toward learning improvement, leaders at this school are addressing their learning goals by mobilizing their efforts along multiple pathways that lead directly to student, professional, or system learning. Improving learning is a complex task, and it is more likely to happen when multiple leaders take strategic action and work together with the same goals in mind.

Defining the Underlying Ideas for Acting Strategically and Sharing Leadership

Leading for learning involves devising courses of action that use support activities, management structures, new or existing policies, and leadership resources to create improved learning opportunities for students, teachers, and the system (see, for example, Berends, Bodilly, & Kirby, 2002; Clune, 1998; Institute for Educational Leadership, 2001; Murphy, 2004). The essential ideas are that these leadership actions are strategic and distributed, and that they utilize multiple pathways to influence learning.

To be strategic, first, leaders must align their actions with the focus on learning that they have established. Second, their actions must be sensitive to the local context and responsive to the most critical learning issues that arise at the site during the particular time period. Third, they should explore opportunities for change in the settings that have maximum leverage over the situation. Thus, in a district with high turnover among teachers, actions aimed at new teacher support (e.g., induction programs and mentoring) might be an especially strategic opportunity for leadership.

Strategic action by this definition naturally implies sharing leadership among different kinds of staff. One thing that makes opportunities ready for action is the presence of individuals who can or are willing to take on leadership responsibility. Leadership is thus distributed when leaders operating from different vantage points in the system, some in formal positions of authority and some not, address related aspects of a commonly held learning-improvement agenda (Elmore, 2000; Spillane, Halverson, & Diamond, 2001). The concept implies more than delegation; rather, it connotes sharing of values and an integration of effort in pursuit of school or district goals.

Acting strategically must begin with getting clear about the problem that needs to be solved. Without a clear understanding of the learning problem or focus, any strategy or action taken to address the issue is just a shot in the dark. When leaders are clear about a specific problem, then different avenues for exerting influence on the problem can be identified.

An extended example from a middle school illustrates the essential underlying ideas for acting strategically and sharing leadership. This school leader's inquiry into the performance of struggling English language learners at her middle school was the starting point.

> Through an examination of her school's standardized assessment data, it was readily apparent to principal Corrine DeRosa that the English language learners (ELL) at Isaacson Middle School were experiencing a more difficult road to achieving academic excellence than the typical IMS student. Overall, 63 percent of Isaacson 8th graders met the standard on key subtests of the state learning assessment; however, only 21 percent of the school's growing ELL population met the standard. But exactly what was contributing to their struggles? DeRosa began reading about various programmatic approaches to ELL instruction, and

she discovered that the model in place at the school, primarily a daily pullout program that removed ELL students from their regular classroom for a period of time each week, was among the least effective of six ELL models typically used at the middle school level.

Going a little deeper, the principal found that aspects of the regular education program, in particular how regular education teachers were assessing the progress of ELL students, may also have been contributing to their difficulties. After leaving their pullout ELL classes, the rest of the ELL student's day was spent immersed in regular education classes. However, the school's staff was using an alternative assessment system to grade the ELL students. Many regular education teachers were essentially passing ELL students along without ensuring that they were learning the curriculum. What DeRosa realized was that, for many of the regular education teachers, working with ELL students was a phenomenon for which they had not been prepared either in their teacher education programs or through school or district professional development.

DeRosa also discovered that ELL students were facing significant challenges in their social interactions with other students, and they were not participating in extracurricular activities at the same rates as other students. In her observations, she noticed many ELL students tended to find other students who knew their own language and were virtually isolated from the general student population. There also was a variety of incidents of bullying and harassment at the school that were directed both from the general population toward ELL students and vice versa (DeRosa, 2004).

The principal in this example recognized that the issues facing her ELL learners were multifaceted and required strategic, distributed activity to address all the areas that needed improvement. Working with her staff, she developed a set of goals focused on improving learning for the school's ELL students. The first goal addressed detected deficits in the overall service delivery model.

Working with district support staff, DeRosa and her ELL teacher researched different approaches to delivering ELL instruction. Budget constraints were considered, along with various approaches that had well-supported success in other schools and districts. Ultimately, the district decided to adopt an ESL model that offered an increase in the maximum amount of services for students within the budget constraints they faced. The new model was designed to provide ELL students with focused English language development concurrent with the regular curriculum in English. The approach had been shown to work well in a multilingual environment, which was an additional concern for Isaacson staff members. DeRosa, in concert with district leaders, also made a personnel decision to maximize the use of the school's ESL teacher by pulling him out of his district coordinator duties and using him in the classroom to deliver services to students full time (DeRosa, 2004).

Revising the ELL program was one key strand of activity that involved leadership from a number of participants (see Figure 6.1). The principal worked from her position in the school system to leverage resources and to get staff members focused on finding a new approach to serving a targeted special needs population. District leaders supported the work by enabling a key personnel change; and DeRosa, the ELL teacher, and the district staff read, discussed, and, ultimately decided on an approach to ELL instruction that would better serve students' needs.

However, redesigning the program for the school's ELL students was only the first step. A second set of goals focused on supporting ELL students in their regular education classes as well as beefing up staff development for regular education teachers working with ELL students.

DeRosa believed that giving her teachers better ways to reach all students within the regular classroom would improve how they served the school's ELL students, as well as other students who were not reached through typical teaching methods. To help her teachers reach this goal, DeRosa arranged for a number of teachers to begin a series of professional development courses focused on differentiated instruction. The school's ELL teacher also began offering professional development designed to help

regular education staff members learn techniques and strategies
for working more effectively with ELL students.

Figure 6.1

Illustration of a Leadership Pathway

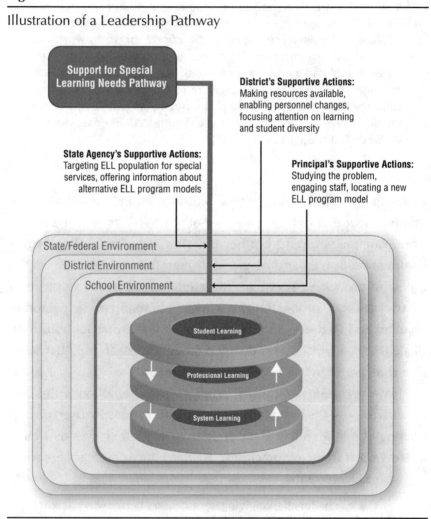

In addition to promoting new teacher learning, DeRosa also
worked with staff members to develop additional classroom supports for ELL students. These supports included training and
using peer mentors, after-school homework help, additional
reading time built into the school's master schedule, and targeted math support for 7th grade students who had not met the
4th grade math standard. The principal also used her influence

as school administrator directly with several Hispanic families whose children exhibited chronic poor attendance to help them understand the importance of being at school every day (DeRosa, 2004).

The strategic work by the principal and her colleagues to support the special learning needs of the school's ELL students now becomes evident. In addition to redesigning the program, the original problem DeRosa identified, improving learning for ELL students in general education classrooms, is also addressed through a new focus on teachers' professional learning and through additional instructional supports for struggling learners. Various educators across the system, from central office leaders to regular education teachers, are sharing leadership along what we call the Support for Special Learning Needs Pathway. At the same time, the principal is working toward creating a friendlier, more welcoming environment for ELL students at the school by providing opportunities for social interactions with the rest of the student body.

> Given the problems she had observed with bullying and harassment, Principal DeRosa believed that improving the overall environment at the school would help all students perform better. A concerted effort was undertaken to stop bullying at the middle school and to help all students learn to celebrate differences. In addition, DeRosa worked with the associated student body (ASB) advisor to find ways to ensure that ELL students had the opportunity to be included in school leadership classes and in the school's student government (DeRosa, 2004).

Strategic, distributed action is most likely to influence learning when it stimulates and supports activities that have a direct, intrinsic relationship with learning and teaching. For example, in the case above, the strategic work to identify the needs of ELL students cut across several levels in the system and involved leadership by multiple participants. Yet, all the work focused clearly on the original problem of improving learning for Isaacson's ELL students. We refer to this full stream of activities as a pathway to learning.

There are many such pathways, as illustrated in Figure 6.2, and they do not exhaust the routes that might be identified. All pathways converge on student, professional, and system learning. Some pathways target content and assessment, others target support for learners, and still others target professionals and their practice. Another set of pathways may influence learning more indirectly by focusing on the workplace or system as a whole. Pathways exist, whether or not leaders choose to act along them, and each one offers potential avenues for leaders at various levels of the system to influence teaching and learning. The act of learning-focused leadership is to select and act on those pathways with the greatest leverage over learning. (For more detailed information on the pathways, please see the Appendix.)

Essential Tasks for Acting Strategically and Sharing Leadership

Acting strategically and sharing leadership includes the following four tasks.

1. Identifying or creating pathways that have the greatest influence. Leaders search among possible sets of pathways that have a high potential to influence interactions between students, teachers, and content in a particular setting at a specific time.

2. Mobilizing effort along more than one pathway. Along selected pathways, leaders allocate resources, motivate participation, guide activity, and otherwise make things happen.

3. Helping others assume and exercise leadership. Leaders find and support individuals in various positions at both the school and district levels who have the potential to guide, direct, and support others' learning.

Figure 6.2

A Range of Pathways to Student, Professional, and System Learning

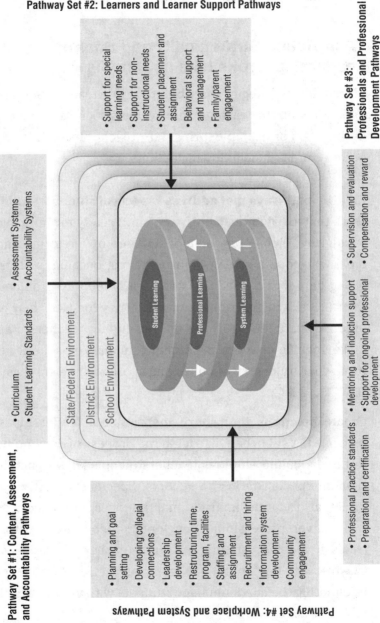

Pathway Set #2: Learners and Learner Support Pathways

- Support for special learning needs
- Support for non-instructional needs
- Student placement and assignment
- Behavioral support and management
- Family/parent engagement

Pathway Set #1: Content, Assessment, and Accountability Pathways

- Curriculum
- Student Learning Standards
- Assessment Systems
- Accountability Systems

State/Federal Environment

District Environment

School Environment

Student Learning

Professional Learning

System Learning

Pathway Set #3: Professionals and Professional Development Pathways

- Supervision and evaluation
- Compensation and reward
- Mentoring and induction support
- Support for ongoing professional development
- Professional practice standards
- Preparation and certification

Pathway Set #4: Workplace and System Pathways

- Planning and goal setting
- Developing collegial connections
- Leadership development
- Restructuring time, program, facilities
- Staffing and assignment
- Recruitment and hiring
- Information system development
- Community engagement

4. Mobilizing support for activity along multiple pathways.
Both internally and externally, leaders build a base of acceptance,
interest, and resources for improvement activities.

What Acting Strategically and Sharing Leadership Looks Like in Schools

In schools, strategic, distributed action can take many forms,
depending on the learning improvement focus and the particulars
of the site. For example, principals, teacher leaders, coaches, and
others can take the following actions.

**Identify pathways that address aspects of students' and teachers'
work that are demonstrably weak and ready for improvement.** A
small, rural elementary school staff, led by a reform-minded principal who took a strong inquiry stance, became experts on analyzing data that helped the staff clearly identify problem areas in
their literacy instructional practice. They focused their efforts on
improving student learning by developing teachers' capacity to
make specific changes in the curriculum. The school now has a
three-year trajectory of improving scores on the state assessment
(UWCEL, 2004).

**Create positions that share instructional leadership with the
principal.** A suburban district in the process of developing its own
K–12 curriculum employs teachers on special assignment as curriculum specialists in the schools. Specialists work closely with
principals to model instructional practices for teachers, help plan
and deliver professional development consistent with the district's curricular planning, and guide teachers in grade-level teams
to work with one another to learn instructional strategies for differentiating the curriculum for students with various special needs
(UWCEL, 2004).

Develop multilayered, ongoing school improvement efforts to improve teaching and learning in a key content area. The principal of a suburban elementary school made improving writing instruction a major goal for professional development for his staff. He embarked on this goal after he analyzed trends in achievement data that reflected weaknesses in students' writing abilities. The staff began by identifying the status of student writing and related classroom teaching across the school through a yearlong process of shared, ongoing examination of student work. Staff meetings were altered to focus on learning issues for both teachers and students. Nuts and bolts organizational issues were handled through daily e-mail and a weekly update. In the second year of the project, additional strategies were developed to keep the instructional focus on writing. Time was built into professional development meetings for staff members to write in personal reflective journals. Monthly schoolwide writing prompts were developed and used with all students to provide a common assignment for focusing on student work. A schoolwide writing hour was established to give teachers time to try out and assess new writing instructional strategies with students. Peer observations between teacher pairs and triads were arranged, and the principal provided substitutes to cover every teacher's classroom to allow at least one classroom visit per month. Finally, the principal asked staff members to establish specific writing goals that they would work on with students, and he used these goals as the basis for formal and informal classroom observations. As a result, writing scores on the state assessment have shown marked improvement over the course of the two years of work thus far (UWCEL, 2004).

What Acting Strategically and Sharing Leadership Looks Like in School Districts

At the district level, leaders may exercise strategic, distributed leadership in ways similar to those just illustrated for the school.

For example, district leaders and others (including school staff members) may identify pathways of activity that are especially pertinent to areas of weakness in school performance. They may create positions that can alleviate some of the districtwide leadership burden for particular issues, content areas, or functions. They may launch initiatives to improve teaching and learning in a key content area through activities that fall along a number of pathways. But the challenge of being strategic and effectively distributing leadership at the district level is complex, particularly in larger settings, given the number and diversity of participants and the many connections between the district and the outside world. With these complexities in mind, several other examples offer a fuller picture of strategic, distributed leadership actions at the district level. District leaders might take the following actions.

Develop and implement policies with teacher leaders and unions that provide additional support and clarify expectations for new teachers and struggling veterans. Administrators and union leaders from a large urban system worked together to implement a policy of peer assistance and review, which made teachers responsible for supporting, coaching, and evaluating identified colleagues. Oversight of the program, including decisions on whether to renew teachers, was conducted by a panel of the district's teachers and administrators. A group of consulting teachers—all district employees who had demonstrated outstanding instructional abilities—was hired on special assignment to coach, mentor, and evaluate a large group of new teachers and a handful of struggling, veteran teachers. The consulting teachers worked with building principals to establish expectations for the new role they played. Teachers who participated, received coaching, and experienced improvement in their classrooms credited their success to their work with the consulting teacher. In addition, 15 teachers were either counseled out or not renewed for employment as a result of this evaluation process, a marked increase over prior years in the district (Goldstein, 2003).

Seek out and support university-school district arrangements to develop school-level leadership aimed at improving learning. School districts from across one Western state supported 33 principals to participate in an ongoing, job-embedded professional development program focused on defining and closing gaps in student and teacher learning. The program, conducted by a university-based center for educational leadership, engaged principals in yearlong inquiry projects conducted in their home school sites and supported by monthly cohort meetings on the university campus. Each principal developed a project focus in his or her own context that was linked to improving teaching and learning. From the first group of 33 principals, 22 voluntarily returned for a second year of study that enabled them to continue the supported inquiry work (UWCEL, 2004).

Seize opportunities to develop leadership with other local initiatives to improve instruction in specific content areas. The National Science Foundation awarded 28 partner districts a five-year, $12 million dollar grant to improve science instruction and learning in their schools. The director of curriculum in one small city district, who was also on the partnership's leadership team, knew that in order for the collaboration to be successful, the principals would have to play a critical role in helping their teachers achieve the partnership's goals. However, his initial attempt to promote his principals' professional development through the grant was minimal. Eventually he designed a series of professional learning opportunities to guide principals in their work with science teachers. After one year, the partnership's leadership team realized the importance of supporting the principals as they worked to accomplish the science education reforms targeted in this complex project (UWCEL, 2004).

Processes and Challenges for Acting Strategically and Sharing Leadership

Leading for learning involves finding or creating opportunities along pathways that lead directly to student, professional, or system learning. Fashioning strategies that exert specific influence on these learning agendas raises questions for leaders regarding where to start, who exercises initiative, and how an initiative is shared between the school and district.

Where Can Leaders Start?

With so many possible courses of action available, school and district leaders face a major strategic puzzle. What will give them leverage in addressing a learning improvement agenda? No single answer applies equally in all settings. Essentially, the answer is to start somewhere that relates to the learning focus and takes full advantage of local circumstances, events, and leadership resources. External mandates may set the stage, as in this case.

> One district put together a yearlong series of workshops that persuaded schools to create a portfolio of standard-bearing work for every child. This request was based on an external mandate that encouraged teachers to use portfolios to assess their students' work. Teacher leaders from each school were invited to these workshops and were expected to become in-school experts on using portfolios and related assessment techniques, including creating explicit rubrics regarding standard-bearing work. These ideas were simultaneously introduced to principals and became a focus of school visits by district staff. Teachers had different responses to this innovation. Some teachers concluded that rubrics were a useful tool for assessment and instruction and tried to create them, while others felt that traditional grading was a sufficient representation of students' work quality. By year's end, due to increased opportunities for teachers to learn and collaborate, coupled with increased classroom-level scrutiny from administrators that was focused on developing and using portfolios, many teachers had altered their classroom assessment practices (Center for the Study of Teaching and Policy, 2003).

In this instance, leaders saw an opportunity along the assessment pathway to bring additional support for their vision of individually differentiated instruction. Had circumstances been different, they might have started with a different activity, but the external mandate provided a convenient point of entry. By taking advantage of external assessment pressures, the leaders led many teachers in inquiring about assessment methods and encouraged others to reconsider their classroom assessment practices. They accomplished this task by combining activity along multiple pathways (e.g., assessment, professional development, accountability, and leadership development). Through a combination of persuasion, modeling, strong arming, resource allocation, and other inducements, these leaders moved the district toward a broader repertoire of student assessments and different ways of using evidence to improve educational practice.

Who Is the Leader When Leadership Is Distributed?

Strategic, distributed action implies finding people who are in a position to mobilize and sustain efforts and assume responsibility for a learning improvement agenda. In the example above, district leaders involved teacher leaders who were positioned to persuade their colleagues to think critically about useful and preferred forms of classroom-based assessment. Effective leaders at the school level understand both the issue and the potential for many staff members to exercise leadership, as noted by this principal.

> Principals don't have enough time to be involved in all the decisions, so we have to disaggregate the jobs and fit them where they go. Consequently, every staff person in this school has some form of leadership role. For example, we have grade-level leaders, and during our grade-level meetings, they assume a leadership role to make sure that the agendas are organized and that the work that needs to be done progresses. We also have content leaders in science, technology, mathematics, literacy, and social science. There are many different leadership roles that function

across the school (Center for Research on the Context of Teaching, 2002).

Who Initiates Leadership? The School or the District?

An extension of distributing leadership involves how the learning improvement agenda is shared between the school and district. Extremes in either direction may compromise learning improvement. For instance, when leadership in centralized systems is exercised too aggressively from the top of the system, it may be disempowering to teachers and provoke counteractions in the schools. At the other extreme, decentralized districts that transfer most instructional leadership to the schools may risk substantial unevenness and inequities among schools. A solid middle ground exists, however, when school and district leaders take joint responsibility for learning improvement, develop goals, and mobilize their efforts accordingly.

Mobilizing Effort Along Strategic Pathways

As the previous examples and discussion suggest, leading for learning requires strategic action and sharing of authority. Streams of activity exist in schools and school systems that converge on teaching and learning, whether or not leaders choose to guide, direct, or support these activities. Personnel decisions are made, curriculum choices are implemented, and teacher evaluation processes are cycled on and off the radar screen. However, the extent to which any stream of activity actually matters in improving teaching and learning is largely dependent on leaders' abilities to exert leverage from their particular vantage points in the system, and enable others to also support their specific learning improvement goals.

7

Creating Coherence

Administrators in Mr. G.'s school and district have not looked closely at how teachers and students are interpreting their mathematics curriculum, assessments, improvement programs, and policies. Nor have they looked for ways to link one function to another (e.g., assessment of mathematics learning and professional development for math teachers). While they work hard at managing their schools, they have yet to imagine how their disparate efforts can relate to one another or help Mr. G. to see new possibilities for his practice.

Critical to leading for learning is the fifth and final area of the Leading for Learning Framework, *finding ways to develop a sense of clarity and coherent support for improving instruction.* When leaders stimulate and guide activity along multiple pathways, two questions arise: How well are the activities linked to one another, and how effectively do they connect student, professional, and system learning? The case below illustrates one answer to these questions.

> One middle school uses biweekly, two-hour faculty study groups to examine samples of student work for evidence of learning progress and areas of need, and to identify future instructional steps to take with specific students. In these sessions, staff members are learning about high-quality student work as well as planning ways to produce this type of work in their classrooms.

Nothing is allowed to interfere with this standing commitment. Each study group posts a public record of their work, to which the principal provides feedback, questions, and affirmation. In addition, study groups report their progress and evidence of student learning improvement to the whole staff at staff meetings. Student achievement is steadily increasing (Center for Research on the Context of Teaching, 2002).

Here, activity along multiple pathways focuses on all three learning agendas: student learning, by considering special learning needs and the quality of particular students' work; professional learning, by engaging faculty members in study groups to learn about their students' learning and gathering ideas for better teaching; and system learning, by generating data and insight into school performance that is shared publicly with other staff members and school leaders. The activities bring coherence to learning improvement through mutually reinforcing connections among the three learning agendas.

Over a longer span of time, coherent activities reinforce how teachers and learners work in the classroom. The next example shows how one district pursued this idea.

One district, known initially in a large metropolitan region as a dumping ground for low-performing teachers, created a teaching quality improvement strategy that included active recruitment, extensive mentoring, explicit teaching standards, opportunities for teachers to assume leadership roles, and support for the ongoing work of the teaching forces. Ultimately, these activities were linked to a new set of student learning standards. This strategy, patiently developed over a period of years, provided the foundation for a transformation in this district's performance and ultimately its image (Snyder, 2002).

Defining the Underlying Ideas for Creating Coherence

The actions of leaders, in combination with other schooling conditions, present learners and teachers with a set of messages about their work that vary in how they cohere with one another. Initially applied to systemic reform policies, coherence has several meanings (Fuhrman, 1993; Fullan, 2001; Newmann, Smith, Allensworth & Bryk, 2001). At one level, coherence refers to *alignment* (i.e., how various activities relate on different pathways, what the connections are between activities, and what resources are needed to carry them out). The more aligned, presumably the more coherent. But merely aligning activities with one another and their resources is insufficient to ensure coherent support for good instruction. After all, a system's improvement activities could be fully aligned and based on an ineffective teaching model. Therefore, at another level, coherence means alignment and accepting a *link between leadership activities and a compelling vision of learning and teaching* that teachers understand and acknowledge. At a third level, coherence implies a *sufficient working consensus* so that teachers' efforts to improve student learning are consistent with the efforts of other grade-level teachers, as well as teachers in other district schools. Ultimately, coherence is about learning agendas making sense: Does the work of improving learning and the strategies for achieving that goal make sense to all or most participants? Figure 7.1 shows an example of a coherent learning agenda in action.

The quest for coherence takes place against a typical backdrop of substantial incoherence in public schooling, especially in larger districts. Many conditions—including staff turnover and the division of labor in a large, complex bureaucracy—have a tendency to diffuse the focus, disconnect one function from another, and make it difficult to develop working relationships or consensus. Environmental constraints further complicate leaders' efforts to build cohesion into the agenda for powerful and equitable student learning. State policies, as one obvious example, may be at odds with local visions, priorities, and practices. But promising evidence from a growing number of cases suggests that, even in the face of adverse circumstances, districts can successfully establish coherent reform strategies. Districts that have reorganized themselves

Figure 7.1

Examples of Connectivity Between Learning Agendas

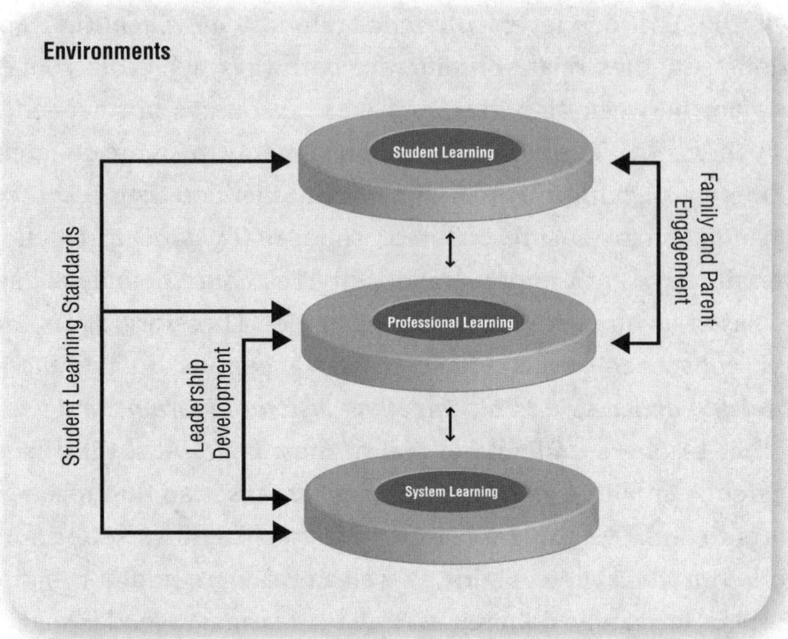

into multilayered nested learning communities (see Chapter 4) have created an infrastructure that supports learning for students, teachers, and leaders and have produced modest to impressive student achievement scores (see, for example, Hightower, 2001; Learning First Alliance, 2003; Resnick & Harwell, 2000).

Essential Tasks for Creating Coherence

Creating coherence means doing the following actions.

1. Use pathways that intentionally address student, professional, and system learning. Coherence is more likely when leaders can forge connections between what students are learning about in classrooms, what teachers are learning about in professional development (e.g., their classroom work), and what administrators are learning about system performance as a whole.

2. Align activities with one another, their respective resources, and compelling visions of learning and teaching. Leaders look for and make operational connections between activities along different pathways that are informed by an overarching vision of improving learning.

3. Create structures and incentives for system learning that are mutually supportive of student and professional learning. Leaders devise methods for understanding system performance that support student and teacher learning when they have a clear learning focus in mind.

What Creating Coherence Looks Like in Schools

School leaders create coherent connections among student, professional, and system learning when they take part in the following actions.

Develop coherent school structures that support teachers' learning. As principal of the Manhattan New School, Shelley Harwayne created structures with her teachers that supported their mutual learning on a daily basis. One structure included formal demonstration lessons carried out by colleagues for one another. These lessons incorporated follow-up time to discuss the lessons and informal interclass visitations that were encouraged by an open-door policy. Harwayne also worked to make whole-staff and grade-level meetings prime-time quality. She considered each session together as a time to solve problems and explore issues that mattered for teaching and learning. She also encouraged and supported teachers in their efforts to submit work for publication. Professional reading and book groups that focused on teaching and learning issues were standard practice at the school. Harwayne also assembled a professional videotape library, consisting of both in-house videotapes of teaching and published material. Other strategies included mentor relationships for all new teachers, informal collegial breakfast and dinner dates, visits to other schools, and opportunities for reflection on professional practice. These activities were aligned with one another, both formally and informally, and with a rich picture of the learning that students and professionals in a high-performing school need to do (Harwayne, 2003).

Develop strategies for improving learning that give teachers opportunities to lead and to analyze hierarchical school role boundaries. The International High School at LaGuardia Community College brings ESL, bilingual, and content teachers together in interdisciplinary teams to assume leadership for the academic success of all students. International High is an alternative high school that serves students who are new to the United States and who have varying levels of English language proficiency. Professional development is built into the governance and instructional organization of the school. The overarching goal is to guarantee that all staff members have the tools to support students in meeting rigorous graduation requirements. All staff members must continually improve their ability to manage a student-centered classroom, accommodate classrooms with a mixture of students with different backgrounds and languages, and integrate first and second languages into the content areas. Interdisciplinary teacher teams work collaboratively to develop and revise curriculum, plan schedules, discuss student learning, and share successful practices. Staff members hold one another accountable through peer coaching, peer evaluation, and teacher portfolio presentations (Clair & Adger, 1999).

Work from a clear theory of action that is focused on improving instruction and is reinforced through supervision and evaluation. A principal serves a suburban elementary school with a population that includes 52 percent of students receiving free or reduced-price lunch and more than 50 percent of students speaking a first language other than English. She leads the schools with a clear set of reinforcing strategies for improving students' literacy and math achievement. The principal's efforts have provided for smaller class sizes in the early grades, high-quality teachers in those classrooms, and a concerted focus on increasing the instructional capacity of all teachers. She also has worked with district personnel to support new student initiatives at the school, especially activities that emphasize students' math learning. The principal encourages teachers to participate in professional development activities that introduce them to new instructional strategies. Staff members regularly discuss an ongoing inquiry approach that highlights student assessment data. The data allow the school staff to continue to readjust and refocus instruction if outcomes are not as expected. As a result, the school has accomplished a four-year trajectory of growth on standardized assessments of student learning (UWCEL, 2004).

What Creating Coherence Looks Like in School Districts

District-level administrators and staff can create coherent improvement efforts through similar means as leaders at the school level. However, district leaders need to keep in mind that coherent bridges need to be built between the school and the central office. These activities are likely when leaders take the following actions.

Create structures that encourage and support new avenues of communication between central office leaders and school leaders. A new superintendent for the Oakville School District focused on creating a more coherent approach to leadership. He instituted several types of meetings to encourage collaboration among administrators. A central office administrator in the district explained that instead of just having meetings with staff at the central office, the superintendent has his monthly meetings with the administrative council, which includes central office staff members and principals. "I have monthly meetings with the curriculum coordinators. I also have monthly meetings with the elementary principals. On many occasions, we've brought the directors' meetings and the administrative council together, and this just helps to make the administrative group more cohesive in the sense [that we work] together rather than working in competition with each other" (Johnson, 1999, p. 78).

Focus ongoing professional learning for principals on improving instruction. District leaders in New York District 2, under the leadership of Tony Alvarado, developed a number of organizational practices to ensure that principals would continually learn about how to lead for powerful instruction. These practices permeated every aspect of the principals' work life. District leaders regularly scheduled for principals to visit other schools to view and discuss instruction. They also organized monthly conferences with district instructional leaders to analyze leadership strategies and progress toward district goals, and they established mentor-coach relationships for new or struggling principals to develop their practice, both individually and collectively. District 2 supervisors also made routine supervisory walk-throughs with school building leaders to observe classrooms and discuss the instruction taking place. These walk-throughs addressed the individual needs of schools and provided guidance to principals (Fullan, 2001).

Use external experts to help teachers and leaders build capacity in particular content areas and link professional efforts to ongoing assessments. District leaders from a small, rural Kentucky district are clear about their focus on strengthening instruction. They provide activities that develop and support principals as instructional leaders and offer opportunities for principals and teachers to learn about instruction. Principals and teachers also have access to professional development in key content areas. In addition, the district has brought in nationally recognized presenters in writing and mathematics to build the capacity of the district staff on an ongoing basis. The district measures progress on these initiatives by tracking teachers' instruction plans, assessing high-quality instructional practices reflected in their lesson plans, and evaluating the quality of student work over time (McDiarmid, David, Corcoran, Kannapel, & Coe, 1997).

Restructure central office leadership responsibilities to serve learning-related goals. A reform-minded superintendent sought to fill a recently vacated position for a personnel director. Some members of the school board argued that the responsibilities of the position were more clerical than professional, and they were opposed to filling it with a new administrator. However, the superintendent recognized the importance of the position and saw possibilities for expanding it to include responsibility for professional development—a priority of her administration. She convinced the board to create an expanded position with greater influence. The administrator who was subsequently appointed redefined the job to focus centrally on supporting teachers, curriculum, and schools (Johnson, 1999).

Processes and Challenges for Creating Coherence

Coherence is often difficult for leaders to achieve because there is such a broad span of activities and there are several people who may be involved. The resistances, as previously discussed in other areas of the Leading for Learning Framework (*establishing a focus on learning, building professional communities. engaging external environments,* and *acting strategically and sharing leadership*), are among the many efforts that make creating coherent working environments complicated. Potential threats to coherence include making difficult decisions and trade-offs regarding the pace of change, evaluating the degree of professional autonomy and discretion, and responding to environmental turbulence.

How Quickly Should Leaders Make Changes?

There is a temptation for the pace of reform to move faster than schools and teachers are ready to internalize it. As the next example shows, if there is any lesson from sites that have narrowed their focus and stuck to it over a period of years, it is that deep change in any aspect of the instructional program is a long-term matter.

> In one well-documented case, an urban district's campaign to instill balanced literacy teaching in its elementary and middle schools stretched more than 10 years. Only after a period of time did a second subject area, mathematics, become a part of the district's strategy. A byproduct of the continuing focus on literacy was the district's ability to project and reinforce a stable set of messages and support for more powerful forms of literacy instruction. Whether or not teachers agreed with these messages (some didn't and left), they were clear and consistent. The district's approach to reform had considerable coherence (Elmore & Burney, 1999). The trade-off, however, was that other subject areas were not given as much attention or support. But, had the district sought to address other subjects all at once, there would have been some risk to the coherence of the messages the teachers were receiving, not to mention their sense of being able to make all the desired changes.

How Much Autonomy and Discretion Should Leaders Allow?

A second trade-off emerged from the case described above. Other valid approaches to literacy teaching were not honored in the same way as the initial set of ideas and techniques were embraced for the district's vision of balanced literacy. In effect, in the district leaders' quest for a coherent approach to reform and professional practice, they limited professional autonomy at the same time that they sought to boost professional competence. While the trade-off may have been worthwhile in this case, there may have been a temptation to equate coherence with control. Alternative scenarios can be imagined, in which the reform theory of action places greater emphasis on school-level invention, initiative, and discretion. If these values are consistently promoted and supported, a different form of coherence is possible, as the following case suggests.

An urban district made considerable progress in improving performance for its 50,000 students. In recent years there have been explicit attempts to empower schools and encourage entrepreneurial activity at the school level. Schools were given budgetary control, latitude in hiring, and encouraged to develop professional development strategies as part of school-specific transformational plans. The overall direction for the schools' work was guided by a districtwide set of student learning standards and teaching practice standards. Many schools responded and, although varied, progress was made. But schools were not always sure what messages the central office was sending. For example, professional development dollars allocated to the schools were to be used to purchase services solely from the district office. Yet, the district office didn't always have the requisite expertise or offer what the schools were looking for. Some school-level initiatives were stymied as a result (Center for the Study of Teaching and Policy, 2003).

In this case, some coherence had developed at the district level around a more decentralized approach to improving student learning. But at the ground level, coherence was not always experienced because the district sent contradictory messages. Whatever the theory of action, leaders are likely to struggle with some basic tensions between the purpose and direction of a specific initiative and whether or not professionals are willing to pursue that path.

Coherence, or the attempt to achieve it, can clearly be threatened by other circumstances. No amount of careful planning or environmental scanning will head off major, unpredictable events in the often turbulent world surrounding schools and districts. In the next example, a consortium of professional development organizations discovered that the changing environment in their city could substantially alter the coherence of the strategies they were implementing in schools.

A professional development consortium provided instructional leadership to a group of partner schools in a major city district. They had built a strategy to emphasize student-centered practice that aligned with the district's curriculum and policy stance. However, they discovered a sudden change in district leadership, accompanied by governance changes and new pressures in the city, led to an abrupt turnaround in policy. Before, the district had embraced student-centered practice and related approaches to professional development. After the abrupt changes, the district shifted to a strict accountability strategy that was tied to basic skills testing. The district would now face heavy consequences for schools and principals who exhibited low performance. Partner schools responded by retreating from forms of teaching that they feared would not be captured well in the testing program. The consortium dealt with the situation by becoming strategic intermediaries between district pressures and the schools' practices. Members of the consortium reached out aggressively to sympathetic staff members at the central office and to important constituencies outside the district (e.g., the mayor's office). At the same time the consortium worked with school staff members to help them visualize responses to accountability pressures that went beyond justifying test scores as the bottom line. Within a year, principals and teachers in the partner schools had begun to see new possibilities in inquiry-based teaching that could help students do better on tests while learning valuable habits of mind (Burch, 2002).

In this instance, leaders were able to overcome a major environmental disruption to further their original learning improvement agenda. School and district leaders are not always fortunate to accomplish this effect. But their best hope lies in combining strategic relationships with key leaders and attempts to help participants make sense of changing conditions. During a crisis, it is the leaders' responsibility to help principals and teachers see new ways of attending to a learning agenda.

Making Leadership More Coherent

Ultimately, coherence occurs when leaders coordinate their actions across all five areas of the Leading for Learning Framework. Initially, school and district leaders can seek to achieve coherence by focusing persistently and publicly on learning (Area 1), and subsequently by zeroing in on ways that link activities along and among pathways. In the process, leaders can develop linkages by creating teams and other mechanisms for encouraging dialogue, expectations, and support for collaborative work. These linkages can be further enhanced by building strong professional communities (Area 2). Leaders can solidify their learning improvement agendas and stall many adverse circumstances by judiciously engaging external environments (Area 3). Over time, the results can create a consistent set of activities and resources that are focused on improving teaching and learning. Leaders create coherence by working intentionally along and across various pathways in the system aimed at learning improvement, and by distributing leadership for learning improvement among many others (Area 4).

Leaders who seek to create coherence in their schools and school districts face a voluminous array of potential school reform initiatives. Coherence in leading for learning implies that there are efforts at multiple levels designed to make the leader's daily work serve a clear set of goals for students and professionals. Through it all, learning-focused leaders seek to build a durable consensus around a specific learning agenda for student, professional, and system learning.

Part Three

The Leading for Learning Framework in Action

To understand and use the Leading for Learning Framework ideas more fully, developing leaders need to see the actions manifested in different contexts over time. In the examples that follow, leaders across discrete school and district settings work to improve learning from various vantage points over time. The work of these leaders gives concrete, cumulative meaning to the principles underlying the Leading for Learning Framework. When viewed retrospectively, these stories illustrate various ways to put learning-focused leadership into action. With these long-term views of how learning-focused leadership emerges, leaders are then in a better position to use the Leading for Learning Framework as an effective tool for advancing their practice.

This part of the book will help the reader visualize the meaning and the use of the Leading for Learning Framework in two ways. First, this section offers extended case descriptions of four schools in Chapter 8 and three districts in Chapter 9. Each case shows how learning-focused leadership is embodied in each educator's efforts. These case accounts go well beyond the brief vignettes that appear in preceding chapters to present a continuous story of leaders who struggle to effectively improve teaching and learning. The leaders in each case faced unique sets of challenges and circumstances and executed their work differently, yet their starting points were similar. Each school or district struggled with major problems like low staff morale, operations difficulties, or low performance. But, these leaders resolved to do something about it. Their stories offer glimpses of how leaders can begin and build their initial efforts, and how they can make changes to shift the attention, energies, and resources in schools toward a focus on improving learning. Though these leaders were unaware of the Leading for Learning Framework, they *lived* these principles in their daily practice.

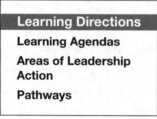

Learning Directions

Learning Agendas

Areas of Leadership Action

Pathways

To help the reader grasp how the case stories exemplify the Leading for Learning Framework, we have annotated the cases with boxed notes indicating which learning agenda, area of leadership action, and specific pathways of learning were central to the leadership strategy at that point in the case story.

Second, in Chapter 10, we question how the Leading for Learning Framework might be used by leaders who are new to the concepts of the framework. In this chapter, rather than using the Leading for Learning Framework as an analytic tool to understand what leaders are doing, we show how it can act as a guide or toolset. This section will assist leaders who want to develop their leadership practices so that they are more oriented toward learning. As we will show, the Leading for Learning Framework can be used in the context of leadership practice, professional preparation, or ongoing leadership development.

The discussion and examples in Chapter 10 differ from those in the preceding two chapters in several respects. First, in the latter instances, leaders were making conscious use of the Leading for Learning Framework while trying to learn the ideas themselves. As such, they were only beginning to see the possibilities that the framework affords. Second, the span of time is much shorter—the educators in Chapter 10 had only a short period of time to put the ideas into practice, unlike the earlier cases, which spanned a decade and more. This discussion will help the reader visualize the initial application of the Leading for Learning Framework to different kinds of uses. The story of using the Leading for Learning Framework over the long haul has yet to unfold.

8

Leading Learning in Schools

In the extended examples that follow—four brief cases within a middle school, high school, and two elementary schools—we use the Leading for Learning Framework to give meaning to particular leadership actions. These actions, which occur in these schools over a period of years, are aimed at improving learning. The Leading for Learning Framework helps to point out strengths, strategies, and coherence in the work of these school leaders, as well as illustrate the evolution of their work over time. As the stories unfold, we loop back through the five areas of the Leading for Learning Framework and link them to concrete, practical actions taken by leaders in these contexts.

We recognize that learning-focused leadership does not operate in the same way in every school. Leadership approaches to improving learning differ in emphasis and how leaders leverage different strategies. Essentially, *leadership is bound by context*. As with every school, each case is unique. The Leading for Learning Framework helps us to explore how each of these schools work to connect leadership action and learning in context and to identify common principles in these different contexts. The stories highlighted here offer potential insights for school leaders who are asking "How do we begin? What do we do? Where do we go from here?"

Falls City Elementary School: Engaging a Community of Leaders

Leadership for learning doesn't just magically happen without an individual leader or leadership group having the will to say, "We can do better." The tale of Falls City Elementary School illustrates what can happen when a community wakes up to the idea that the status quo is not working.[1] With this realization as catalyst, various individuals began to exercise leadership that was more coherent and effectively focused on learning.

A Necessary Catalyst for Change

At Falls City Elementary School, a school with a population that includes almost 90 percent of students at or below the poverty level and 20 percent of students as English language learners, that realization came from an article in the local newspaper, *The Falls City Herald-Review*. On February 28, 1993, the paper proclaimed that the school's children were unable to learn and that the staff was incompetent. The article also detailed the 4th grade students' abysmal Comprehensive Test of Basic Skills (CTBS) test scores. While this event was a humiliating and demoralizing episode for the school, it served as a catalyst for meaningful and sustained change for what the school staff believed about children's learning and how they acted on those beliefs. The community and staff of Falls City came together to evaluate their failings and challenges and to identify and build on their strengths.

---

[1] This case was constructed with considerable assistance from Dr. Lorna Spears. This account is based on an original description of the school's work. Dr. Spears has deep familiarity with this school, and she was instrumental in planning and leading much of the history recounted here.

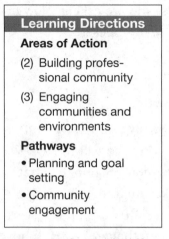

Learning Directions

Areas of Action

(2) Building professional community

(3) Engaging communities and environments

Pathways

• Planning and goal setting

• Community engagement

For the 1993–94 and 1994–95 school years, an emergent learning community, composed of staff, parents, central office personnel, and community members, surveyed all stakeholders to find out what they believed about children and their learning. The staff formed focus groups and began researching promising practices. Several parents came together with the staff to create the Falls City Site Council. This group was actively involved in gathering information and research. From their in-depth self-study and review of the research, stakeholders came to consensus on a set of core beliefs, a mission statement, and a short list of schoolwide learning goals.

Learning Directions

Areas of Action

(1) Focus on learning

Learning Agendas

Student learning

The belief that all children could learn at high levels, and the goal of helping every child achieve at or above state standards in literacy and mathematics remained at the center of Falls City Elementary School's mission from that point forward. The changes, stimulated and guided by the community's agreement on what they wanted for children, have been substantial. Children, their parents, and the community once considered Falls City to be a low-performing school that should be avoided at all costs. Now, the school is known across the state for academic excellence. Students understand that they are capable and can be successful. They enjoy the many visitors who come to talk to them about how they learn at such high rates, and they can articulate the strategies that teachers use to help them learn.

<table>
<tr><td>

Learning Directions

Areas of Action

(3) Engaging environ-
ments (community
and city politics)

</td></tr>
</table>

Parents take ownership of the changes in the school because they have been an integral part of articulating the school's program. The Falls City Site Council is not only the school's parent decision-making body, but it is the official neighborhood council sanctioned by the Falls City government that represents neighborhood citizens in citywide decision making. In this capacity, parents and neighboring community members participate in governing Falls City Elementary School and the broader city government. The Falls City Site Council is the only group that serves both roles in the city. The council monitors test scores, discipline referrals, and after-school programs. Parents who once were concerned about sending their children to Falls City now recruit new families to the school.

Eight years after the school set forth its new course of action, a parent explained the impact of the changes.

<table>
<tr><td>

Learning Directions

Pathways

• Family and parent
engagement

• Community
engagement

</td></tr>
</table>

I've been a Falls City parent for around 12 years. I've seen a lot of changes since my oldest daughter, who is now 19, first started school here. There was not a lot of opportunity for parent involvement back then. I was never invited to participate in anything at my daughter's school. There were no family nights, workshops, or extended learning opportunities for children. As my other three kids started school, I wanted to be more involved, so I volunteered in their classrooms not knowing what to expect. I felt very welcomed to the school by the teachers, and then principal Dick McClellan and assistant principal, Lillian Sparks. I was invited to be a part of the Falls City Site Council. The school also had a Parent Educational Assistant Program that I was interested in because parents received training in reading and math. This training helped me help my kids at home the same way they were being taught at school. I was also able to read and work with other students in the classrooms and was able to attend the Title 1/LAP conference. Falls City started an extended learning program so kids can have help with their homework after school. The school now has some great family nights, evening workshops such as Love and Logic, and computer classes for adults. I've seen a lot of changes at Falls City over the years that benefit our community, kids, and adults.

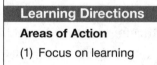

Learning Directions
Areas of Action
(1) Focus on learning

The halls at Falls City Elementary School used to be cluttered with chairs and desks that were used for pulling students out of classrooms for remediation. Now, the halls are shiny and clean and the walls are filled with student work that invites visitors to learn more about the academic pursuits of Falls City students. The front hall proudly displays the school's Title I Distinguished School banner, and students and guests can sit on a park bench and chairs under the banner and choose a book from the bookcase. If the bench is full, the book nook is just around the corner. In an area where carts and extra desks were stored, students can now sit on sofas, put their feet up on the coffee table, and read.

Building a Professional Community in Falls City

These changes did not come by accident nor did they happen overnight. The Leading for Learning Framework suggests that improvement in student learning is inextricably tied to how the instructional practices are carried out. When a community of professionals is committed to improving instruction, they are in an excellent position to stimulate and guide their improvement processes. Through a deep examination of their own assumptions about the challenges facing their children, teachers at Falls City began to come together as a professional community, and they became determined to improve their practice.

Learning Directions
Pathways
• Support for professional development
• Support for special learning needs
• Assessment systems
• Student learning standards

Falls City teachers have always worked hard. Even during the 1992–93 school year when the CTBS scores were low, it was not due to staff laziness. Teachers, however, were not as focused on academic success then as they are now. If teachers taught mathematics, the lessons included only basic arithmetic or number sense, and instruction was very tied to the textbook. A basal reading textbook and basic science textbook was used. Then, as now, almost all of the students at Falls City lived in deep poverty. Teachers knew that students were not coming to school ready to learn. Many of these children possessed few of the readiness skills that were needed to be successful in school. Most parents lacked the skills or time to assist their child with homework. In response to these challenges, the principal and leadership team formed an early intervention focus group and an assessment and instruction focus group. These groups began researching instructional strategies and classroom environments that could increase the learning of all children, especially children who lived in deep poverty.

The district supported the school by placing a Title I early childhood facilitator at Falls City. This early childhood literacy specialist was an in-house professional developer who planned lessons, coached, team taught with teachers in their classrooms, and worked with students. With her expertise and coaching, new teachers had their first opportunities to try out some of the instructional strategies they had been researching. However, it was not easy for veteran staff members to invite an expert into their classrooms. But through examining student learning data, the staff recognized that it was time to try something different.

Learning Directions

Areas of Action

(4) Acting strategically and sharing leadership

Pathways

- Recruitment and hiring
- Support for professional development

As teachers began moving from old methods like fixed reading groups, textbook-based teaching, and "one size fits all" instruction, the state was beginning a reform movement of its own by identifying essential academic learning requirements for all students. Fortunately for Falls City, two certificated staff members, who just happened to be playing important roles at the state level in defining the standards for reading, writing, and science, were able to help other staff members do research and make changes in their instructional strategies to help students meet the new state standards.

As a school community, Falls City leaders decided to use their Title I funding to hire three more instructional facilitators who were content experts in mathematics, literacy, and professional development. This decision coincided with a change in philosophy concerning instructional improvements aimed at struggling learners. The staff shifted from assisting a few of the lowest performing students to providing in-depth professional development for all teachers in their classrooms that would improve their quality of instruction for all children. Teachers became learners and, as their students began to engage in new forms of instruction focused on the state standards, the students' achievement soared.

Learning Directions

Areas of Action

(5) Creating coherence (connecting student, professional, and system learning)

Pathways

- Assessment
- Curriculum
- Support for professional development

The Falls City leaders and staff began researching and creating assessments that informed their instructional decisions. All children in the primary grades were assessed with common assessment tools four times a year. These analytical tools gave teachers and facilitators the information they needed to plan whole-group, small-group, and individual instruction in reading. In several years' time, teachers moved from basic instruction to instruction that was more flexible and focused on students' interests, needs, and capabilities. In the 1998–99 school year Falls City applied for and received a K–2 reading grant from the state. This grant, which was used to integrate phonics instruction into kindergarten through 2nd grade classrooms, enabled the school to offer additional professional development, acquire phonics-based literature, and secure materials designed to promote letter-sound and word-chunk skills and other kinds of direct phonics instruction.

> **Learning Directions**
> **Pathways**
> • Mentoring
> • Support for special learning needs
> • Developing collegial connections

At this same time, two reading recovery teachers were hired to offer direct instruction to struggling 1st graders at the school. After two years of this intervention, the number of primary students being referred to special education was reduced from an average of eight students each year to only one. The literacy facilitators and one of the reading recovery teachers spent a year collaborating with the other kindergarten teachers to examine current instructional practices. To guide improvement in these practices, the reading recovery teacher shared the new knowledge she was gaining from her weekly professional development activities, while the literacy facilitators assisted teachers in implementing the new instructional strategies into their classrooms. Before, few Falls City kindergartners (never more than 16 percent) left kindergarten with the ability to read. After only six months of implementing the instructional changes introduced to kindergarten teachers, almost half (49 percent) of the kindergarten students were reading. During the next two years, teachers continued to refine their literacy instruction skills, and now nearly three-quarters (74 percent) of Falls City kindergarten students leave as readers.

No longer do Falls City staff members make excuses about their students' lack of readiness. Instead, they assess their students' reading skills and then systematically teach them to read. Before, teachers used to know that children were coming to Falls City several years delayed and felt defeated before they began; now teachers know that they can make up for that delay with focused, developmentally appropriate teaching.

Making Dramatic Changes in Mathematics Instruction in Falls City

The Leading for Learning Framework suggests that improving learning requires intentional action that is focused on identifiable goals. Building on their early success in literacy, Falls City leaders and staff members turned their attention to mathematics. In this area, leaders actively used results from standardized assessments to inform areas of instructional need. The assessments helped staff members focus their improvement activities and document their progress.

Learning Directions

Areas of Action

(1 Focus on learning (mathematics)

(4) Acting strategically

Pathways
- Student standards
- Assessment
- Curriculum
- Support for professional development

Mathematics became one of Falls City Elementary School's greatest successes as teachers worked to improve student performance after the 1992–93 CTBS scores. At that time, the school's 4th graders performed far below national norms. They only ranked in the 14th percentile for computation, the 16th percentile in concepts and applications, and the 14th percentile for a total mathematics battery score.

Falls City leaders and staff members helped their 4th graders raise their performance on the CTBS by aligning their mathematics instruction to the new state mathematics standards. After a five-year period, 4th graders at Falls City scored in the 62nd percentile for computation, the 47th percentile for concepts and application, and the 55th percentile for a total math battery score.

After disaggregating the results from the CTBS (and in later years the new state assessment) the mathematics facilitators planned problem-solving workshops and led study groups based on the state standards and standards from the National Council of Teachers of Mathematics (NCTM). Although most teachers had a firm grasp on teaching number sense, the 4th grade teachers made changes in their instruction, based on data from the CTBS and the Washington Assessment of Student Learning (WASL) assessment scores. The assessments emphasized more practice for students to explain their mathematics thinking in writing, explicit teaching of problem-solving strategies, critical reading strategies to improve comprehension in mathematics, and encouragement for children to think in divergent ways about mathematics.

Learning Directions

Learning Agendas

Student learning

System learning

Meanwhile, 3rd grade teachers began using a norm-referenced test, the Iowa Test of Basic Skills (ITBS). This test allowed teachers to examine and demonstrate the impact of the instructional changes for students at this level. In the spring of the 1998–99 school year, when students took the ITBS for the first time, teachers found that, slowly but surely, the changes they had been initiating were taking hold. Students were able to transfer learning from one grade and from one classroom to the next. This was dramatically demonstrated when the 3rd graders ranked in the 61st percentile for mathematics on the CTBS. The entire community was thrilled! High-poverty students were demonstrating that they were capable and could learn when provided with the opportunity. In mathematics, the school's students scored two percentage points ahead of the district average and one percentage point higher than the state.

The dramatic changes in mathematics suggested a pattern of continuing and cumulative impact that was also apparent in other parts of the school program. For example, the leaders had confidence that reading achievement would continue to improve as teachers planned and implemented balanced literacy in their classrooms. They also were encouraged as more children left each primary grade reading at grade level. Teachers and administrators began calling this increase "the Falls City wave." Each year as students were exposed to the new instructional strategies based on the state standards, the more prepared they became for the next grade and the more the students' overall achievement grew.

Sustaining Success Through a Leadership Transition

Of all the killers of school renewal efforts, transition in formal leadership is perhaps most pervasive. Countless school reform strategies have gone by the wayside with a change in the principalship. Many of these efforts, most likely, were too dependent on the skills and artistry of an individual gifted leader. Mindful of this danger, Falls City leaders negotiated a transition in the principalship with strong support from the broader community for hiring an insider. The new principal would already be trusted by the staff and passionately devoted to the school's improvement effort.

> **Learning Directions**
>
> **Areas of Action**
>
> (3) Engaging environments
>
> (4) Acting strategically and sharing leadership

At the time of the principal's retirement in 1999, all Falls City classrooms were focused on the state's essential academic learning requirements and the associated grade-level learning targets set up by the district. Teachers and key parents understood that no child could afford a year without these added values. Therefore, the team welcomed the former assistant principal, Lillian Sparks, as the new principal. She had worked as one of the school's instructional facilitators, and she came to her new role with five years invested in the leadership changes at the school. This investment and her connection to the school community enabled her to step into the top role and continue work that was already underway without disruption. The Falls City community recognized the importance of this transition and was actively involved in supporting Sparks's hiring. This was yet another signal that the staff and parents valued the changes that had been implemented in the school, and they recognized how these changes benefited the community's children.

One of the first tasks the new principal and staff undertook was writing and implementing a schoolwide progressive discipline plan. Staff, students, and parents were provided with a copy

---

Learning Directions

Pathways
- Behavioral support and management

---

of the plan and discipline records were kept. For the first time, everyone knew what acceptable behavior was in school. The leaders began ensuring that all children would have the opportunity to learn by not tolerating any disruption of the learning process. Eventually, parents were called any time a child was referred to the office. Three years into this policy, discipline referrals decreased and suspensions went down by 44 percent. Parents were supportive and student achievement as measured by test scores and classroom work remained high. This was a great accomplishment for a school located in a neighborhood with high transience and deep poverty.

The school that had once been in the news as a place where children could not learn and teachers could not teach now was in the news for being a high-poverty, high-performing school. As of fall 2002, eight years after setting out to improve the school, 65 percent of students were meeting the standards set by the state's 4th grade reading assessment. This figure was comparable to the state and district averages. Seventy-two percent of Falls City children met the mathematics standard and nearly half of the students went beyond being just proficient to exemplary.

As with most successful school improvement processes, the progress at Falls City Elementary occurred inside a larger district context, and without a doubt, was supported by district leaders who allowed these positive changes to happen.

Parkside Alternative Middle School: Building Coherence Through a Joint Curriculum

Parkside Alternative Middle School illustrates a different leadership dynamic.[2] Leaders at this school demonstrate other ways to connect student and professional learning at the school level (see Gallucci, Knapp, Markholt, & Ort, 2003). Here, in the midst of a large city, the school engaged in a substantial restructuring effort that fell in line with tenets of the small schools movement (Cotton, 1996; Meier, 1995; Raywid, 1996). The primary focus for the staff and for rebuilding the school program was centered on innovative curriculum development. The results of these restructuring efforts, now in their 10th year, suggest that the school has found a viable way of serving a highly diverse, high-poverty, urban student population. Once viewed as a school that few parents would want their children to attend, the school is currently sought out by parents who can opt for enrollment under the district's school choice plan. As the current principal put it, over the past seven years, the school changed from very rough to

> A school that working families would consider putting their kids in...[A school for] families who want their kids in school every day and don't expect their kids to fight....[Now you see] kids who are polite and carry a notebook and aren't embarrassed of it, and kids who think school is important, regardless of how well they perform.

The school continues to serve a student population that reflects the character of diverse neighborhoods in a segment of the city with relatively few resources. Parkside serves approximately 200 students in grades 6 through 8. The school accepts about 60–65 new students each year. The student population is ethnically diverse—almost

---

[2]   This case description has been jointly constructed by Chrysan Gallucci and Mike Knapp. It is based on field work and case materials developed by Dr. Gallucci as part of research conducted in New York City by the Center for the Study of Teaching & Policy. A recent account of this work appears in Gallucci, Knapp, Markhout, and Ort (2003).

half of the students are Latino, 40 percent are black, and about 10 percent are white or other. Approximately three-quarters of the students receive free or reduced-price lunch. The students come from primarily stable housing projects and neighborhoods. The transience rate in the school is low and the students tend to stay through the three middle school years. Attendance at the school is also high (approximately 93 percent of students are present each school day), and absenteeism, which is relatively rare, is handled personally by the teachers, the school counselor, or the principal.

Changes at this school and how they were enacted can be understood by considering the Leading for Learning Framework's concepts for learning agendas, areas of leadership action, and strategic pathways.

Roots of the School's Evolution

The school's shift from a traditional to alternative school structure in 1995 was abrupt and involved dramatic changes from what had been in place before. Located in one subdistrict of a large city,[3] Parkside had served a relatively small student population for years, (approximately 200 to 300 students), and the students had produced low test scores. Dissatisfied with the school's performance and the direction it was heading, the superintendent transferred Renee LeJeune to Parkside. At the time, LeJeune was a principal at another school in the district that was slated to be closed. As the district sought to establish all of its middle schools as distinctive small schools of choice, the new principal of Parkside was given wide latitude to reconstruct the school program as she saw fit, and she also had considerable influence over hiring at the school.

Several features in the surrounding environment set the stage for the evolution at Parkside. First, there were many examples of small schools in the city at that time. Some schools were located

---

[3] Parkside was located in one of the 32 community school districts. This was the basic organizing unit of the New York City Schools until 2003, when a new organization condensed these districts into 10 larger, regional districts. In this description we refer to the host subdistrict, District M (pseudonym).

in District M, while others were in adjacent subdistricts. District M recognized this advantage and the presumed promise that these schools might have for addressing the educational needs of urban youngsters. The district had formalized its intention to encourage such schools several years before LeJeune arrived at Parkside. But developing Parkside into a distinctive school community was not a blank check for school-level reformers to implement a new school vision in a vacuum. Rather, the district made it clear that the school had to meet the recently revised and demanding learning standards adopted by the city, and district leaders would remain active observers of the school's work. Meanwhile, the school was encouraged to develop unique qualities for an alternative school of choice while also adhering to city and state reform policies. Although the district and state standards could be potentially intrusive, school leaders also had to decide whether these standards could be a useful stimulus and resource for the school's development.

Reculturing, Restructuring, and Rebuilding the Staff at Parkside

Learning Directions

Learning Agendas
Professional learning

Areas of Action
(2) Building professional community

Pathways
• Collegial connections
• Restructuring time and programs

Parkside began in 1989 as Parkside Academy. The school was originally created to extend an urban elementary school into a middle school. The program was directed by the elementary school's principal. Early on, district officials viewed Parkside as chaotic. They recognized that the school had both instructional and disciplinary problems and that the program lacked close attention to its needs as a middle school. The first target for Parkside's new principal was improving the qualifications and composition of the staff and creating a collegial community. With the district's approval, Principal LeJeune brought a core group of staff members with her. This team worked with LeJeune when she was a teacher leader, and this group developed an alternative, arts-based high school program in the same school district. LeJeune and those four teachers were given the charge to revamp the middle school, and they had a relatively free hand in hiring new replacement staff members to augment their ranks.

LeJeune's first year as principal was one of cultural change aimed at creating an atmosphere that said, "This is a school and it's about learning." At the end of the first year, the staff agreed to develop a family model that involved three teachers teaming up to teach language arts, social studies, math, and science to a group of students. This structural change helped the staff be more accountable to one another. By the third year, as the changes began to substantially affect curriculum and associated teaching responsibilities, many of the original staff members opted out of the program and LeJeune began filling the staff with young, bright, and like-minded professionals.

The school brochures, the principal, and even the teachers themselves note that high-quality, creative, and intelligent staff members are at the heart of the school's work. As she hired new staff, the principal looked for people who traveled, were worldly, took courses, and did other things outside of education. The teachers she found tended to have varied backgrounds (e.g., artists, writers, editors, museum educators.), and most candidates had degrees in the humanities as well as in education. More than one teacher explained that the group is intellectually demanding and noted this as one of the positive features of working at the school.

Learning Directions

Areas of Action

(2) Building profes-
     sional community

Pathways

• Recruitment and hiring
• Restructuring time and
  programs
• Curriculum
• Staffing assignment

The district supported LeJeune in a school-level interview process, which meant that she did not have to hire teachers that she did not want teaching at the school. In her fifth year at the school, the staff officially voted for a union-supported plan that formalized the role of school-level stakeholders in the hiring process. From this point forward, a team of teachers, the principal, and parents would interview and hire new staff members. (From this plan, all newly hired staff members had to "reapply" for their jobs. However, with this mutual agreement, their job descriptions were written in such a way that these staff members would be assured to return if they chose to do so.)

As new staff members were hired, the program at Parkside began to assume a new and structurally different form that was characterized by block scheduling, team teaching, and small classes. Each grade-level team of three to four teachers worked together to develop and teach an interdisciplinary humanities block. All staff members were responsible for teaching a literacy block that focused on reading and writing. Teachers also teamed up for other curricular offerings, including science and the arts. Mathematics instruction was delivered in a more traditional structure. The net effect was that all staff members in the school taught several subjects. Most staff members who stayed accepted this task. However, the newer teachers often expressed some conflict regarding the challenges of teaching outside their content areas.

Using Collaborative Curriculum Development as the Centerpiece for Improvement

Learning Directions

Learning Agendas
Student learning
Professional learning

Areas of Action
(4) Acting strategically and sharing leadership

Pathways
• Curriculum
• Collegial connections
• Restructuring time and programs
• Planning and goal setting

The first five years of LeJeune's transformation at Parkside were spent developing the interdisciplinary curricula and team teaching model that characterize the current school program. Simply put, outside of teaching and working with students, the staff at Parkside spends most of its faculty time developing a common humanities-based, project-oriented curriculum. LeJeune made it a point to construct the weekly schedule so that there was ample time for the discussions implied by this curriculum development process. Faculty members were given time each day to meet in grade-level teams or in subject-matter teams. The schedule was arranged so that on one day a week students were excused early to enable staff members to meet to work on curriculum and associated instructional strategies. Once strong norms emerged about the importance of the curricular work, team members often supplemented the scheduled meeting times with additional conversations during their lunch hours and even after school.

The principal made curricular work the main focus of the periodic staff development days that were provided by the district. LeJeune also began requiring some institute-based curricular work in the summer. The summer curricular work also included discussing required common readings, preparing detailed unit plans for the next year's teaching, or tackling other big issues on the school's developmental agenda (e.g., one summer, the staff learned about creating portfolios as an assessment tool).

The principal and teachers at Parkside concentrated their curricular efforts on two courses—an interdisciplinary, project-based humanities class called Connections and a small-group literacy block that integrated reading and writing called Readers & Writers. Each course was taught by grade-level teams of three to four teachers. Students were grouped in various grade-level configurations across the teams depending on the goals of particular projects or activities.

Teachers openly note the challenges of developing and teaching in this format. One teacher said, "The teaming complicates it...there is more room for disagreement and it requires a great deal of communication and feedback between team members." In this regard, it was not unusual for a large portion of a staff development day to be devoted to issues related to teaming. The other half was often spent discussing issues of curriculum content and approach—(e.g., the meaning of terms such as "project, activity, and lesson" in relation to the project-based curriculum that integrated history, language arts, and the arts and sciences).

Learning Directions

Learning Agendas
Professional learning

Areas of Action
(4) Acting strategically and sharing leadership

Pathways
• Collegial connections
• Leadership development
• Support for ongoing professional learning

The joint curricular work is about far more than the content of instruction. It focuses, instead, on all facets of instruction including the students, the work they do, the way they interact with one another and the faculty, and the norms that guide their work. Thus, staff time is spent focusing on goals for developing and implementing the curriculum. LeJeune defined the dialogue that goes on as a source of the innovations that take place at the school. All of the teachers spoke of the importance of the interdisciplinary, project-based curriculum that creates several entry points for students of varying abilities. Several teachers referred to having high expectations for students' behavior and schoolwork. One teacher said,

We are very focused on getting students to really dig deep into their studies and to be serious [about it]. We have high expectations for their behavior. And we spend a lot of time and thought on making sure that they behave in a way that is appropriate for working productively. We try to celebrate student work that's excellent and give them opportunities to share and present. And, [we emphasize that] it's cool to be smart here.

The Growth of a Vibrant Professional Community

Learning Directions
Learning Agenda
Student learning
Professional learning
Areas of Action
(1) Focus on learning
(4) Acting strategically and sharing leadership
(5) Creating coherence

While the never ending curricular development work at Parkside defines the content and academic tasks for student learning, it also supports collective professional learning among the school staff. As the school's instructional leader, the principal sees the importance of building capacity from within the staff through developing shared knowledge and ideas about teaching and learning. Initially, LeJeune and a part-time staff developer conducted classes and workshops to encourage interaction among staff members.

In subsequent years, classroom teachers began to take the responsibility for making presentations at staff meetings and on staff development days. Several staff members subsequently did presentations for the rest of the group. These presentations often left a clear effect on their colleagues' practice. LeJeune explained,

I would see things that Sam did that would blow me away, and I wanted people to know about them, so I'd ask him to present. And, then at the retreat, two years ago, Sam did a number of really interesting presentations, so we started getting into presentations. The first year we were all reading *In the Middle* together, but we didn't do anything with it [as a group]. This summer we read *Nonfiction Matters* and I assigned [grade-level leaders] to make presentations to the rest of the staff on parts of the book. I told them teaming is like getting married...and this is a good way to get to know each other.

In response to a presentation about teaching memoirs, several teachers developed memoir units for their Readers & Writers classes. LeJeune commented on what ensued in one teacher's classroom after a presentation.

[One teacher] completely restructured his classroom...he used to be the center of the room. All children and all instruction revolved around him. You walk into his room now and you can't find him. He's seated somewhere and the kids are all working at different levels with different pieces. They're either engaged in some form of writing or reading from a menu of items that they can work from. He's gone into the workshop model. He does mini-lessons. . . . He is willing to respond to where the kids are and move through things as a literacy program, not as the "English teacher with the lesson plan". . . . I think that was a big change for him. That was the biggest bang I got from that presentation.

LeJeune also conveyed her thoughts about how the teachers at Parkside were beginning to make their shared knowledge transparent.

[After reading] *Nonfiction Matters,* our teachers began marking text and analyzing visual images. . . . [The teachers were encouraged to] take each other's rubrics and [use] each other's lessons.

Learning Directions
Pathways
• Leadership development
• Curriculum
• Restructuring time, program, and facilities

The staff at Parkside is small and, as noted in the discussions about teaming, the work is intense, demanding, and definitely *not* private. One does not get the impression that anyone at the school is being made to work in a way that they have not chosen. At the same time, however, there is an air of honesty about the difficulties inherent in maintaining the high quality of teaching and learning that both LeJeune and the staff expect. She commented on the difficulty of collaborative work.

> I think that they're much further along than they [believe] they are. And I think that they wouldn't like being in their own rooms with the door shut. But this is really hard; and it's also very rewarding. I think that they've accomplished a whole lot. Here team members stay in a room together, teach and mingle there [and share] their materials and their space. You don't have your own territory to go back to, you don't have control over your own curriculum, and you don't have control of your time. But it always comes down to the kids. They're getting a better experience because of this. I think the teachers know that, so even if they are frustrated, they would not go back [to the old way of doing things].

The teachers that came with LeJeune from her former school function as co-leaders with her at Parkside. When interviewed about the school, they uniformly identified the important features of the program. They detailed the changes that they were leading, and they named teaming, developing the project-based curriculum for Connections, and emphasizing middle school literacy as priorities for the staff. One of these veteran teachers said that strong leadership and democratic processes for making decisions were defining features of the school. Other teachers who were newer to the staff referred to the pressure of working at Parkside, but they generally felt supported by LeJeune in their work.

LeJeune has been clear about her priorities as the school leader. "To me the biggest and most important job as a principal is to be the staff developer. Everything else can get thrown out, but not that." She has not spent as much time in classrooms modeling instructional practice as she has supporting her teachers in curriculum development. (Modeling instructional practice is primarily the job of the in-house staff developer). She stated,

> I do a lot of writing of or editing curriculum. [I also help teach-
> ers] find the books and resources [they need]. In the morning,
> they will come and tell me what they need...and I try to deliver.
> But, I would say that I'm intricately involved in the curriculum of
> all the teams.

LeJeune noted that she is aware of how instruction is going because she sees it happening, but that she doesn't have the time to devote to that type of staff development. "I wouldn't say that I have the luxury of sitting in classrooms for long amounts of time. Our in-house developer, Lydia, focused on a new teacher who was having problems. She could devote a month to him. I could never do that." The principal does feel, however, that she models a certain inter-action style with students by the way that she talks to them and spends time with them during their lunch.

Navigating Increasing Accountability at Parkside

Learning Directions

Learning Agendas
Student learning

Areas of Action
(3) Engaging external
environment

Pathways
• Student learning
standards
• Assessment
• Accountability

Parkside does not carry out its academic program in a vacuum. Pressures from district, city, and state are ever present. Many of these pressures concern assessment, performance, and accountability. One of LeJeune's essential functions is to respond to these external demands, act on them in ways that serve the interests of the school's students and teachers, and deflect them when appropriate and feasible. Here, the school's collaborative culture enables LeJeune and her staff to be responsive to a demanding environment while staying true to its principles and distinctive mission.

One example is Parkside's response to the district's push for a portfolio-based assessment system. After attending several summer institutes at Harvard University, the Parkside staff had developed and implemented their own process-based portfolio system for the school. When the district chose to participate in a city-sponsored pilot of a standards-based portfolio system, a move that district leaders saw as supporting its instructional improvement agenda, the staff at Parkside strongly resisted the change. They felt that the district's presentation of the new system was a poor fit with their well-developed understanding of performance-based assessment systems. However, LeJeune saw an opportunity to think more deeply about the school's portfolio process. Under her leadership, the staff reconsidered the district's standards-based system and worked hard over a two-year period to integrate it into their own process. As a result, students in all grades were guided in presenting two portfolios at the end of the school year. The students were aware of the difference between the two portfolios and were able to articulate the differences. One system showcased their best standard-bearing work and the other highlighted their learning in several thematically-based areas of growth. The district, to their credit, showed respect for Parkside's efforts. They let LeJeune take the lead with her staff in developing a response to the district's policy. In the end, LeJeune and her staff were invited to present their process to school leaders and staff developers across the district as a model for thinking deeply about assessment practices.

It is not easy to navigate these kinds of pressures productively, but, so far, Parkside has found a way to do it. To date, its performance on externally mandated measures of success is sufficient to attract a continuing clientele of students and parents. Parkside's success also has stalled more intrusive threats by a system that is not patient with low performance.

Manchester High School: Distributing Leadership to Improve Student Learning

For most of its 50-year history, Manchester High School had the reputation as the lowest-performing high school in its midsized suburban district. Significant improvements for a failing school don't happen overnight. More than 10 years of teacher-driven reform efforts have transformed Manchester High School from one of the surrounding region's lowest performers to an academically rigorous institution that offers students a choice of six theme-based academies. These academies include a program with a traditional schedule, a challenging freshmen academy, and junior/senior academies in communications, environmental studies, engineering, and leadership. At the heart of this renewal process was a carefully crafted leadership strategy initiated by an incoming principal.

Manchester enrolls just under 1,000 students. The school's student population is 82 percent white, 2 percent black, 1 percent Native American, 6 percent Hispanic, and 3 percent Asian. Relatively few Manchester students (3 percent) qualify for free or reduced-price lunch. While Manchester's demographics are basically unchanged, its students are currently outperforming their wealthier peers at neighboring schools on national, state, and district assessments.

Manchester's reform plan focused on four design principles—personalization, instruction, support, and creating a learning community. This has led the school to become a nationally recognized leader in project-based learning, integrated curricula, applied technology, and professional development. Academy students take classes with the same teachers and peers for two years. These close relationships provide personalized support that is pivotal to student success.

In recent years, Manchester has demonstrated a strong, multi-year trend of improved student achievement across a range of indicators and a high degree of teacher and student satisfaction. The graduation rate is 100 percent as compared to 88.4 percent in 1996, the dropout rate is zero, and the attendance rate has improved. More than 80 percent of students enroll in college. Sixty-two percent of students meet the rigorous requirements to attend state universities as compared to just 40 percent in 1993.

How did Manchester dramatically improve student learning outcomes? Where did they begin? Over time, what leadership action spurred efforts to improve learning?

The Many Sides of Manchester's Leadership Story

Learning Directions
Areas of Action
(4) Acting strategically and sharing leadership
(5) Creating coherence

Reforming a comprehensive high school is a particularly messy and complex endeavor. Manchester's story involves leadership and funding changes at the school and district level, distribution of leadership among teachers, parents, and administrators, and instructional and structural reforms to improve student learning opportunities. The process also included hiring and inducting new staff members, improving facilities, and communicating the school's vision with the staff, students, parents, community, school district, and the wider public.

The original impetus for change at Manchester came from an unpopular district mandate. Fed up with chronic low performance at Manchester, the superintendent at the time sent a private foundation with a specific program to help save the school. The foundation established a small school-within-a-school program called the School for Integrated Studies that was facilitated by outsiders. This development was met with a lot of negative response from veteran staff members and school leadership. Although the program had produced some success, its influence did not spread across the school as funders had hoped, largely because the program was being mandated.

When the district hired a new superintendent and the school hired a new principal the following two years, there was plenty of room for change. The new principal, Bob Perkins, had a 26-year history as a teacher and as an assistant principal at one of the more prestigious high schools in the district. His prior experience was respected by teachers. He entered the job with a determined learning focus—to help the Manchester staff and students meet or exceed learning levels of other high schools. The new superintendent approached leadership as a shared enterprise. His leadership style was less top-down than the previous administration. The superintendent sought ways to support Manchester's existing reform projects and build on the new principal's commitment to excellence for the school.

Learning Directions
Areas of Action
(1) Focus on learning
(4) Acting strategically and sharing leadership

Even though the Leading for Learning Framework paints a comprehensive picture of learning-focused leadership, getting there requires leaders to first figure out how to get started. For Manchester, as in many school renewal efforts, structural changes provided a place to begin.

Upon his arrival, Principal Bob Perkins recognized a rift between a subgroup of staff members who were involved in the School for Integrated Studies (which experienced student success through an instructional approach featuring small groups and project-based learning) and those who were not. Very early on, he facilitated a staff exercise around the following questions: "What do you want kids to have when they leave us? What do we teach? What are the ingredients of a good learning experience?" Perkins noted, "The idea was to get everybody to agree to some generic idea about good instruction." He wanted the reason for the tension between the programs to surface, and he wanted teachers to realize that they had a lot more in common. After six months of doing this exercise and applying conscious leadership around these issues, the rift was over.

Perkins and teacher leaders also encouraged staff members to celebrate the successes going on in the original School for Integrated Studies program. They made the program their own, and they worked to create personalized learning communities and theme-based instruction. They continued to use the original funding and sought additional funds to support the staff's instructional vision for what skills they wanted the kids to have as they left Manchester.

Around the time of leadership transition, the school received additional funding from the state and outside grants due to a revised funding formula. At first, the school's leaders focused some of these resources on structural reforms like scheduling and improving the school facility and grounds. At the same time, however, Perkins and teacher leaders began to focus in a more long-term, systemic way on improving instruction and student learning opportunities and on distributing leadership for these improvements more widely within the school staff.

Learning Directions

Areas of Action

(1) Focus on learning

(2) Building professional community

Pathways

• Hiring and induction

• Supervision and evaluation

Over his seven years as principal, Perkins focused heavily on the triangular relationships between teachers, learners, and content. Having taught for 26 years, the principal put great stock in the power of high-quality instruction to improve student learning. He emphasized this as he hired and oriented new staff members and during his regular teacher evaluations. During his tenure, he was able to hire approximately 70 percent of the teaching staff due to retirements. This allowed him to select and train teachers who were committed to the importance of the relationship triangle.

Perkins and his staff hired teachers who were committed to creating personalized, integrated learning opportunities for students and teachers who were willing to experiment with these ideas outside the School for Integrated Studies program. As teachers took ownership of their teaching experience, the reform that had begun initially with a top-down, foundation-funded project was picked up and spread throughout the school. Academies were set up for juniors and seniors in addition to expanding the integrated program for freshmen and sophomores.

Building Manchester's Leadership Capacity

Learning Directions

Pathways
- Leadership development
- Support for ongoing professional development
- Developing collegial connections

Consistent with current thinking in the field, the Leading for Learning Framework underscores the importance of distributed leadership. A failure to pay attention to the need for distributed leadership would likely have resulted in a disappointing ending to the Manchester story. Literature on school reform foretells the demise of change efforts when strong formal leadership departs and leaves a vacuum at the top. Perkins was a strong, trusted, powerful formal leader; however, he was wise enough to recognize that sustaining learning improvement efforts was predicated on shared ownership and leadership. As learning improvement efforts began to take hold, Perkins strategically took steps to remove himself from the spotlight and build the capacity of those around him to carry the efforts forward.

In order to focus on instructional improvement, Perkins and a core group of teachers secured additional grant funding to create time for teachers to meet, plan, and take official leadership roles. Perkins and his team made their reform successful by paying significant attention to building a professional community and by setting aside time for teachers to lead and meet. Now, at least eight Manchester staff members are paid as teacher leaders.

> **Learning Directions**
>
> **Areas of Action**
>
> (2) Building profes-
>   sional community
>
> (4) Acting strategically
>   and sharing
>   leadership

At staff meetings, it is now difficult to tell who the leaders are. The process of sharing leadership was initiated in the first weeks of Perkins's tenure. One of the first things he did was bring the department chairs together to talk about governance. They created one leadership body and displaced two other groups with a long history of conflict. They wrote bylaws in one morning and created the Manchester Leadership Council, which was composed of the nine department chairs, parent and student representatives, and classified staff representatives. Over time, they added teacher representatives from each of the instructional initiatives that were underway at the school.

It was with these initiatives that leadership began to be distributed across the school. Perkins's role in the leadership council was to facilitate meetings but not to vote. The principal defined his role as follows: a communicator for the school's vision to the public, a coordinator who creates space to help others lead, a liaison with the district and superintendent, and a negotiator who balances the relationship between the teacher, the student, and student learning through hiring, induction, and evaluation.

> **Learning Directions**
>
> **Pathways**
> • Leadership
>   development
> • Compensation and
>   reward

Furthermore, Perkins and the council members defined the role of teacher leaders as follows: creating and spreading the vision at the school level, facilitating staff meetings, and helping staff members contribute to reforming student learning at Manchester. As one teacher leader noted, "Developing multiple leaders depends on people having something real and authentic to do and [having] considerable support to do it. You can't just assume a leadership role on top of all your other responsibilities." Through grants and other funding, Manchester created a compensation scale that included either extra pay or additional classroom release time for a wide spectrum of teacher leaders. Perkins and his staff saw this investment as having long-lasting positive effects on the way staff members work regardless of their official positions at the school. Instead of following someone else's reform agenda, Perkins and his staff established their own agenda and then consciously communicated it to crucial constituencies.

> **Learning Directions**
>
> **Areas of Action**
>
> (1) Focus on learning
>
> (3) Engaging environments (community)
>
> (4) Acting strategically and sharing leadership

One teacher leader recounted how the leadership group had searched for effective ways to communicate the vision to the staff. They worked to get it down to a one-minute version that would help everyone be able to articulate the vision and direction for the school. They consciously set up opportunities for staff and community members to question, disagree, and contribute to the dialogue about the school's direction.

> **Learning Directions**
>
> **Areas of Action**
>
> (3) Engaging environments (district)

Perkins was responsible for communicating the vision to communities outside of the school, especially the school district. He helped the school tailor its vision to support the district's goals, while at the same time guiding district policy and receiving supportive treatment from district leaders. For example, teacher leaders asked for and were given permission to be absent from district meetings so that they could have school-based time to work on their instructional reforms. The school's teachers were also able to affect the district's direction by facilitating the district's summer institute for all employees.

Enabling Student and Professional Learning
Through Inquiry Processes

Learning Directions
Learning Agendas
System learning (school level)
Pathways
• Planning and goal setting
• Accountability

Contrary to some prescriptive reform programs that view change as a destination rather than an ongoing process, Manchester's approach invites continual renewal and growth. The school embraced new accountability expectations for learning progress. These measures included an inquiry process designed to promote ongoing improvement of instructional practice through careful examination of data collected at the school. The district was supportive in collecting and analyzing data on student achievement for the school.

Looking at student data has been a central piece of Manchester's strategy for growth over the years. Five years ago, Manchester became involved with a reform program that helped staff use data and inquiry to create the optimal experience for students. Using a support structure and funding from a reform organization, Manchester staff members continued to pursue their vision for improved student learning by using a cycle of inquiry to study, plan, act, and evaluate their progress.

Over time, as students have experienced greater success at Manchester, the school became a popular choice for area students. The student demographic mix has not changed significantly. However, Manchester's staff has managed to create improved student learning opportunities and outcomes for the very types of students who were present during its decades of low performance. They have done this by focusing on student learning, instruction, and distributing leadership.

Douglass Elementary School: Developing Capacity to Close Achievement Gaps

Some readers may ask, how does a school get started with a learning-focused agenda that is designed to close identified achievement gaps? The case that follows provides an opportunity to use the ideas from the Leading for Learning Framework to analyze one elementary school principal's learning improvement efforts. Her initiatives start to answer the question "Where to begin?"[4]

Principal LaToya Washington said, "There is an achievement gap at Douglass Elementary School, particularly for students of poverty and color." Over the past three years, Washington and the Douglass faculty members have begun an intensive effort to close the identified learning gaps among students at the school by using a variety of strategies and interventions revolving around restructuring the school's Title I program. They have focused their work on achieving specified district literacy benchmarks at each grade level. To support this process, the school has institutionalized team collaboration, professional development, ongoing assessment, and reflection as part of everyday practice. The school also changed the delivery of remedial services from traditional pullout sessions to in-class support using teacher facilitators. In general, staff learning is more specific, and it targets teacher capacity and instructional skills that relate to literacy. This also has created significant new learning for the principal—her personal professional development is now centered on learning how to lead instruction about literacy for her students and teachers.

---

[4] This case description has been created with assistance from Kathleen Poole. Her personal knowledge and leadership work at this school were invaluable.

Identifying a Clear Focus at Douglass

Learning Directions
Areas of Action
Focus on learning
Pathways
• Support for professional development
• Curriculum
• Restructuring program

During the 2002–03 school year, Douglass Elementary School staff members, under the leadership of Principal Washington, began to focus their attention on the achievement gap between students from low-income and minority backgrounds and their wealthier counterparts. Although 55 to 60 percent of Douglass students were achieving at expected levels on standardized assessments overall, the vast majority of students not achieving those standards were students of color, students living in poverty, or students with both characteristics. Washington said,

> As a staff, we identified the students, and we confronted our own responsibility to them. Much of last year was spent in analysis and reflection. We met, we read, and we discussed. By the end of the year we had formulated a plan that we thought would assist our students. What we came up with was primarily a technical change in the delivery of remedial services from a pullout model to an in-class model of support for students and teachers. We hired three facilitators to work on literacy with students and the teachers in a coaching model for the 2003–04 school year. Our theory of action was that by changing the delivery of remedial instruction and focusing on specific reading goals we would improve student achievement in literacy.

Learning Directions
Areas of Action
(1) Focus on learning
(2) Building professional community

Through plans to increase teacher collaboration, teaming, professional development, ongoing assessment, and reflection, school leaders realized that all students could achieve at high standards. Most important, Washington began to understand that teacher learning was crucial if student learning issues were to be addressed. She said,

While we established specific goals for students during our entry into the work last year, the real goal of the work this year has become improving teacher capacity to deliver high-quality, dynamic, effective instruction to all students in the content area of literacy. In hindsight, looking back over the past 18 months, I believe the greatest change that occurred last year was not in the progress of the students but in the belief system of the teachers. We are moving from a culture of frustration to a place of hope [and] accepting our own responsibility as educators in the successful development of our students.

Improving Literacy Learning at Douglass

Drawing on research and her own experiences, Washington led her teachers in an improvement effort that was rooted in a clear theory of action. Washington's work is founded on the fundamental belief that students are successful when they have outstanding teachers who are well-versed in instructional strategies and can meet a variety of needs within one classroom. Washington and the Douglass staff also worked from an understanding that more students are successful when the cognitive demand in a classroom is high and when the climate of the school supports high academic achievement. Washington's working theory of action was to improve the quality of the classroom experience. She believed that Douglass's students would be more successful when teachers had appropriate professional development and opportunities for observation, interaction, and conversation with other teachers.

> **Learning Directions**
> **Areas of Action**
> (1) Focus on learning
> (2) Building professional community
> (4) Acting strategically and sharing leadership

Professional development quickly emerged as a key vehicle for change at Douglass. Washington arranged for the Douglass staff to host an intensive, weeklong, job-embedded professional learning opportunity that featured a well-known and respected literacy teaching and learning expert. This effort, coupled with a number of other similarly focused activities, has already led to more teacher learning in the area of literacy instruction. Washington said,

> We have engaged in significant staff development, not only [during] the intensive week with [the expert on teaching literacy] but in other district-sponsored workshop and trainings as well. We have read four different books in book groups including *Professional Learning Communities at Work, Because of the Kids, Reading Essentials,* and *Conversations.* We used several articles on literacy from the March 2004 issue of *Educational Leadership* to focus on vocabulary development, training, and disseminating the information at staff meetings. We used all staff meetings for professional development, focusing on comprehension within fiction and nonfiction text, with topics ranging from vocabulary to ESL. We engaged our staff experts as teachers of teachers, and used our after-school kids as volunteers.

Learning Directions

Areas of Action

(4) Acting strategically and sharing leadership

Pathways

• Support for ongoing professional development

• Developing collegial connections

In addition to a focused set of professional development activities, Douglass staff members have begun to develop an organizational culture that emphasizes teaming. This involves teachers working with each other in grade-level and cross-grade groupings. These efforts also entail intensive work with district curriculum specialists and developers who provide ongoing, job-embedded support for improvements in literacy instruction. Washington said,

> The entire school team is focused on meeting the specific reading goals for our kids. Grade-level teams meet every week with a facilitator [to discuss] student progress and strategies. Teachers routinely observe each other teaching [and give] feedback and ideas. Vertical teams meet to discuss the coordination of content areas, specifically writing and math. Facilitators are in classrooms every day for extended lengths of time [to assist

with] team teaching, coaching, or providing services to students. The curriculum developer for literacy in our district visits once a week to work with one student and observe teachers [and to provide] feedback and support. Our district curriculum specialist is in the building one day per week to focus on those teachers who struggle with implementation. She teaches, models, and provides support. Our literacy leaders assist teachers with the effective implementation of balanced literacy. We have moved from what I would describe as a closed culture (i.e., I'll teach my students and you teach yours), to a much more open one. The rooms are open, our practice is open, our results are open, and we routinely share and receive feedback on our progress. In contrast to the old model, teachers are doing a significant amount of discussing, examining, and speculating both about students' progress and their own practice.

Assessing Douglass's Progress

Part of learning-focused leadership is helping the principal and the teachers know what kind of progress is being made and how well their theory of action is working. When questioned about measuring evidence of progress so far, Washington said,

> It's tricky. All year long I've wrestled with the question, how do you measure capacity? How do you track progress? What are the criteria that would exemplify excellence? Do we look at student success as an indicator of teacher success? Certainly, but if a student isn't succeeding how does that tell us what to do to help the teacher? I have used professional development, observations, interactions, and conversations with teachers to improve their practice, but I have found quantifying that progress challenging. I have also been in the classrooms much more frequently than in years past and for longer periods of time, observing both formally and informally. I know each teacher's skill level much more deeply as we approach the year's end.

A group of Douglass teachers who were charged with leading the changes for the Title I programs at the school surveyed the staff in the spring of 2004. The purpose of the survey was to gather input for the next year's plan. One question asked for each teacher to perform a self-assessment. Staff responses to another survey question, "How did the professional development activities in the area of literacy increase your capacity as a teacher in addressing the needs of your students?" illustrated the growth that teachers perceived in their own professional learning. When commenting on the focused professional development, individual teachers said, "the professional development gave me new strategies for shared readings, emphasizing comprehension, holding kids accountable for comprehension, and [helping them] enjoy reading." Another teacher said, "the sessions deepened our knowledge and understanding of how students learn and what new tools we could use to get them to our targets." Teachers were uniformly clear in expressing that their work together had added value to their daily literacy teaching practices. One teacher noted, "I am more able to assess my students' reading ability and to design instruction to address their needs."

Even though the evidence is early and arguably limited, the data do suggest some progress and growth toward building teacher capacity as literacy instructors. In response to the revelations from teachers, Washington said,

> I was surprised at the general nature of the teachers' comments, and I'm going to push for more detail during my year-end conferences. I intend to use a literacy teacher continuum that offers a developmental view of literacy teacher development [and I'm going to ask] staff to place themselves on the continuum. I am interested in pursuing more vehicles to document progress next year. My intent is to tie in the idea of increasing capacity to individual teacher goals as well as the observation process. I would like the goals to be specific.

Finally, in late spring 2004, Douglass teachers assessed students to generate end-of-the-year data regarding their grasp of literacy. The students were assessed based on a balanced literacy reading program that gauged what level the students could read independently.

Across all grade levels, teachers reported excellent progress, both in terms of student learning across the year and when compared with learning levels in prior years. Washington said,

> As an example, a 1st grade teacher reported that 84 percent of all her students are testing at or above a level 16 (the target). She has two more students who are at a level 14 and may be at 16 by June 21st. Comparatively, last year's 1st grade class had only 61 percent of the students at or above a level 16.

Future Work at Douglass

Even though a number of promising events can be noted from the efforts at Douglass thus far, much work remains to be done. When asked to describe the future work at Douglass, the principal succinctly replied,

> Close the gap! All of this has been preliminary stage setting for the actual results of the work—all children achieving at high levels, all children being engaged in learning, [and] all students having confidence in their own intelligence and capacity. In essence, we want all of our students to be knowledgeable about many things, to be well read, to think with sophistication, [and] to problem solve with more tools. We want their minds to be rich with ideas, goals, and curiosities. We want them to be able to access any part of the system, higher-level classes, and a college education.

As of this writing, Douglass's principal and teachers are in the process of once again revisiting and refining the plans they established in light of their progress. Washington anticipates a limited number of changes in the curriculum facilitator model with small modifications. Ideas discussed include assigning facilitators to specific content areas rather than grade levels, allotting more time with upper grades, and adding more refined specific goals at some grade levels. Washington expects the staff to develop a much more

cohesive and explicit set of goals and an even richer understanding of specific instructional practices that meet particular student needs. Washington remains confident that she can guide the
school's process to reflect that thinking. She said,

> I expect us to focus on comprehension in fiction and non-
> fiction, as well as the reciprocal action of the writing process.
> [The expert on teaching literacy] is already booked for January,
> so we will be able to continue our work with her. I believe my role
> as an instructional leader has expanded as a result of this class
> and the work we do together. I continue to experiment with my
> own understanding and influence on the literacy instruction in
> the building. I continue to be interested in this notion of capacity,
> and in refining what an effective instructor of literacy looks like
> in the classroom. I plan to spend even more time with teachers
> in classrooms. I am going to become an ad hoc member of every
> grade level team, dedicating my time to attending their meetings,
> and participating in their efforts. I have modeled some lessons
> myself, and plan to continue to do so.

The future goal for Douglass is for staff members to remain focused
on student achievement in literacy and to continue openly examining both district and classroom assessments of student progress.
Washington said,

> The data does drive the action, and we can get into such
> trouble if we don't keep it in the center of all we do. I struggle
> with that to some degree, primarily logistically. I think teachers
> are beginning to use the data to drive their instruction, but it's
> not always the case. How can I support them to do that regularly,
> as an individual, as a grade level, as a staff?

In addition to the literacy emphasis, the Douglass staff has suggested a pressing need to also focus on math learning and teaching. As they increase their skill level in literacy, teachers report
that they notice gaps in their math instruction. Douglass also faces

some new budget challenges moving forward. Due to declining enrollment, the school's Title I funds have been cut by $20,000 next year, triggering reductions in special education hours and classified staffing as well. Washington believes she can continue to make the facilitator model work, but she will need to be creative to stay the course.

Washington's year-end reflections offer a hopeful tone for what is to come at Douglass Elementary School. She said,

> It's been a remarkable year by any measure. Students are achieving at higher levels and as we learned from our teacher survey, the staff is united behind the broad ideas. We are responsible for the success of our students. If we are excellent, effective teachers, they have a chance to realize their dreams.

Learning-Focused Leadership in Schools

As these school cases demonstrate, leadership for learning involves work in all five action areas of the Leading for Learning Framework. School-level leaders who work for success focus their efforts not just on student learning, but they also focus on developing teacher capacity to deliver high-quality instruction and creating systems to supports those efforts. A number of pathways appear prominently in these stories, but perhaps most visible is the strategic emphasis leaders place on teacher learning that focuses on students' needs.

9

Leading Learning in School Districts

District leadership aimed at powerful and equitable learning depends on district leaders' ability to engage and respond to multiple environments. The variety of environments across district settings is enormous, and these differences have important implications for any attempts to improve teaching and learning. However, as in schools, district leadership begins with creating a focused learning agenda and maintaining that focus when negotiating in a broader environment. District leadership also entails encouraging support, fending off counter pressures, and buffering schools from conditions that would pose a barrier to a learning agenda. The success of these efforts depends on leaders' ability to perceive opportunities in complex and often adverse conditions.

We explore three cases in contrasting environmental settings in which districts have attempted to exert leverage over learning in different ways. The leaders' efforts reflect the nature of their environments. These examples show how they grapple in contrasting ways with forging a collective will, building a high-quality teaching force, and balancing discretion and initiative across levels. In each case, we use the Leading for Learning Framework as an analytic tool to help pinpoint where and how district actions can reach student learning.

Northern Valley School District: Leading for Learning in a Rural Setting

The Leading for Learning Framework ideas and tools offer an analytic framework for understanding the efforts of learning-focused leaders in the Northern Valley School District (NVSD). Northern Valley, a small rural district near the Canadian border, serves approximately 1,800 students across a high school, middle school, three elementary schools, and a birth-through-five Center for Children and Families.[1] Superintendent Michael Jones and Assistant Superintendent Shelley Ames comprise the central office administrative team and have worked together in Northern Valley since the early 1990s.

Financial Challenges in Northern Valley

The Northern Valley School District is made up of three communities: Eversville (population 1,800), Summertown (population 880), Northern (population 825), and the Northern Indian Reservation (unincorporated). It is a very rural, beautiful, and isolated district with families spread out across one of the largest transportation areas of any of the surrounding county's seven districts. The student population increased over 60 percent from 1989–2000 but has since leveled off. Fishing, logging, and farming have been the stable occupations of this area for many generations. But all three have declined dramatically, leaving workers searching for alternatives, which are usually low-paying service jobs. Unemployment and unemployment claims are 6 to 12 percent above the state

[1] This case draws extensively from the experiences of Mark Johnson and Sandy Austin. They are doctoral candidates in the University of Washington's Leadership for Learning Ed.D. program. The authors wish to acknowledge their leadership and expert assistance in constructing this account.

average, and wages and per capita income are 80 to 84 percent below the state average.

Northern Valley is also a place where families migrate to seek seasonal employment. Many of these migrant families are not of the dominant culture, and their children are at risk for failure in the public school system. Families identifying themselves as Hispanic have increased 249 percent in the school district since 1990. Parallel to this growth, there has been a 30 percent increase in families qualifying for free and reduced-priced lunch (almost 50 percent of total district enrollment). Recent demographic data further illustrate the changing population and identify Northern Valley in the top three of 33 districts in the region with the highest percentage of low-income families. In addition, the percentage of adults living in the district who did not complete high school is well above the state average.

Complicating the situation in Northern Valley has been the lack of financial resources needed to develop, implement, and sustain initiatives to ensure students' success. Northern Valley's annual district property tax levy is only $1,017 per student. With this amount, Northern Valley ranked 29th out of 33 school districts in the region for per student capita distribution, and it ranked the lowest out of seven school districts in the county. NVSD also has the least advantageous tax base among the 33 regional districts as measured by the assessed value of property per each full-time equivalent (FTE) student. Moreover, while the district collects the least levy revenue per FTE in the county (4th lowest in the 33 districts in the region), local taxpayers pay the second highest levy tax rate in the county.

Evaluating Positive Learning Trends in Northern Valley

Despite these numerous challenges, the district has made considerable progress on several initiatives over the past few years. A clear theory of action focused on student, professional, and system learning guides the district's work in assessment, accountability, curriculum development, leadership development, parent involvement, and creating coherence in staff development.

For student achievement, NVSD's results suggest that the district has experienced significant progress relative to other districts, despite its fiscal challenges. As of 2003, Northern Valley's student performance data on the 4th and 10th grade state assessments ranked well above the state averages. This data also show that these students have a continuous trajectory of improvement across all assessed subject areas. Notably, the scores for Northern Valley students in reading, writing, and mathematics were at or near the top scores when compared to the seven surrounding school districts in the same county. NVSD students also ranked either first or second in every subject matter category.

Additional Northern Valley data show trends toward more students meeting state standards over time (as measured by the Washington Assessment of Student Learning (WASL) and improving on grade-level assessments. For example, the percentage of 4th grade students at or above the state standard in math increased 50 percentile points between 1997 and 2003; 10th graders were proficient in or exceeded their writing performance by 17 percentile points between 1999 and 2003. In 7th grade math, the percentage of students who were at or above the state standard jumped 29 percentile points between 1998 and 2003. Comparisons within a single student cohort show gains that are no less compelling across three state assessments conducted in 1997 (grade 4), 2000 (grade 7) and 2003 (grade 10). Over this six-year period, the percentage of students in the cohort who met or exceeded state standards increased 20 percentile points in reading, 38 percentile points in writing, and more than 30 percentile points in math. As these trends indicate, Northern Valley students show improving trends in achievement on annual standardized tests, between different groups of students at the same grade level, and within cohort groups over time. Reflecting on the ongoing improvement trends in student achievement data, Superintendent Jones and Assistant Superintendent Ames recognize that they have learned a lot since their work in Northern Valley began. They continue to have zeal as they work with other principals, teacher leaders, coaches, and external consultants in the district to move to another level. Ames said, "We are aware of what we're doing, but we're still working to understand how it all connects coherently."

Learning Directions

Learning Agendas
Student learning
System learning

Areas of Action
(1) Focus on Learning

Pathways
• Planning and goal setting
• Leadership development

Part of the ongoing work involves a cyclical revisiting of the district's strategic plan. The planning process, initiated by Jones early in his tenure as superintendent, has evolved as a way to keep the district focused on learning improvement. Recent work on the strategic plan, which last occurred in 2003, has helped to support a continual commitment to leadership efforts, as well as expand the scope of the work designed to improve learning. The revised plan opens with a mission statement that focuses on learning for all students. When leaders in this district are questioned about this language, their depth of understanding and their commitment to focusing on learning becomes clear. A middle school principal who serves on the planning team noted,

> All kids? What does that mean? The leadership team spent a lot of time talking about what [this term] means, and [we] realized we had to fully understand its meaning as leaders before we tried to explain it to staff and faculty. For us, at the middle school, we decided it means very simply that all kids have an equal opportunity to meet the standards we've set for them. I think other [principals] would say the same.

The coordinator for the birth-to-five Children and Family Center further clarified how Northern Valley's leadership team implies learning for every student, and how leaders make the necessary connections across levels in the system. She said,

> Ensuring [that] all kids learn is a great idea, but at the center we needed to align this with what we want to accomplish in the K–12 system. There was a real need to bring [more intention] for the early years so that what we are hoping to accomplish in student learning at that level aligns with what we ultimately want throughout the system. So, when we create assessments for language and literacy development, for example, there is the intention that what we are assessing in our early learners matters for what comes next.

Northern Valley's leaders recognize that strategic planning needs to be backed up with actions that are designed to improve learning. Using the Leading for Learning Framework brings clarity to analyzing the district's leadership action. All five action areas are evident in the work that Jones, Ames, principals, and other leaders in the district strive to accomplish. For example, Jones and Ames are clear about the importance and specifics of engaging environments that matter for learning. They said,

Learning Directions

Areas of Action

(1) Focus on Learning

(3) Engaging Environments

Jones: At the middle school, engaging environments means the middle school principal [has] focus groups with 8th grade parents to ask them what went well for their kid's school experience and [to ask for] their recommendations for improvement. At the elementary schools, it means developing family nights, partnerships with 4H, or developing a health focus grant to work with the local hospital on tracking children's health needs. It [also] means building community partnerships for the early childhood center. Our children and family center coordinator has probably 20 such partnerships going including everything from the local community college to the hospital.

Learning Directions

Learning Agendas

Student learning

Professional learning

System learning

Pathways

- Professional practice standards
- Support for ongoing professional development
- Planning and goal setting

Ames: What we've done so far to engage environments primarily involves physical partnerships. Intentionally, we've called these learning partnerships to signal that we are really learning and growing together.

Through working with the principals and teacher leaders, Jones and Ames see that the district has accomplished much with regard to student learning so far. Recently, they moved into a new stage of learning that primarily focuses on adults in the system. Jones and Ames believe that focusing on professional learning is the key to moving the district to even greater levels of accomplishment. So far, their professional learning has involved a broad array of teachers designing and delivering professional learning for themselves and colleagues. Professional learning is also increasing the student learning goals as evidenced by ongoing data assessment. Jones said,

> In reading, we've been working to get our head around the work that we're doing. If you look at the kids in our district, probably 70 percent of them are meeting our standards up through [8th grade.] We're doing pretty well, but we're not done with this work. We've done a number of things that focus on the students—working on curriculum and assessment issues, extending the learning day for kids, building our center for early childhood learning, putting school accountability measures in place, working on student accountability, creating improvement plans, and seeking additional funds. I see all this work as a part of traditional student learning systems. So, we've been asking ourselves, what is going to push us to all kids learning? What we've realized is that we've got to talk about adult practice and adult learning in the same way that we've focused on the kids. We see the need to

focus on teaching and learning standards for our teachers and principals, understand the attributes of successful classrooms and successful schools, build professional learning communities in our schools, and delve deep into cycles of inquiry focused on individual teachers' practice. We also need to build system supports around internal accountability, reciprocal relationships, distributed leadership, and additional opportunities for professionals to learn.

Learning Directions
Areas of Action
(5) Creating coherence

For Northern Valley leaders, the work continues to be about developing coherence across efforts designed to improve student, professional, and system learning. Working for coherence means that leaders try to always maintain a focus on the "big picture" while still attending to the daily tasks of running a school or a system. One middle school principal in Northern Valley said,

> Work goes on while we try to refine our approach to achieving the vision and mission. There is an increased commitment to make sure that everything is aligned with that vision [and] that it makes sense. [We're ensuring that] we're not doing that knee jerk thing and off running with another good idea over here or the next research thing over here. There's been a constant focus on "how do we build a plan that always is aligned with that vision for learning?"

Highland School District: Data-Driven Cultural Change

The Highland School District is a K–8 suburban school district in a large metropolitan area with well over 7,000 students in roughly a dozen schools.[2]

---

[2] This account is based on research from the Center for Research on the Context of Teaching in collaboration with the Center for the Study of Teaching & Policy. The case materials draw heavily on fieldwork and case summaries constructed by Dr. Julie Marsh. (See Methodological Notes for details on the research base.)

One long-time administrator explained that in the 1950s and 1960s the area used to be "a little bedroom community" serving predominantly white, English-speaking, middle-class residents. From the 1970s through the 1990s, the district's population became more diverse as increasing numbers of Latino and Asian families moved into the area. Highland has become an increasingly diverse district, both ethnically and economically. As one board member commented, "We have kids who come to school in limousines and kids who come to school barefoot and live in cars." Approximately half of Highland's students are white, one-third are Latino, and one-tenth are Asian, while the remaining students are a mixture of other ethnicities. About one-fourth of all Highland students are English language learners, and one-third of students receive free or reduced-priced lunch.

When Deborah Gerstein was hired as superintendent of the Highland School District in the mid-1980s, she faced challenges that were typical for many districts in the state. The student population was becoming increasingly diverse, and the district's scores were slowly declining. However, the causes for the decline in achievement were not obvious at the time. According to the former associate superintendent, "I remember discussions [during this time] that our reading scores aren't what they used to be."

Implementing Strategic Planning and Data Analysis

Inspired by her personal interest in strategic planning, Superintendent Gerstein dragged a couple of board members to a conference on the topic. Encouraged by what they learned, the superintendent began engaging district leaders in conversations about strategic planning. She used shared goals and joint analysis of student achievement data to guide their future

---

Learning Directions

Learning Agendas

Student learning

System learning

Pathways

• Planning and goal setting

• Information system development (data and analysis)

action. Before, disaggregated data analysis was the norm in most school districts. Now, Gerstein encouraged the district leaders and provided them with the training to examine data more in-depth. By using this analytic mindset, leaders were prodded to ask exactly which students were doing poorly on these achievement tests. This data analysis also helped leaders explore the programmatic and societal features that may have contributed to students' low achievement levels. Through sustained inquiry, observation, and discussion, it became clear to Gerstein and her staff that the district's teachers and instructional programs were not adapting to its changing student population, despite the district's excellent reputation for teacher support and professional development.

Highland's leadership team focused on the district's common values and data analysis skills before launching any major curriculum or professional development initiatives. When Gerstein and her staff focused on what they wanted students to learn and developed data-analysis tools to identify the causal problems affecting student learning, the team was able to diagnose the problems more accurately and devise effective solutions. While many districts are preoccupied with crisis management and do not have the luxury of establishing a core set of values or analyzing their data, these can be crucial first steps in developing a positive professional culture that can inform decision making and improve coherence.

After Highland's leaders established their data-analysis strategies, they focused on strategic planning. From the late 1980s into the early 1990s, Highland staff members became more skilled at strategic planning. They improved this process by using third-party facilitators, stakeholder representatives from across the district, and a collaborative process that created a broad base of ownership. The superintendent noted the importance of broad involvement in the process. She said,

> There have been some wonderful things that have come out of strategic planning from the heads of the people in our community [because] they look at schools and schooling with a different perspective. We have always felt that [this] was [valuable]

because, otherwise, we talk to ourselves, and you're doomed to repeat the same dumb stuff you've done before. But people make you look at yourself when you bring them in from outside and have a different perspective. That's been very, very helpful to us.

Learning Directions
Areas of Action
(3) Engaging environments
Pathways
• Planning and goal setting
• Community engagement
• Accountability systems

Although this process received very positive reviews from participants, there were some complaints regarding stakeholder representation, most notably from the ELL constituency. A group of teachers and school staff continued to be unaware of the district's strategic planning and data analysis efforts.

Another important piece of this planning process was aligning resource allocation with strategic planning priorities. Changes in resource allocation that resulted from strategic planning processes signaled to the administrators, teachers, parents, and community members who helped develop the plans that the district intended to be responsive to their priorities. Along these lines, the superintendent made an agreement with the board to tie her performance evaluation to the district's progress on its strategic planning agenda.

Encouraging Collaborative Leadership at Highland

Learning Directions
Areas of Action
(2) Building professional community
(3) Engaging environments (through school board)
Pathways
• Leadership development

As she helped district leaders identify the primary cause for the district's slumping achievement scores, Superintendent Gerstein also made significant strides towards developing collaborative leadership in the district. She cultivated her relationship with the school board, and she kept them well informed of her goals, concerns, and plans. In addition, Superintendent Gerstein also surrounded herself with capable leaders who complemented her abilities and shared her vision for the district. This group also included leaders who did not always agree with her on the best means of achieving the district's goals. For example, Gerstein was not known as a people person. She was viewed as a very strong-willed leader who was never satisfied with the status quo. However, she hired her associate superintendent to provide a balance. The associate superintendent had 30 years of experience in the district, and she was widely regarded as a people person who did everything she could to support those under her supervision.

> **Learning Directions**
>
> **Areas of Action**
>
> (4) Acting strategically and sharing leadership
>
> **Pathways**
>
> • Planning and goal setting
> • Leadership development

Moreover, Superintendent Gerstein distributed a considerable amount of authority to her leadership team and local leaders. For example, when asked, the leadership team in this district could not produce an organizational chart for the central office. One administrator commented, "We tried this last year and we got so frustrated trying to put a chart on paper because we cross roles so often. [Our] organization is not that compartmentalized." At the school level, principals were expected to facilitate their own independent strategic planning sessions at their sites, rather than having the district's plan handed down to them. In addition, teacher-based curriculum committees empowered teachers to articulate their concerns, participate in identifying problems, and develop solutions with personnel in the central office. This process allowed for greater teacher ownership over the curriculum and cultivated more widespread buy-in for programmatic changes.

Zeroing In on Student Achievement Data and Performance-Based Assessments

The Highland School District continued to narrow its focus to concentrate directly on student achievement. Whereas the original strategic plans had developed 10 or more goals, the strategic plans during this period of time only had a handful of goals that were more closely related to student learning.

Learning Directions
Pathways
• Student learning standards
• Assessment systems

At this stage, the district was developing an increasing appetite for student achievement data. This desire for authentic measures of student achievement prompted the district to develop its own performance assessments. Over the years, the district administrators engaged teachers in discussing and agreeing on district learning standards and quality assessments that the district could use to evaluate student learning. After looking extensively at a variety of assessments including student portfolios, the district decided to develop its own performance-based assessments in reading, writing, and math. This involved an enormous amount of work over several years by teachers and central office staff who generated the data. Everyone saw the resulting assessments as useful and informative.

Learning Directions
Areas of Action
(1) Focus on learning (student learning, system learning)
(2) Building professional community
(3) Engaging environments (Higher Ed)
(5) Creating coherence
Pathways
• Preparation and certification
• Mentoring and induction
• Recruitment and hiring

Eventually, the district gained experience with its performance-based assessments. While these assessment measures were considered an integral part of the district's means of monitoring student progress, two challenges arose. First, the state launched a very public accountability policy that required all students to take a multiple-choice, norm-referenced test. This test would publicly rank all schools according to their students' performance and provide financial incentives aligned to the rankings. Although the district continued to administer its own assessment, the state accountability system clearly overshadowed the district's performance-based assessment. Second, the district assessment scores were inconsistent, which suggested that the test had questionable reliability. For example, the percentage of 2nd graders meeting the standard in writing on the district's assessments went from 24 percent in 1997 to 53 percent in 1998. During the same time, 53 percent of kindergarteners met the district standard in reading, up from 33 percent the year before, and 90 percent of these students met the district standard in writing up from 62 percent. Despite these challenges to the performance-based assessments, the district leadership continued to work with and improve these assessments to create a more accurate and comprehensive picture of student learning.

Learning Directions

Pathways
• Support for special learning needs (ELL)
• Support for professional development

Learning Agendas
System learning

Over time, the strategic planning, collaboration, and data-analysis initiatives during the late 1980s were now engrained as system learning, and they produced additional teaching and learning-oriented program changes. District learning standards, performance-based assessments, and a focus on improving literacy instruction are examples of the district's leadership activity expanding along additional pathways in a coordinated fashion to improve student learning.

Learning Directions

Areas of Action
(1) Focus on learning

By the late 1990s, the stability and consistency of the focus among Gerstein and her staff was paying off. Strategic planning, collaboration, and data-driven decision making were institutionalized, and a professional culture based on these practices existed among the district leadership. Now district leaders were charged with one goal—improve student achievement so that 100 percent of district students meet the district's learning standards.

Building Collaborations That Strengthen the Professional Infrastructure

Another development for the Highland School District during this time was a partnership with a neighboring district and a local university. This collaborative was intended to promote teacher learning and leadership via three major components. First, it provided onsite teacher education and extensive, yearlong internships for prospective teachers. Second, the collaboration provided new teachers with mentors, peer support, and continuing education opportunities. The district's ability to grow their own high-quality teachers has been a positive outcome of this partnership. One of the district coordinators for new teacher support said,

> I think that [this collaboration] has provided us with a wonderful core of interns who are matched with teachers who really have best practices. They are really ahead in terms of pedagogy [as compared to other] first- or second-year teachers.

> **Learning Directions**
> **Pathways**
> • Leadership development
> • Supervision and evaluation

Third, the collaborative offered experienced teachers a master's degree program in teacher leadership that prepared them to be mentors and onsite professional development facilitators. This program has been the most popular of the three with more than 50 teachers presently participating in the program from both partner districts. Similarly, experienced teachers in the district are offered an alternative to the standard principal's supervisory evaluation. The evaluation allows teachers to pursue their own area of interest with a classroom-based action research project.

Promoting Professional Development to Improve Learning

Additional data analysis from the district pinpointed literacy as a major area of need throughout the district, especially among the ELL population. The district administrators and teachers adopted a reading recovery program and devoted extensive resources and training to early elementary literacy in grades K–3. Gerstein and her team pursued grant money vigorously to enhance the organization's capacity to support this instructional initiative, and the district's teachers were provided extensive professional development by external trainers in reading assessment and instructional strategies.

Learning Directions
Areas of Action
(1) Focus on learning (Literacy)

As the literacy initiative gained momentum throughout the district, the program expanded to include full-day kindergarten, substitute teachers to support peer coaching, and offsite training to help teachers become master teachers who would serve as onsite literacy coordinators in every school. Once a month, teachers at all schools participate in literacy training for an hour and a half, with compensation provided for an additional two hours of optional training.

The district also provides substantive professional development to principals. Every other week administrative meetings are devoted to professional development. Often, principals are given reading materials in advance, which they then discuss as a group. The district has also put principals into teams for schools visits. Teams visit one of these principals' schools, conduct walk-throughs, compare their analyses, and provide the host principal with feedback based upon their observations.

Learning Directions
Learning Agendas
Student learning
Professional learning
Pathways
• Leadership development
• Support for professional development

Gerstein and her staff continue to build upon their prior successes. Their leadership actions have continued to broaden to include growing their own teachers, offering meaningful learning opportunities for teachers and principals, and developing the knowledge, structures, and practices to support literacy instruction.

District M: Accountability and Support for Learning in an Urban Setting

District M (pseudonym) was one of 32 community school districts in a major urban center. Diversity in this community spawned both rich cultural resources as well as residential segregation.[3] Enrollment included approximately 15,000 students in preK–8th grade. (High schools were not part of the city's community school districts.) The district was both ethnically and economically diverse, though it lacked a middle class between poor and wealthy residents. Competition from the private schools tended to lure students from middle-class families. More than 80 percent of the students were black and Latino. Approximately 16 percent of the students were English language learners. Of students who were English language learners, the dominant language was Spanish. About 6 percent of the students were enrolled in full-time special education programs and more than 70 percent of the students were eligible for Title I.

Beginning in 1989, the district moved from a ranking of 31 out of 32 community school districts in reading achievement to 10th in 1999. During this same period, the district moved from a ranking

---

[3] This case description relies extensively on fieldwork and case summaries by Chrysan Gallucci, Anneke Markholt, and Suzy Ort, along with Dr. Knapp. This work is part of research conducted in New York City by the Center for the Study of Teaching & Policy. Parts this work are described in Gallucci, Knapp, Markholt, & Ort (2003). The case account presented here concentrates on the last four years of District M's existence before it was incorporated into a larger regional organization of the city's schools.

of 29th in mathematics achievement to 14th. District M administrators attributed the steady increase in test scores to the hard work and focus on professional learning and accountability for learning as it related to how schools spent their money.

> **Learning Directions**
>
> **Areas of Action**
>
> (1) Focus on learning

Between 1997 and 2001 District M's superintendent and deputy superintendent for curriculum, instruction, and professional development were pivotal forces in sustaining a focus on instruction, student standards, and accountability. Superintendent Alicia Rosario had a long established role in the district as someone who cared about curriculum and professional development. Prior to becoming the superintendent, she was the deputy superintendent of curriculum and instruction in the district. Though Rosario moved from that position, she maintained a clear, strong commitment to instructional improvement.

> **Learning Directions**
>
> **Areas of Action**
>
> (4) Acting strategically and sharing leadership
>
> **Pathways**
>
> • Support for professional development
> • Student learning standards

Superintendent Rosario began her position in 1997, and she was an expert in literacy instruction. The deputy superintendent of curriculum, instruction, and professional development, though relatively new to the district at the time, had many years of experience in professional development and leadership roles related to literacy teaching in similar urban settings. Though the superintendent and the new deputy superintendent had fairly different working styles, they saw eye to eye on the basic principles they were trying to establish in their work. On a daily basis, Superintendent Rosario focused much of her attention on shaping professional learning, literacy improvement, and instructional leadership. From the beginning, she designed an elaborate district-led professional development system. The deputy superintendent also honed in on professional development because in her view the "most enormous work [we do] and the work that matters the most [is] the ways in which we learn together [within] a district, a city, [and] a state."

Creating a Policy for Improvement

> **Learning Directions**
> **Learning Agendas**
> Student learning
> Professional learning

The district's overarching learning improvement strategy featured extensive investment in staff development, strong support for principals as instructional leaders, and a focus on literacy instruction. (Mathematics and science were also a matter of concern to the district but to a lesser degree.) At the center of the district's policy strategy were ambitious learning standards that included a blend of state and city standards and sophisticated learning standards derived from the Institute for Learning at the University of Pittsburgh. The district's professional development opportunities converged around beliefs about standards, best practices, and the teaching and learning exemplified in the Principles of Learning [4] from the Institute for Learning. The district's partnerships with institutions of higher education were consistent with the district's goals and efforts around literacy.

> **Learning Directions**
> **Areas of Action**
> (1) Focus on learning
>   (student and
>   professional)
>
> **Pathways**
> • Support for professional
>   development
> • Accountability systems

District M's strategy combined high, explicit expectations for performance by teachers and students with aggressive outreach to schools. Experts in literacy and math instruction were assigned to each school and regularly spent one or more days a week in them depending on the size of the school. Monthly meetings for school leaders

---

[4] The Principles of Learning refer to principles espoused by consultants from the Institute for Learning at the University of Pittsburgh as developed by Professor Lauren Resnick and colleagues. See for example, Resnick, L.B., & Hall, M.W. (2001). *The Principles of Learning Study tools for educators.* [CD-ROM, version 2.0]. Pittsburgh, PA: University of Pittsburgh, Learning Research and Development Center, Institute for Learning (www.instituteforlearning.org).

Learning Directions

Areas of Action

(4) Acting strategically and sharing leadership

(5) Creating coherence

Pathways

- Student learning standards
- Support for professional development

were largely devoted to issues related to learning and teaching. Annual comprehensive plans by each school addressed areas of instructional improvement. The district attempted to maintain a visible connection with each school through annual walk-through visits by the superintendent and other district staff members. The district leaders personally visited each classroom and offered the school leaders feedback on their work and progress toward improvement goals.

Improving Fiscal Planning in District M

During her tenure, Superintendent Rosario strived to get greater control over the district's instructional expenditures. In her view, expenses were poorly guided and not focused on student learning. She began to require all school purchase orders be reviewed by her first. If she thought they had nothing to do with instruction, she would not approve them. She said,

> For 12 years the schools looked so poor, it was depressing to visit [them.] There were no library books in classrooms, there were no materials for children, no manipulatives. Now our schools look very, very rich....My first year [as superintendent] I listened. We were pouring money into schools and I saw no evidence in terms of practice, in terms of materials and supplies.... As I started the second year, there were radical changes in this district. In terms of resources, our schools will never be richer. [But] if we don't deliver to the kids, then shame on all of us.

The superintendent combined intense professional development efforts, pressure for results, and more accountability for school leaders. Between 1986 and 2001, the district consistently garnered $4 million to $7 million annually from outside funding sources. Many of these funds were used to support the district's onsite model for staff development. Even during severe budget shortfalls, district officials stayed the course. Their messages were aligned on familiar themes of standards-based education and professional learning.

Creating Effective Collaborations

> **Learning Directions**
>
> **Pathways**
> - Leadership development
> - Support for professional development
> - Restructuring meeting time
> - Support for special learning needs

Superintendent Rosario considered herself a learner and engaged in opportunities to deepen her own understanding of powerful and equitable student learning. One prominent example of both her commitment and focus on learning was her participation in a study group with the Institute for Learning. She brought her four top district administrators, two directors of staff development, and three principals with her to these meetings. Her goal was for all of these people to spread the word and create a direct pipeline between the Institute for Learning's ideas about principles of learning and the district's efforts to enact instructional policy. Not surprisingly, given the immersion of key district players in these activities, learning became an overarching concept for what educators in the district were expected to do. More specifically, district leaders were encouraged to learn about learning and instruction.

> **Learning Directions**
>
> **Areas of Action**
> (4) Acting strategically and sharing leadership
> (5) Creating coherence
>
> **Pathways**
> - Student learning standards
> - Support for professional development

Fueled by their exposure to these ideas from the Institute for Learning, the superintendent, the deputy superintendent, and other district staff members stimulated and guided the learning for administrators and teachers in the district in a variety of ways. Principals' meetings, held every other month for a full day, were devoted almost entirely to topics related to learning and instruction, especially in literacy. Leaders from schools that were identified as struggling received additional attention. District administrators provided advice and technical assistance for these leaders. Leaders from struggling schools also attended an additional school leaders' meeting once a month to further focus on instructional priorities.

Assessing Accountability for School Leaders in District M

Learning Directions

Areas of Action

(1) Focus on learning (district staff in schools)

Pathways
- Accountability systems
- Leadership development

The superintendent's regular walk-throughs of school buildings emphasized the principles of learning as well as various messages about curriculum and pedagogy. The superintendent viewed her walk-throughs as an opportunity to serve as a critical friend to specific school leaders. The superintendent moved through a school, went into every classroom, and actively interacted with people in the classroom. She had a particular agenda of things that she looked for like word walls, leveled classroom libraries, and abundant displays of student work. She freely talked to students to figure out how they were engaging with the material.

These walk-throughs sent clear messages about particular things that the district valued. At the same time, they indicated symbolically that the district was watching what was going on and would not be a passive player in what happened within the school. Each walk-through was followed up with a detailed letter to the principal that included the superintendent's impressions and suggestions for improvements. School leaders appreciated the letters, which were detailed enough to suggest to schools that the superintendent was knowledgeable and attentive to their work. For school leaders, the superintendent's letters served as models for teacher evaluations.

School-based staff developers were also expected to engage teachers in professional learning guided by the principles of learning ideas. They met with the deputy superintendent once a month to talk about standards, principles of learning, and how to prompt teachers. The district sought to build capacity at each building through school leaders and staff developers.

Defining Standards for Professional Learning

The district used several sources to build standards, assessment, and accountability measures. Those sources included: the New Standards project, which was adopted and adapted by the city as a reference point for students' performance; activities from the city's Chancellor of Schools to form measures for high standards and clear accountability; and state mandates for new assessments that were aligned with state standards, district standards, and strict student and school accountability for student performance.

Learning Directions

Areas of Action

(1) Focus on learning

(2) Building professional community

(5) Creating coherence

Pathways

- Curriculum
- Student learning standards
- Accountability systems
- Assessment systems

The district's concepts for good teaching and curriculum were also aligned with national standards from the National Council of Teachers of English and the National Association for the Education of Young Children, specifically as they related to language arts instruction and developmentally appropriate instruction in early childhood education, respectively. For this district, meeting standards, practicing the principles of learning, and being aligned with current best practices were exemplified in a balanced literacy approach to teaching students to read and write. Balanced literacy was a strong district push and an explicit target of the superintendent's walk-throughs.

School leaders and teachers in District M perceived district leaders to be supportive of students and staff. They also viewed the district leaders as supporters of change. Many principals and teachers also commented on the quality of the staff development and the district's generosity with resources. Opinions about specific initiatives were varied across the district's schools, although there were some commonalities. For example, nearly everyone was aware of what the district's initiatives were, and *most* people in this district seemed to view themselves as learners. There were, however, dissenting opinions at the school level. Although the district had a strong hand in the schools, it did take school-level resistance into account. At times the resistance by some schools was simply attributed to the healthy tension that results from the district's bottom line expectations. District administrators listened to the responses from school leaders and worked to adapt their strategies to take school-level concerns into account.

Combining Theories of Action in District M's Middle Schools

District leaders had their own learning to do with respect to their middle schools, all of which were relatively small, distinctive schools of choice (Parkside Alternative School, described in Chapter 8, was one of these schools). For all schools serving grades 6 through 8, district leaders opted for a combined strategy that rested on two theories of action. In essence, leaders combined a proactive, district-approved approach to improving literacy and mathematics teaching and an existing policy for supporting small schools of choice for middle schools.[5] The strategy for improving literacy and math featured an activist role for district central office members to be instructional leaders. The strategy also pushed for high performance for a common set of standards, promoted a specific curriculum for these standards, and emphasized accountability. On

---

[5]   For a more extended description of this combined strategy and its consequences see Gallucci, C., Knapp, M. S., Markholt, A., & Ort, S. (2003). *Standards-based reform and small schools of choice: How reform theories converge in three urban middle schools.* Seattle, WA: Center for the Study of Teaching & Policy/University of Washington.

the other hand, the theory of action underlying a small school strategy emphasized a distinctive character and mission for the school, collaborative development of the academic program and curriculum, initiative for change and improvement within the school, and accountability to colleagues and parents.

One reason for the district to institute a small school choice policy was because the movement had deep roots in the city. Small alternative schools in the district over the years had offered a potentially stronger learning experience for urban school children. Furthermore, the small school choice policy appealed both to middle-class parents who appreciated schooling options that more closely mirrored their youngsters' interests and needs, and to less affluent parents who appreciated the neighborhood schooling options at the middle-school level. Rising enrollment and test scores appeared to support the district leaders' contention that the small schools option helped the district maintain enrollment while responding proactively and equitably to parents' desires for their children's education.

But, embracing both small schools of choice and proactive district-guided instructional improvement activities created anomalies and resistances among middle school teachers. Initially, the district leaders found themselves getting a cool reception from middle school principals and teachers. At the root of the schools' response was the perception that the district leaders were pushing an elementary school solution on them. In response, Superintendent Rosario and her staff adapted their ideas about literacy teaching to the unique circumstances for middle school grades. They also took into account what was already being done effectively at this level.

Prompted by this insight and by continuing questions from leaders from the lower performing schools about how to help their struggling readers, the deputy superintendent gathered a group of school people together to help her invent a middle school reading piece. She said,

I did shared reading lessons [in the middle school]. Now a shared reading lesson is seen as [something you do with younger kids using] the large text "Big Books" in grades K–2. You read aloud and the kids join you and you may teach a strategy. But here I am using this is at the 6th and 7th grade level. We used an overhead projector. You [wouldn't] use a big book [in this setting], because it's insulting [to young adolescents]...It was such fun to figure it out together [with the teacher]. The teacher wrote me a thank-you note; she had never thought of it. The principal is all excited and she is making a literacy block in the morning.

This vignette illustrates a pattern that was pervasive in the district. By taking the time to figure out what their audiences knew, needed, and valued, the district was able to stay true to its goal of standard-based instructional improvement while respecting the position of each individual school. In this sense, the district didn't deviate from its long-held belief that small schools would provide the student population with greater opportunities than they would receive from traditional, large urban middle schools. At the same time, the superintendent looked at the district's push for standards-based instructional improvement as a means to enhance the value of small schools of choice. As she put it, "School cultures are important, but you also have to embrace a districtwide effort, develop a community of learners, [and take] pride in your community."

Learning-Focused Leadership in Districts

As these district cases demonstrate, leadership for learning involves work in all five action areas noted in the Leading for Learning Framework. District-level leaders who work for success focus their efforts on student learning, develop the teacher capacity necessary to deliver high-quality instruction, and create an effective system that supports both teachers and students.

10

Using the Framework in Practice and in Leadership Development

The Leading for Learning Framework distills the complex work of educational leadership into a coherent set of ideas that help leaders orient their actions toward improving learning. Once internalized, these ideas provide a vocabulary for thinking about the leader's work and a set of tools for making leadership a greater force for student success. In carrying out that work and the thinking that accompanies it, educators can make intentional use of the Leading for Learning Framework to assist with diagnosing needs, formulating strategies, and gaining perspective on their actions.

In this chapter we describe and illustrate several ways to use the Leading for Learning Framework to enhance one's own leadership practice and to develop effective leadership in others. First, we will briefly review the most common uses for the Leading for Learning Framework. Then, we will discuss daily leadership practice in schools and districts, and leadership development in higher education institutions, districts, and regional support organizations.

Applying the Leading for Learning Framework in Practice

How the Leading for Learning Framework applies to leadership practice or development depends on how leaders think about their professional work. Some people depend on a big picture or a conceptual map to derive implications for their practice. For these educators, the overarching picture of possible ways to connect leading with learning (e.g., as presented in Chapters 3–7) is likely to provide a template for their thoughts about leadership challenges. Others work more comfortably from a piece of the puzzle or an immediate problem to solve from which they can move backwards to a larger sense of the whole. For these educators, a single concept, vignette, or extended case study may prompt new thinking or help them articulate possibilities for action.

Whether a leader uses a big picture or just a piece of the puzzle, the Leading for Learning Framework offers tools for three distinct purposes. First, the framework can be used as a *reflective tool*. The ideas can serve as a starting point for individuals in leadership roles who are trying to reflect on past or current leadership activities or problems. Second, the framework can be a *planning tool* to help leaders visualize and organize their action plan for improving learning. Finally, the framework is a *teaching tool* that can be helpful for familiarizing current or aspiring leaders with the complexities and possibilities of their roles. In other words, the framework can teach educators what learning-focused leadership means in practice.

The following situations illustrate some of the ways that the framework can be used for reflection, planning, and teaching.

For Reflection:

• As a guiding document for a self-study process in a school or district

• As a think piece for a staff or school board retreat; educators with leadership responsibilities can reflect on their practice and how to improve

• As a reference tool to spark interactions over time between a school leader and other educators who act as critical friends

For Planning:

• As a conceptual organizer for a series of meetings devoted to developing a strategic plan for a school district

• As a means for starting dialogue to construct an initiative aimed at fixing a challenge in the school district

For Teaching:

• As a foundational part of the curriculum for a continuing education series created for practicing school principals; this can be planned and delivered by a regional education organization

• As a companion resource for a problem-based learning experience during a weeklong summer institute; this can be used for individuals interested in developing their skills in systems-level leadership

These are all occasions in which educators take stock of their actions and look ahead. Though they often have pressing demands and conflicts, busy professionals need to make the time to figure out what they are accomplishing and find more effective ways to exercise their leadership.

The Leading for Learning Framework provides leaders with a shared language and images of successful school leadership. In the next section, we demonstrate how the framework can focus leaders' efforts for planning and reflection, and how the framework can guide leaders' professional learning.

Focusing Efforts to Plan and Reflect on Leadership Actions

At the outset, it helps to be clear about what the Leading for Learning Framework will do (and won't do) for the busy school or district leader. While the framework offers a template of possibilities and ideas about how different leadership actions connect to each other and to a learning agenda, it does not present a sequence of steps to follow or reduce the hard work of figuring out what might work best in a particular context. Rather, the framework becomes a companion to the ongoing thought processes for leaders who wish to develop a more coherent approach to particular leadership issues or overall learning improvement.

How District Leaders Can Use the Leading for Learning Framework

Consider the following example in which a school district superintendent used ideas from the Leading for Learning Framework to guide his reflection on his district's work. Denny Easton has been the superintendent of the Seaview School District for 14 years. His leadership team includes four central office administrators and principals from the district's eight elementary schools, three junior high schools, and two high schools. Seaview serves approximately 7,700 students in a suburban area near a city in a Western state, and the district has built a reputation during Easton's tenure as a successful, thriving place. Yet, for Easton, this wasn't good enough. The framework began offering Easton and his staff a vehicle for scaffolding a yearlong self-study of their leadership practices.

In fall 2002, Easton returned to Seaview from a sabbatical year of graduate coursework. This coursework included immersion in the Leading for Learning Framework and an in-depth study focused on various pathways that connected leadership to learning. This period of study transformed how Easton viewed his role as a superintendent. He said,

> I am committed to serving as the superintendent of learning in the Seaview School District, with a singular emphasis on transforming the district at all levels into a learning organization. My work will be focused on developing instructional leadership capacity throughout the district. I will be a teaching, coaching, mentoring presence in schools and classrooms. My overarching goal is to have our students learn at higher levels, experience success in academics and other activities, and be prepared to do well in whatever endeavors they undertake when they graduate.

Armed with this deep commitment, Easton reengineered his primary work as superintendent toward improving learning. He began the 2002–03 school year with an intention to exert this influence on many fronts. Easton also concentrated on fostering learning-focused leadership in the district's leaders. To reach this goal, Easton organized a yearlong seminar series for the entire leadership team. He served as the facilitator and used the original *Leading for Learning* reports as a means of systematically organizing his staff's reflective work. The work to date has enabled the leadership team to develop a common vocabulary and begin to inquire more deeply into their own practice as leaders. Through this work, Easton and the team recognized a need to focus in on key pathways of influence. He said,

> These pathways, or leverage points, include factors related to the quality of our teaching staff (hiring, training, and retention), the cultivation of distributed instructional leadership, the advancement of professional learning, and the development of efficient and effective support services. Interestingly, our study and research revealed that the pathways connecting leadership and learning laid out two years ago in our strategic plan, entitled Goals 2004, were very closely tied with [practices from] current research. [This research] suggests [that our goals] are the most promising leverage points which will result in higher levels of student learning. Now, it is a matter of figuring out how each of us as

individual leaders in the Seaview system can bring more coherence to our own work and focus in on these key pathways that hold so much potential for positive change.

As Easton's comments suggest, the team members' deep reflection and inquiry using the Leading for Learning Framework validated that they were headed in the right direction. In this case, the framework served to confirm that the existing plan had a clear logic and intellectual coherence rather than providing a source or stimulus for an improvement plan. For the Seaview team, the Leading for Learning Framework provided a way for members to pinpoint areas that needed improvement and to recognize their strengths in supporting learning across the district.

For leaders in the Northern Valley School District (introduced in Chapter 9) immersion in the Leading for Learning Framework prompted new thinking about what was missing from their strategic plan and how to begin their learning improvement plan. Superintendent Jones and Assistant Superintendent Ames discovered the framework ideas shortly before embarking on a new round of strategic planning. Prior to that point, their plan had focused directly on student learning. Their plans were guided by the premise that everything done in the district should point solely toward student learning without regard to professional and system learning. For Jones and Ames the Leading for Learning Framework opened the possibility that professional and system learning were separate entities that were inextricably connected to student learning. Guided by this concept and by the idea that pathways could connect all three learning agendas, Jones and Ames reconceived the district's strategic plan and placed new emphasis on professional and system learning. Their plan was significantly reorganized and the three learning agendas became the overall organizing principle rather than the traditional functional rubrics (e.g., finance and budget, community relations, curriculum, and professional development).

The district is now embarking on a significant round of activity aimed at strengthening professional learning opportunities.

Reflection and planning can easily inform one another, and, as these examples show, the Leading for Learning Framework can help to facilitate their interaction. The framework may also support a more formal teaching function as illustrated by the Seaview case. Superintendent Easton started off the yearlong self-study seminar series with a leadership team academy. During the series he presented his vision for the leadership work in the district. Easton took on a teaching role in this academy and used the framework as his curriculum. During the academy, the entire group was introduced to the Leading for Learning Framework, and participants had their first opportunity to talk about how the framework influenced learning-focused leadership. The session had a powerful impact and was well received by the team. Easton said,

> At our initial leadership team academy, I spoke to members of the team about my determination to ensure that we make the transition from a very good [district] to a great district. I also talked about my goal to focus on leveraging the key pathways connecting leadership to high-quality teaching and enhanced student learning. The framework offered us a way to begin to develop a common vocabulary and to start to see the system we all work in very differently, more holistically. I received very enthusiastic feedback from leadership team members following this academy. Uniformly, members expressed a deep level of commitment to the vision I proposed, as well as to the obvious hard work ahead.

Easton plans to continue using the Leading for Learning Framework with the leadership team for ongoing inquiry and professional development. Thus, in addition to providing a way for him to rethink his own personal vision of leading education, the framework has helped Easton start growing that vision among the rest of the district's administrative team.

The Seaview and Northern Valley cases underscore several points about how the Leading for Learning Framework can be used productively. First, leaders from both districts used the framework beyond a one-time seminar or session, and the leaders weren't expecting the framework to have an immediate impact on thinking and action after a single exposure. Rather, participants *engaged* these ideas over a significant period of time and any benefits they gained reflected their sustained interaction with the framework. Second, the framework can be used to stimulate or guide planning for leadership actions that are already underway. For district leaders in Seaview and Northern Valley, the framework came to their attention midstream. In such instances the framework can be used to embrace a wide range of activities undertaken by leaders. One of the greatest advantages of using the Leading for Learning Framework is that it provides a way to evaluate previous actions and consider new actions.

Using the Framework for Planning and Reflection

At Seaview and Northern Valley, the users of the Leading for Learning Framework were experienced district leaders who already had an established pattern of success. However, as examples later in this chapter will show, the framework can be just as useful for leaders who have yet to create their own vision of leadership. The framework may be utilized to further establish their respective roles or to solidify their plans for focusing energy and resources on improving learning. Listed below are actions from the Leading for Learning Framework that can be useful for new and established leaders.

• Mapping the primary pathways of influence in a current district initiative (e.g., leaders can track specific efforts such as improving literacy within secondary schools or promoting inquiry science at the elementary level). This type of visual planning can show a range of possible pathways identified by the framework.

• Articulating a set of core values that supports student learning and professional learning in a particular school.

• Identifying all the ways that a district leader pays persistent, public attention to teaching and learning.

• Considering how actions along one pathway at the school and district level might connect to other particular pathways (see Appendix).

• Charting how efforts to engage relevant groups in the external environment of a school, as well as building the school's professional community, all relate to an agreed upon focus on learning.

These examples are small glimpses of how school and district leaders might use the Leading for Learning Framework to guide planning and reflection at any stage of their journey. These actions can help them secure learning-focused leadership in any given setting.

Guiding Professional Learning for Current or Aspiring Leaders

As the Seaview leadership team academy exemplifies, the Leading for Learning Framework can be a particularly useful way of introducing new and established school or district leaders to a more comprehensive and coherent way of understanding their leadership actions. The framework offers a way of organizing professional learning activities to supply content and to provide a set of teaching tools that can be readily used by participants.

The Leading for Learning Framework implies a certain kind of pedagogy for professional development. These ideas will not produce substantive learning for current or emergent leaders who don't have a grasp of what the framework means or a sense of connection to their specific leadership problems. Instead, the Leading for Learning Framework invites leaders to be active learners and to connect their learning with their daily activities. Above all, the framework encourages interactive engagement of these ideas in collaborative settings with other colleagues. Leaders become teachers who facilitate learning, prompt their colleagues to think in divergent ways, and structure opportunities for them to carry on their thinking productively.

Using the Leading for Learning Framework in Various Settings

The Leading for Learning Framework can support professional learning for current or aspiring leaders in various settings. These include

• **School-based professional development.** Opportunities can be arranged in multiple sessions that enable repeated engagement with the framework ideas.

• **Districtwide or state-level professional development and support.** At this level, the Leading for Learning Framework can support ongoing learning-improvement efforts rather than a one-time exposure to new ideas.

• **Continuing education for practicing leaders.** The framework is especially helpful in settings that permit leaders from schools or districts to come together repeatedly to examine and renew their practice.

• **University-based degree and certification programs.** The Leading for Learning Framework can be useful in instructional settings aimed at educational leaders in the preK–12 system.

Venues in which educators are able to step back from the daily intensity of their work and reconsider their practice represent a ripe opportunity for using the Leading for Learning Framework as a teaching tool. Consider these two cases.

> The state of Maryland developed a series of summer workshops for school principals in which the Leading for Learning Framework served as a catalyst for professional development. The framework helped the leaders to focus their efforts on learning.

The University of California at Santa Barbara organized intensive summer institutes for educators across the country. Each institute focused on diverse roles within and outside of the traditional leadership system. The institutes were aimed at identifying systems to improve teaching and learning. Institute developers introduced the Leading for Learning Framework as one of several conceptual models for helping system-level leaders understand how to focus their work on learning.

The framework can also help provide a structure for learning in a series of long-term, connected events. The following case shows participants grappling with the framework ideas, experimenting with the ideas at their schools, discussing their use of the framework, and preparing for another round of experimentation.

The Center for Educational Leadership at the University of Washington has sponsored a continuing education series for new principals and experienced school leaders during the school year. This series uses the Leading for Learning Framework to help school leaders imagine what an inquiry-based approach to their work might entail. Participants in this continuing education program meet once a month for a one and a half day session to work on self-determined, school-specific inquiry projects intended to improve teaching and learning at their home school sites.

The next case shows how the framework can also be useful in the design phase of a new leadership preparation program.

The Center for Evidenced-Based Education (CEBE) is in the process of organizing a new Ed.D. program linked to a regional university. The program is heavily based on ideas from the Leading for Learning Framework and on a structure from an established program at the University of Washington, which also uses the framework. The CEBE's program is aimed at training prospective leaders who work in challenging urban school districts. The framework has helped leaders in this program coalesce their planning efforts.

Using the Leading for Learning Framework in a Leadership Preparation Program

In this section, we share a brief description of our own use of the Leading for Learning Framework at the University of Washington. We used the framework as the backbone of our doctoral program for aspiring system-level leaders. This example illustrates how the ideas in this book can provide a larger intellectual structure and some specific learning experiences for a graduate-level program. This example also shows how leaders prepare for exercising significant and responsible influence on teaching and learning in a variety of complex educational systems.

Using the Framework for Program Design

The doctoral program at the University of Washington is a three-year, cohort-based program that leads to the Doctor of Education degree (Ed.D.) and the Washington state superintendent certificate. This program is the result of reenvisioning superintendent and district-level preparation at the doctoral level (see Sirotnik, Kimball, & Copland, 2003). The program is built around a set of core values similar to those outlined in Chapter 3 (see pp. 31–32) and focuses explicitly on the challenge of connecting leadership in school districts, regional entities, and state systems. In this respect, the goal of the program coincides with the framework's central premise of connecting learning with leadership. The program serves a cohort of roughly two dozen practicing leaders. Many leaders in this program are currently running schools or working in district-level offices, regional educational units, or state education agencies.

The program's curriculum and delivery structure was designed to maximize the potential for integrating powerful ideas about leadership practice with leaders' ongoing practice in their daily settings. Program participants also have the benefit of discussing their ideas among a community of leaders. Participants can either meet once a month or during summer institutes. This flexible scheduling allows leaders who work full-time to participate, and it allows them to try out these ideas during the school year. The capstone project is a dissertation that is designed to bring systematic, critical analysis to a leadership problem in the participant's workplace.

This structure sets the stage for continuous exposure to the Leading for Learning Framework throughout the entire program. Participants have numerous opportunities to grasp the meaning of the framework and evaluate its potential in their work. The framework is also a central component in the two "book end" experiences within this program. The initial summer institute exposes participants to all pieces of the Leading for Learning Framework, and the participants work in teams to apply the framework to a problem-based case. During the culminating activity, leaders construct their own theory of action for system-level instructional renewal, and they draw on all their learning in various course modules and learning activities. Modular learning experiences in between these two activities provide material for the culminating project as well as for the capstone project.

Using the Framework for a Summer Institute

Participants are initially immersed in the program during an intensive, weeklong summer session. They are exposed to the big ideas of the Leading for Learning Framework, read the underlying research and theory that supports the framework, and engage in a problem-based exercise (Copland, 2003).[1] This exercise is intended to involve two dozen prospective system-level educational leaders in activities that will cause them to reflect and act on their beliefs about leading learning. The framework and the literature also provide foundational curricular content during the summer institute week. Participants are expected to read the material before the

---

[1]   The published case for the Skyline School District can be found in the *Journal of Cases in Educational Leadership* (see references).

institute and then discuss the content in presentations and small group sessions.

The problem-based case allows the participants to use the framework for reflection, planning, and teaching simultaneously. During the analysis, the participants act as incoming superintendents for the district presented in the cases. Participants work through the case exercise over five sessions during the week, with each session lasting three to four hours.

The cases are developed with the support of local superintendents. The superintendents provide a multitude of data from within their school systems, and they offer insights about the nature of problems they have encountered as a system leader over many years. The Skyline School District provides is an example of a problem-based case study presented during the summer institute.

> The Skyline School District is experiencing some significant issues related to closing achievement gaps. The school district data provided shows discrepancies in student achievement based on race, language, and poverty. The "new superintendent" is replacing a well-liked, long-time administrator whose focus has been on building the financial capacity of the district. His administration leaves behind a significant fund balance that could open the door to some interesting financial possibilities for the new leader. But, the plans don't lend themselves towards a coherent learning focus for the district.

Participant teams are charged with using the Leading for Learning Framework to analyze the current condition of the district, and developing a plan for the future. On the final day of the institute, each team's plans are presented to an actual group of local school board members who are recruited to play various roles on the simulated Skyline board. Board members read the framework in advance and are coached by instructors to ask pointed and probing questions of the "new superintendents" that push the depth of their thinking about leadership. Participant teams use the Leading for Learning Framework in varying ways to think through and set up their presentations to the simulated school board, especially in ways that target their particular action plans on specific learning issues.

Following the problem-based case presentations, participants are given three more weeks to write individual reflections on their work, either by critiquing the framework in light of their experience with the case or by applying the ideas to their current school or educational system. The framework serves as a reference point for reflection.

Using the Framework as a Reference Point

Following the summer institute and during the program, participants return to the Leading for Learning Framework periodically while engaging in extended learning about system-level leadership. The program as a whole features curriculum blocks that address the following:

• Dynamics of educational systems and system change, including matters such as school system finance, legal context, organizational dynamics, system change, and leadership perspectives;
  • Teaching, learning, and instructional renewal;
  • The moral and historical roots of leadership practice;
  • Foundations of action-oriented inquiry; and
  • Interdisciplinary perspectives on leadership practice.

A set of experiential internship and mentorship experiences accompany the learning in the instructional modules. Although the framework is not meant to offer comprehensive guidance on all aspects of system-level leadership, it nonetheless provides a useful organizing structure for participants' learning throughout the program.

What Leaders Gain From Using the Leading for Learning Framework

Through using the Leading for Learning Framework in different kinds of practice and leadership development settings, leaders who learn the framework ideas have much to gain. Several participants in the leadership development program at the University of Washington commented on how the framework influenced their work. Although they were experienced educational leaders, these participants said that the framework increased their ability to clearly see what was going on around them and to imagine how they can improve their learning agendas.

One district administrator in charge of curriculum, instruction, and professional development said,

> I am fortunate to be in a time of great change and possibility in my district. With the recent passage of a large bond measure [that we] will [use to] construct a second high school, [the leadership of a] superintendent [who is] in his second year with us, and the retirement or departure of a number of administrators in the last year or two, I feel we are [ready to face] the challenge of maintaining a clear focus on learning. I am excited to have learned everything I have this summer and am eager to put my learning into action. It is now clear to me that maintaining our current level of focus on learning is not sufficient and that enhancing it is imperative. I believe this begins with the perpetuation of a consistent message about what we expect our students to be able to do and what we are convinced they are able to do. We need to be clear that all students can and will achieve at high levels and be granted equitable opportunities to do so. This is a moral obligation that we bear. We need to continue [to] enhance our efforts to reach out to parents and the larger community [so] that we might open the system to them in ways that enable them to embrace our shared mission of making every child successful.

For this leader, the Leading for Learning Framework helped him express his district's need for a more singular focus on learning as a central strategic goal and as a moral obligation. In the next example, an administrator reframes her district's work through the framework's emphasis on a persistent, public focus on learning (Action Area 1). After reading examples from the framework and actions from leaders who make their commitment to a learning focus visible, she decided to make her presence in the schools more frequent. She said,

> I believe that in my role as curriculum director, one of the most important things I can do is to be in buildings [and] classrooms and [be] in dialogue with teachers. Many of our readings [in the summer institute] emphasized that high visibility and leader success go hand in hand. Being accessible to staff does a number of things. First, it models the value of listening to and honoring one another's insights. It demonstrates a commitment to and an interest [about] what's going on [and] where it is important, [especially] at the classroom level. Second, I believe this will build trust throughout the system and enable us to communicate more clearly and from the same point of reference. I also hope it will demonstrate that I, too, am a learner in our system and that our department is there to work in tandem with teachers and [to] build staff to help them achieve their goals.

Her thinking extended to other action areas in the framework including Action Area 3 of the framework, engaging external environments. She said,

> If our system is to be "of" the community rather than "in" the community, we will need to continue the outreach we have begun. I see the notion of engaging external environments as critical to our success in the coming years. My district is steeped in tradition and building a second high school has been met with much opposition in the past. To continue our current forward momentum, it is critical that we keep the community on the inside of the system and that we nurture the idea of a whole community existing as a resource for learning.

The framework in this instance was not the original inspiration for the actions that this administrator and her team had taken to advance their instructional improvement goals. But, it did provide a vocabulary for understanding what she and others had already begun to do to reinforce the value of these actions. In this sense, she was articulating and enacting what Michael Fullan calls a "theory of change." She and her colleagues tried to nudge the system in new directions. At the same time, they connected these efforts to a clearer "theory of education" that included a compelling set of ideas about high-quality teaching and its impacts on learning (Fullan, 2005).

When leaders use the Leading for Learning Framework as a reflecting tool, it helps them evaluate the workings of their current educational system, discover what is not working optimally at present, and imagine possible solutions. In the following example, another summer institute attendee, a district administrator without an extensive instructional background, came to see critical weaknesses in his district's approach to instructional improvement. He said,

> The other day my superintendent walked into another administrator's office and said, "I feel like I'm not quite getting it." The administrator asked what "it" was. He said, "I'm doing everything right. I talk about student achievement as the number one goal—it's right there on my wall—but test scores just haven't taken off like I thought they would. What do you think is wrong?" The administrator encouraged the superintendent to review the agendas of the 2003–04 meetings for principals and the administrative team to see how much time key leaders devoted to learning-related issues. An hour later, the superintendent returned. "You're right," he said. "Only about 10 to 15 percent of those meetings focused on teaching and learning. We've got to do better." I listened to this story with great interest earlier this week because it mirrored many of the issues we discussed in the summer institute. I've come to see that in our district, we have a superintendent who seemingly aspires to be an instructional leader but lacks the tools to get there. As a result, the district lacks a coherent focus on teaching and learning despite the pockets of excellence.

Here, this district administrator, newly sensitized by the framework ideas, was able to spot the critical lack of an operational focus on learning and teaching in the day-to-day workings of the central office, despite a genuine, albeit rhetorical, commitment by the superintendent to enhancing student learning. Prior to his exposure to the framework, this administrator might have missed the significance of this incident because he, like the superintendent, lacked expertise in teaching and learning. This administrator was able to pursue the matter further by identifying particular ways in which interactions among district staff members tended to diminish the possibility of creating a culture of academic excellence. As his comments below suggest, he was beginning to see the superintendent's role in building a professional culture (Action Area 2).

> While the superintendent aims to focus on instruction, he has yet to create a common culture in which powerful teaching and learning dominate conversations. His natural interest lies in the management and operations field. As a result, senior staff meetings often become a laundry list of facilities concerns. Thus, when the superintendent visits schools, he focuses more on facilities than learning. His approach is to ask principals, "What do you need? How can I help you do the job you need to do?" He occasionally visits classrooms but rarely discusses instructional practice with principals or teachers. In short, he takes on the role of a business manager. A more focused approach by the superintendent to learn about teaching and speak the language of educators might go far in creating a culture of academic excellence.

The district administrator recognized that even the physical arrangement of the central office could contribute to the problem, and he suggested that if reorganized, it might point toward a solution. He said,

> Another key area in which leadership action might move the district forward is the structure of the central office itself. The curriculum and assessment departments are housed in a far corner of the building, far away from the superintendent's office.

While the executive director of the department works in an office near the superintendent, support staff members remain out of the picture. The configuration leads to a lack of cohesiveness, as assistant superintendents rarely meet [with] the directors of assessment and professional development. That leads to very little critical conversation about school improvement among senior district leaders.

Through such rearrangements and other ways of exercising learning-focused leadership, this leader was able to visualize new possibilities for the district. In effect, he was starting to apply notions that he previously reserved only for the work of schools and professional development events to the district office itself. He said,

The district's award-winning professional development director puts together two large summer weeklong events every year for educators to polish their skills, discuss pedagogy, learn new technology, and talk about life. Turnout is always high. It is often the only time of the year that faculty members in different buildings come together to share ideas. At the district office, however, there is little sense of a professional learning community. Senior staff members don't read and discuss papers together. While there is certainly no lack of brainpower in the office, there is a lack of inquiry and shared exploration. The superintendent could lend leadership by creating a study group or another mechanism to get district leaders talking critically about school improvement.

Other summer institute participants heard different things during their exposure to the framework. For example, one school administrator used the notion of multiple, converging pathways as a helpful tool to understand what he had been doing to initiate a school-directed improvement agenda. These ideas helped him organize three related pathways of activity that he and his staff have been engaged in over the past several years, including planning and goal setting, engaging community, and forging collegial connections. This idea also helped him imagine a fourth pathway: support for ongoing professional learning.

In particular, he was able to note how one pathway's activities connected to another, which is a key idea for creating coherence (Action Area 5) in the framework. He was also able to understand for the first time how activity along a pathway could involve the strategic sharing and development of leadership resources. He noted this discovery as he used the community engagement pathway to describe his efforts to develop a collaborative community/ business project for the Powerful Partners school coalition.

He said,

> Powerful Partners, originating in 1998, is a six-school coalition attached to a nonprofit organization. [Their] purpose is to acquire resources and [to] develop programs aimed at addressing the achievement gaps in the member buildings. What is possibly the most salient feature of this project, based on framework ideas, is the development of distributed leadership among community members who serve on the Powerful Partners' board of directors, as well as among the paid staff who direct programs as well as fundraising efforts. This increase of community leadership capacity has led to a sizable flow of monetary resources, but more significantly, has proven to be an element leading to the sustainability and growth of programs serving students.

Although these administrators are still relatively new to the Leading for Learning Framework, their use of the framework reflects their emerging practice and suggests that they and their colleagues have only begun to tap the possibilities that the ideas of the framework afford. But as they make the time or find the occasions to reflect on their work, individually or collectively, this beginning familiarity with the framework will prompt further ways of seeing new dimensions and possibilities in their practice.

How the Leading for Learning Framework Can Help Leaders Focus on Learning

In sum, when the Leading for Learning Framework is used in the ways described above, the ideas and tools presented in this book can serve several different functions. First, the framework synthesizes a lot of thinking and research about the complicated work of leading learning organizations and presents these ideas succinctly. The framework does not offer a summary of what is often referred to as research-based best practices—i.e., the framework does not provide a neat summary of leadership actions that are proven to work. Rather, the book presents different lines of thinking and examples of leadership practice in such a way that the complexities of a particular leadership problem come into focus and the larger leadership landscape becomes clearer and easier to grasp. Second, the Leading for Learning Framework presents a map of existing or potential connections between leaders' actions and learning processes or outcomes. These actions help users see possible ways to traverse the leadership landscape, but without prescribing any particular route. Third, the framework validates steps leaders may have already taken and offers users a vocabulary and schema for understanding, articulating, and organizing what they are already doing. Finally, the framework challenges new and established leaders to face their unsolved problems, evaluate the configuration of resources and constraints in their own settings, and develop viable theories of action for addressing these issues. Because the Leading for Learning Framework is not a change theory, it invites users to form and adjust their own theories of action and to tailor the ideas to the unique circumstances of their own working setting.

But to fulfill these functions, exposure to this kind of framework needs to happen during professional development sessions that are specifically created for this purpose. These sessions should be guided by informed facilitators (i.e., leaders who know and understand the framework) and should be extended over time with multiple occasions to consider and revisit the ideas. The following principles illustrate the most effective use of the Leading for Learning Framework.

Recognize that the framework ideas are not digested quickly. In order for learning leaders to maximize benefits of the Leading for Learning Framework, they need extended time with the ideas. A weeklong immersion experience is a good beginning, but users need chances to return to the ideas and time to work more fully toward developing their understanding through repeated exposure to the framework's ideas over time.

Appreciate the value of building collegial interactions around the framework ideas. In isolation, the ideas in this book are limited. But, when using these ideas with a collegial planning group, particularly among those who already have leadership responsibilities or who aspire to obtain more responsibility, leaders can create rich conversation and build a deeper understanding of the framework ideas and their implications for practice.

Encourage leaders to use the framework to make connections between theoretical and practical leadership actions. The ideas in the Leading for Learning Framework are conceptual, yet applying them to the real world is a primary and worthy aim. Leaders' efforts to analyze existing educational plans through the lens of the framework and to apply the ideas to a particular learning agenda are crucial steps in translating theory to practice.

Understand that leading learning is difficult work. The Leading for Learning Framework doesn't make leading for learning any easier. However, after engaging the framework, leaders find it easier to imagine new possibilities and to visualize and articulate their vision to others. New possibilities come into view, and they reveal potential avenues for solutions to problems that previously seemed intractable. Yet, we recognize that there is an ongoing struggle for incorporating knowledge obtained from the framework into existing educational organizations.

Ultimately, the Leading for Learning Framework invites users to selectively use the framework as they discover new possibilities, confirm some of their current practices, and confront their challenges. All of the ideas presented in this framework will not apply or be helpful to leaders who are trying to make sense of particular challenges. But, interacting with these ideas may provoke users to develop a better framework that more effectively captures the relationship between leadership actions and learning in a given setting.

Epilogue

Hector and Mr. G. Revisited

There are many students and teachers like Hector and Mr. G. who struggle in their respective settings. For all of them, the educational leaders' task is to create and sustain systemwide conditions that enable all learners—both young people and professional adults—to fulfill the promise of public education in every school.

Viewing Leadership Actions in Hindsight

In light of all that has been discussed in this book, we ask the following—what could have happened to make Hector's schooling more satisfying and Mr. G.'s teaching more supportive of Hector's learning experience? What might leaders at this school and district have done to recognize the different realities for Hector and Mr. G.? In this case, it is easier to see the possibilities for improvement in hindsight. The leaders in Hector and Mr. G.'s story, similar to many school and district leaders, were not in a position to guide improvement because they didn't know what was going in the present.

One thing is certain—changing the situation of Hector and Mr. G. would not have happened all at once. Informed leaders, guided by core values and thoughtful planning tools, might have started in a small way with one curricular area or with an emphasis on one aspect of student learning. Or, they could have started working on how well the teaching staff understood the cultural roots of all learners at the school. Another tactic may have been working on the nature and content of collegial conversations. Whatever the entry point, leaders in this school and district, if equipped with a clear picture of where their schools and system were headed and how to get there, could have worked to make learning opportunities far more powerful and equitable. Had they been prompted to reconsider and renew their practice in ways that mattered for individual children and for the student population as a whole by using a framework such as this, they could have started down another path. Had these actions taken place, the story of Hector and Mr. G. may have been presented differently than the way it appears at the beginning of this book.

Imagining the Possibilities for Effective School Leadership

In order for educators and educational leaders to realize alternative, more successful ways of addressing their challenges, they need images of what is possible. In some schools that serve populations of students like Hector, leaders are fostering education that is more attentive to the needs of learners who have not been well served (Haycock, 2001). Consider what leaders are doing in the following school with a population similar to Hector's classroom.

> The principal of an urban elementary school promotes discussion about teaching practice and equity. She strategically draws together efforts in curriculum, professional development, and hiring, and she focuses on school structure, culture, and leadership development. In an effort to make teachers' practice more public and open to scrutiny, she strives to create a context where they can talk openly about their teaching and the challenges they face. In the process, the principal pushes them to consider their

teaching in light of race, class, and language diversity. She has refocused staff meetings from discussing procedures and logistics to discussing instructional practice. She has also created times for teachers to explore research on effective teaching in high-poverty, high-diversity schools. Along with several teacher leaders and in conjunction with district-level staff members, the principal has focused the staff's attention on improving literacy teaching in primary grades. At the same time, she renegotiated the use of federally funded Eisenhower funds to support a year-long study group for upper elementary teachers on approaches to mathematics teaching that responds to state standards (Markholt, 2002).

This principal and others on her staff are bringing coherently related activities together to influence students' educational experiences and outcomes. While she builds a professional community, she is also helping her staff engage with a diverse student population. Through her presence and prompting, she has established a focus on powerful and equitable student learning.

The efforts of principals like this sometimes happen in isolation, but they are more likely to take place in districts that proactively address improving learning and teaching. The principal described above is working in a supportive districtwide environment. In the next example, a district director addresses a literacy improvement effort in her district.

The district's director of elementary education, who is an expert on early literacy, is deeply concerned about the pattern of low reading performance in six elementary schools, three of which (including the one described above) are on the state's list of schools required to receive extra assistance and adopt a prescribed, structured approach to reading instruction. Seeing an opportunity in a state grant program for early literacy improvement, she secures extra resources for the six schools, sets up a literacy resource network to support the staff, and requires each school to participate. Several are eager, while others reluctantly agree to try.

The literacy resource network fits nicely with the district's advocacy for professional learning, school accountability with support, a focus on the literate child, and related initiatives for promoting classroom-based assessment techniques. In collaboration with two other departments and with the schools' principals, the director has formed a professional development strategy that combines school-based study groups and district-level workshops on new and powerful reading approaches modeled after reading recovery techniques. Drawing on her knowledge of the schools' staff members from periodic visits, the director taps several teachers with strong expertise in literacy teaching to lead the study groups. Two years after the inception of the literacy resource network, four of the six schools saw a rise in their reading scores (A. Markholt, personal communication, November 16, 2004).

These developments result from district-level activity along several pathways, a distributed pattern of leadership at both school and district levels, and engagement with external demands and resources. Districtwide commitments, such as the literacy emphasis and the insistence on school accountability with support, create the conditions for focused strategies to emerge. This school and district are living examples of the ideas set forth in this book.

How to Begin Learning-Focused Leadership

Imagining possibilities is one thing, but imagining feasible movement toward those possibilities is quite another. A frequent response to the conceptual possibilities and the practical examples laid out in this book is—"Okay, it makes sense, but in my school and district, we are nowhere near the kinds of learning-focused practice presented in this framework. How do we get there? Where do we start?"

Our answer to these important questions is—you have to start somewhere. You must pick some aspect of the local instructional renewal challenge. The bottom line is that the starting point needs to involve or imply a publicly acknowledged focus on learning

(Action Area 1), and the three learning agendas (student, professional, and system) need to be involved. When these matters permeate thinking, talking, and ultimately action, one is already on the way toward learning-focused leadership. From there, it is a matter of imagining new courses of action, initiating the actions, and finding the time to reflect on how they are working. Preferably, leaders will use a systematic reflective tool or process, such as the Leading for Learning Framework.

As leaders struggle to make leadership more learning-focused, a healthy tension will always exist between the concepts proposed in the Leading for Learning Framework and the messy business of trying to realize that kind of leadership. New teachers and new students enter our schools and districts every year, and the real work is about continually renewing one's commitment to leading for learning.

There is no one right place where anyone might start to learn their way into this framework. Rather, the Leading for Learning Framework points a leader toward thinking about the variety of promising possibilities that exist within their particular contexts and suggests routes and strategies for realizing them. But imagining possibilities is not all it will take to achieve the promise of education that continues to elude Hector and other school children like him. Leaders must examine their own teaching and learning practices and reach out to professional communities and groups outside of the school system to gain perspective and the emotional strength to persist. The framework has no magic to make the hard work disappear or right the wrongs that may have deep historical and societal roots.

Hope and Caution for School and District Leadership

Emerging work and new evidence gives leaders hope that what the Leading for Learning Framework describes can be realized in many kinds of leadership settings. However, we caution leaders to realize that pursuing learning-focused leadership will not be easy and to recognize that achieving this goal will be a collective effort. For the many districts and schools that have yet to develop the kinds of leadership illustrated in this book, the framework offers perspectives and tools to help them move forward. It also can help educators visualize powerful, equitable student learning, and create and support the professional and system learning that is necessary to get there. The framework clarifies the core values that bolster these efforts and emphasizes the need for professional communities that share those values. The ideas in the framework also prompt leaders to take a hard and careful look at their internal conditions and external environments, and they also point to places where leaders might search for solutions appropriate to their local settings. Ultimately, it is the work of motivated leaders and their colleagues that will advance educational systems that support powerful and equitable education.

Appendix

Pathways to Learning

Chapter 6 briefly notes 23 different pathways to student, professional, and system learning (see Figure 6.2). Each pathway comprises a stream of functionally related activities, such as direct services, policymaking, and program design work that are undertaken by different people across various levels of the educational system. These activities occur whether or not leaders capitalize on these actions as a means of positively influencing learning. School and district leaders' opportunities for exerting specific influence on the quality of learning and teaching lie along these pathways.

This appendix briefly describes each pathway and notes the potential participants who are in a position to exercise learning-focused leadership. The tables illustrate

- Opportunities for exercising leadership along a specific pathway;
- Points of connection with other pathways; and
- Implications of leadership actions for student, professional, or system learning.

The pathways appear as follows:

Content, Assessment, and Accountability Pathways   205
Student learning standards
Curriculum
Assessment systems
Accountability systems

Professionals and Professional Development Pathways   214
Professional practice standards
Preparation and certification
Mentoring and induction support
Support for ongoing professional development
Supervision and evaluation
Compensation and rewards

Learner and Learner Support Pathways   230
Support for special learning needs
Support for noninstructional needs
Student placement and assignment
Behavioral support and management
Family and parent engagement

Workplace and System Pathways   242
Planning and goal setting
Developing collegial connections
Leadership development
Restructuring time, program, and facilities
Staffing and assignment
Recruitment and hiring
Information system development
Community engagement

These pathways are meant to illustrate key functions of a public education system that have the most impact on student, professional, and system learning. While other functions such as purchasing, accounting, or managing transportation have implications for learning and teaching, their impact is largely indirect and does not have as much influence. However, functions such as resource allocation and governance are so intimately linked with every pathway that little is gained conceptually in treating them as separate pathways.

There is more than one way of defining pathways. Related pathways, like mentoring and induction and support for ongoing professional development, could easily be combined into a broader pathway related to professional development. Conversely, pathways described here, like support for special learning needs, could be subdivided into a larger number of more narrowly construed pathways. Yet, still other pathways not mentioned here could be imagined. The arrangement of pathways presented here tries to strike a balance between breadth and differentiation. It captures functional pathways that are widely recognized within public schools and districts. Readers are strongly encouraged to develop their own pathway maps that better represent the functional arrangement of work in their respective settings.

The clustering of pathways is also somewhat arbitrary and at first glance may obscure the natural connections among them. (The figure on the next page, introduced in Chapter 6, draws attention to these connections.) The current arrangement groups pathways by whether they are aimed primarily at the content, the teacher, or the learner. (These three elements are part of the instructional triangle as discussed in Part One.) An additional set of pathways aimed at workplace and system features is more cross-cutting. Thus, pathways should be thought of more as overlapping and interconnected than as discrete streams of activity. The disconnection of one function from another, as in some large, bureaucratized school districts, has obvious negative consequences for system coherence.

Figure 6.2

A Range of Pathways to Student, Professional, and System Learning

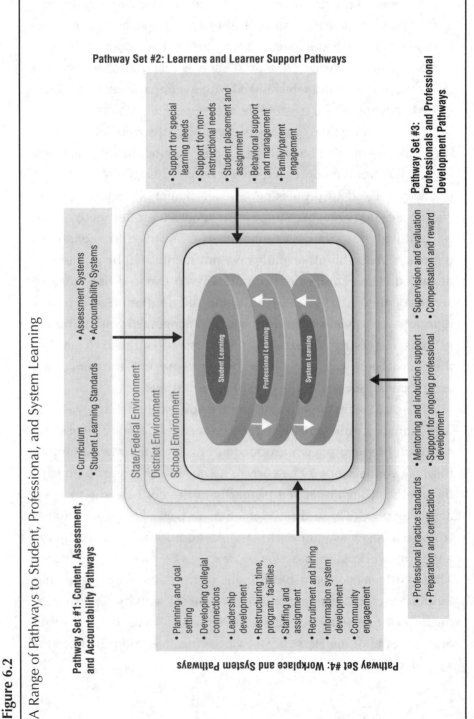

Pathway Set #2: Learners and Learner Support Pathways

- Support for special learning needs
- Support for non-instructional needs
- Student placement and assignment
- Behavioral support and management
- Family/parent engagement

Pathway Set #3: Professionals and Professional Development Pathways

- Supervision and evaluation
- Compensation and reward
- Mentoring and induction support
- Support for ongoing professional development
- Professional practice standards
- Preparation and certification

Pathway Set #1: Content, Assessment, and Accountability Pathways

- Curriculum
- Student Learning Standards
- Assessment Systems
- Accountability Systems

Pathway Set #4: Workplace and System Pathways

- Planning and goal setting
- Developing collegial connections
- Leadership development
- Restructuring time, program, facilities
- Staffing and assignment
- Recruitment and hiring
- Information system development
- Community engagement

State/Federal Environment

District Environment

School Environment

Student Learning

Professional Learning

System Learning

Content, Assessment, and Accountability Pathways

Student Learning Standards Pathway

The *student learning standards pathway* includes activity to develop and promulgate standards for student learning in particular subject areas and in skills sets such as problem solving, citizenship education, and health. Such standards often emanate from state educational agencies and district central offices, but they also come from national professional associations such as the National Council of Teachers of Mathematics or from staff members in a particular school (see Meier, 2002). At the district level, assistant superintendents who are responsible for curriculum and instruction and others with content expertise are likely to take the lead on developing and interpreting learning standards. At the school level, principals, department heads, teacher leaders, and school-based coaches are also responsible for creating student standards. Others outside the local educational system such as staff members with content expertise at state education agencies or professional associations are also likely to be active in setting and interpreting student learning standards.

Leadership Opportunities for Schools and Districts

School Leadership Opportunities

- Encouraging conversations about the meaning of school or district learning standards
- Establishing school-specific standards for particular subjects and other areas of learning
- Developing links between standards, curricula, and assessments

District Leadership Opportunities

- Engaging schools and community in conversation about the purpose of learning standards
- Aligning district learning standards with state standards

Connection with Other Pathways

Related Pathways	Linking Questions
Curriculum pathway	Are student learning standards embodied in curriculum materials?
Assessment systems pathway	Are the assessments addressing the standards? Are the assessments mapped onto standards? What counts as evidence of standards being met?
Professional practice standards pathway	Should standards become a main focus of professional development?
Information system development pathway	What information can be gathered to show progress toward standards?

Leadership Actions for Student, Professional, and System Learning

Student Learning	Professional Learning	System Learning
Defines what students will learn	Provides content focus for professional development	Provides reference point for systemwide data gathering
Establishes reference points for decisions about curriculum and for instructional planning	Provokes consideration about standard-bearing work	Codifies expectations for students between and across schools

Curriculum Pathway

The *curriculum pathway* includes activity to define and select curriculum frameworks, plans, and instructional materials or equipment (e.g., texts, workbooks, equipment, kits, technology, and disposable materials). Curriculum enacted in classrooms is the joint result of activity at many levels. These include individual teachers and teacher groups who adapt or develop their own curriculum; school staffs who decide on or develop schoolwide curriculum; and district personnel who create scope-and-sequence frameworks, select materials, and construct them for districtwide use. State educational agencies also play a big role in establishing curriculum frameworks and other forms of curriculum guidance, not to mention creating preferred textbook lists. Professional associations, the textbook industry, and community groups also define and create curriculum options for teachers.

Leadership Opportunities for Schools and Districts
School Leadership Opportunities

- Engaging school staff in developing or adapting curriculum to meet learning improvement goals

- Reviewing curriculum for its relevance to a diverse student population
- Connecting school curriculum across grades in relation to standards and improvement goals

District Leadership Opportunities

- Developing curricular guidance and professional development to help schools focus on learning improvement
- Aligning district curriculum with learning standards and improvement goals

Connection with Other Pathways

Related Pathways	Linking Questions
Student learning standards pathway	Are student learning standards embodied into curriculum materials?
Assessment systems pathway	How well are assessments captured in the curriculum?
Support for ongoing professional development pathway	What areas of the curriculum should school-level and district-level professional development focus on? What pedagogical content knowledge is required to teach the curriculum?
Supervision and evaluation pathway	What critical curricular areas should supervisors observe?
Restructuring time, facilities, and program pathway	Does the current school or district calendar allow time for learning experiences in the curriculum?

Leadership Actions for Student, Professional, and System Learning

Student Learning	Professional Learning	System Learning
Establishes specific content for what is taught and learned Adapts academic learning tasks to student learning needs	Signals content and pedagogical learning needs for professional development Provides natural content focus for instructional supervision and evaluation	Provides reference point for systemwide data gathering Contributes to coherence in program planning

Assessment Systems Pathway

The *assessment systems pathway* includes selection, construction, administration, and interpretation of assessments of all kinds, ranging from assessments used by teachers in their daily work to annual systemwide standardized testing. Teachers are active players in the assessment pathway, as well as other school colleagues including school coaches, teacher leaders, and sometimes school administrators who have assessment expertise. At the district level, individuals working in a research or assessment office, along with decision makers responsible for curriculum or accountability, are likely to be involved in the design and construction of district-wide assessment systems. Those who design and administer state-wide assessment systems are also major players, as are outside groups such as testing firms and professional associations.

Leadership Opportunities for Schools and Districts
School Leadership Opportunities

- Interpreting state and district assessments to identify improvement targets for the school

- Convening schoolwide conversations about the meaning and use of assessments, both internally and externally
- Using assessment results to pinpoint improvement goals, creating a sense of urgency for learning among staff and parents
- Developing robust school-level assessment databases that can inform decision making over time

District Leadership Opportunities

- Selecting or developing an array of assessments that fully capture what is to be taught
- Aligning assessments with learning standards and the curriculum
- Engaging constituent groups in critical conversations about what students are learning and how we assess their learning
- Using assessment data to create urgency for student learning throughout the community

Connection with Other Pathways

Related Pathways	Linking Questions
Support for special learning needs pathway	Can disaggregating assessment help to pinpoint special learning needs for particular groups of students?
Support for ongoing professional development pathway	What can professionals learn about their practice from a close examination of assessment data?
Student learning standards pathway	Are we assessing what we expect students to know and be able to do?
Curriculum pathway	Are we assessing what we teach and how we teach it?
Information system development pathway	What systems can make assessment information available to teachers and administrators in a timely way?

Leadership Actions for Student, Professional, and System Learning

Student Learning	Professional Learning	System Learning
Defines operationally what students are expected to learn by using curriculum, pedagogy, and standards	Provides content focus for professional development	Provides one set of information on system performance
Demonstrates what students know and know how to do	Provokes a reexamination of curriculum and pedagogy	Communicates student- and school-level progress to constituencies and public at large
Communicates student progress to families and other constituencies	Offers a tool for teachers' inquiry into their practice	Updates benchmarks, creates opportunities for coherence in planning, goal-setting processes
Uncovers inequities in learning across student subgroups	Catalyzes equity and social justice agenda	

Accountability Systems Pathway

The *accountability systems pathway* includes activity to encourage internal responsibility for performance and establish external controls to ensure that individuals assume their respective responsibilities. Controls typically mean attaching consequences to measures of student or professional performance for individuals, schools, or the district as a whole. Most accountability systems emphasize "vertical" controls imposed on subordinates by leaders (e.g., teachers or students) such as accountability mechanisms created by the state for districts, schools, and students, or the corresponding ones created by districts. Accountability systems may also be "horizontal" among colleagues to emphasize mutual accountability to the system and vice versa.

Leadership Opportunities for Schools and Districts

School Leadership Opportunities

- Establishing professional accountability as a norm in the school
- Making professional scrutiny a regular feature of school life
- Inviting routine, critical community feedback on the school's progress toward established goals
- Establishing expectations for reciprocal accountability between leaders

District Leadership Opportunities

- Embracing, adapting, or buffering external accountability systems to serve the district's learning improvement agenda
- Establishing reciprocal criteria for district accountability to support teachers and schools
- Communicating credibility and seriousness of purpose to district stakeholders
- Establishing expectations for reciprocal accountability between the leader and subordinates

Connection with Other Pathways

Related Pathways	Linking Questions
Developing collegial connections pathway	What norms can be developed among professionals that support mutual accountability for professional practice?
Assessment systems pathway	How and why are assessments and accountability structures connected?
Planning and goal setting pathway	Can accountability systems be based on joint goal setting at the school or district level? Who is ultimately responsible for achieving these goals?

Professional practice standards pathway	How can explicit standards for professional practice be the basis for accountability norms and systems?

Leadership Actions for Student, Professional, and System Learning

Student Learning	Professional Learning	System Learning
Motivates student performance (if basis for accountability is understood and fair)	Creates an operation for professional responsibility for quality practice	Attaches action implications to what is learned about system performance
Creates an operation for student's responsibility for the quality of learning	Provides a catalyst for new professional learning	Invites regular feedback from constituencies
Clarifies underlying theory of action at the system level	Creates incentives to attain high-quality professional work	

Professionals and Professional Development Pathways

Professional Practice Standards Pathway

The *professional practice standards pathway* includes activity to make a vision of good practice for teachers and administrators explicit (i.e., declarations of what professionals should know and be able to do). As with student learning standards, state-level bodies, such as professional standards boards and state educational agencies, and professional associations, such as the National Board for Professional Teaching Standards, the Interstate New Teachers Assessment and Support Consortium, and the National Association of Elementary School Principals, are a common source of such standards statements. However, some districts have opted to create their own standards. Although not usual, a single school might also create its own standards. Whatever the source of standards for professional practice, school and district leaders are in position to bring one or more sets of these standards to their staff members and make the standards integral to the working life of their institutions.

Leadership Opportunities for Schools and Districts

School Leadership Opportunities

- Creating conversations about the meaning of district professional practice standards
- Using professional practice standards to recruit and induct new staff members and to supervise and evaluate all staff members
- Establishing a vision for professional practice within the school centered on equity and excellence

District Leadership Opportunities

- Developing district-specific teaching or administrative practice standards
- Identifying models and examples of exemplary professional practice in and outside of the district
- Creating district accountability systems that acknowledge professional practice standards

Connection with Other Pathways

Related Pathways	Linking Questions
Support for special learning needs pathway	Does our vision for excellent practice meet the needs of all children?
Support for ongoing professional development pathway	How can professional practice standards help define the agenda for professional development? How can we productively link with external support providers who focus on developing high-quality, professional practice (e.g., National Board for Professional Teaching Standards [NBPTS], universities)
Student learning standards pathway	How well are professional practice standards reflected in student learning standards?

Mentoring and induction pathway	Are mentors available to demonstrate professional practice standards? How can a school or district encourage professional practice for new or struggling teachers?
Assessment systems pathway	What information can be gathered to show progress toward professional standards of practice?
Compensation and rewards pathway	How can schools or districts reward excellence in professional practice?

Leadership Actions for Student, Professional, and System Learning

Student Learning	Professional Learning	System Learning
Captures how teaching can effectively contribute to student learning	Provides content focus for professional development	Provides a reference point for systemwide data gathering
Defines skills and knowledge that teachers need to enable them to reach all students	Establishes a basis for assessing professional work	Focuses on building systemwide instructional capacity
	Creates a vision for high-quality practice	Creates a local and regional reputation for quality
	Creates an operation for high-quality instruction	

Preparation and Certification Pathway

The *preparation and certification pathway* includes activity to admit teacher or administrator candidates to preparation programs through traditional or alternative routes. This pathway also includes preservice preparation in these programs, verification of professional knowledge and competence (including entrance and exit assessment), and licensure for professional practice. The pathway also consists of recertification at later stages in a professional career, as well as activity to attain a higher level of certification (i.e., teachers seeking the next level of certification in states that have a multitiered certification system). Much of the activity along this pathway takes place outside the purview of schools and districts in conjunction with professional associations, state government, and institutions of higher education. However, actions by school and district leaders can give meaning and value to certification (e.g., encouraging National Board certification), assist with formal preparation (e.g., entering into professional development school programs), or otherwise contribute to professional preparation and certification.

Leadership Opportunities for Schools and Districts

School Leadership Opportunities

- Setting up internship and student teaching arrangements with higher education institutions; making arrangements for quality, onsite placements
- Supporting mentorship for uncertified teachers, including support for mentors
- Actively participating in the hiring process for new teachers

District Leadership Opportunities

- Creating incentives and other supports for teachers seeking higher levels of certification or education
- Seeking strategic partnerships with training institutions in preparing new teachers and leaders, including high-quality, alternative route programs
- Valuing appropriate certification and preparation in hiring and assigning professionals

Connection with Other Pathways

Related Pathways	Linking Questions
Curriculum pathway	In what ways are new teachers prepared to teach the curriculum in use? How can the curriculum take full advantage of staff preparation?
Mentoring and induction support pathway	Can mentors prepare staff members for higher levels of certification (e.g., NBPTS) or leadership?
Professional practice standards pathway	Is the school or district seeking staff with qualifications that match high standards for professional practice?

Leadership Actions for Student, Professional, and System Learning

Student Learning	Professional Learning	System Learning
Establishes a baseline of "look fors" in teacher knowledge, skills, and belief related to improving student learning	Shapes early professional learning and formation of professional identity	Provides a reference point for systemwide data gathering
	Motivates and guides steps toward future professional learning	Develops ongoing, reciprocal relationships with regional institutions of higher education
Ensures the highest possible floor for teaching quality	Builds and contributes to leadership capacity in the school or district	

Mentoring and Induction Support Pathway

The *mentoring and induction support pathway* includes activity to help new teachers or administrators solidify their skills at an early stage in their careers. These activities usually occur through extended, focused interaction with more experienced peers. Such arrangements span a continuum from informal individual mentoring to formalized induction programs, sometimes undertaken in conjunction with an institution of higher education. Within schools, experienced teacher leaders, department heads, administrators, staff developers, or coaches may guide mentoring and induction work. Assisting them may be union staff, faculty from higher education institutions, or individuals working in professional development organizations outside the formal purview of the schools. District-level staff, individuals responsible for professional development, or assistant superintendents may also design and lead activities along this pathway. While states are not typically involved, they may play a role in supporting or encouraging mentoring and induction.

Leadership Opportunities for Schools and Districts

School Leadership Opportunities

- Cultivating a cadre of mentors and connecting mentees with suitable mentors
- Mentoring and developing skills of school-level mentors
- Explicitly acknowledging issues of induction and making these part of schoolwide conversation and problem solving

District Leadership Opportunities

- Creating expectations for school- and district-level mentorship for teachers and administrators
- Identifying suitable sources of mentors and other forms of induction support in and out of the district
- Setting up and implementing mentoring arrangements for leaders and others in mentoring roles
- Establishing and allocating compensation to support the mentoring function

Connection with Other Pathways

Related Pathways	Linking Questions
Curriculum pathway	How can mentors be found with the appropriate subject-matter expertise and grounding in the curriculum?
Restructuring time, program, and facilities pathway	Is regular time set aside for mentors and mentees to interact with each other or other induction support activities?
Support for ongoing professional development pathway	How well are mentors reinforcing what teachers (or leaders) encounter in other professional learning experiences, and vice versa? To what extent are mentors focusing mentees on developing identified areas of need in their professional practice?
Staffing and assignment pathway	Can staffing assignments be used to encourage and solidify mentoring relationships? Do staffing assignments provide the greatest possibility of early success for teachers new to the profession?
Developing collegial connections pathway	How can mentoring and induction activities build collaboration among staff that might not otherwise occur?

Leadership Actions for Student, Professional, and System Learning

Student Learning	Professional Learning	System Learning
Provides immediate intervention and assistance when a staff member's inexperience limits student learning Spreads promising and tested practices supporting student learning	Connects inexperienced staff with immediate assistance; strengthens leadership skills of experienced staff Encourages mutual responsibility for learning among teachers Builds professional community; recognizes and capitalizes on instructional expertise	Helps establish institutional memory with regard to high-quality, instructional practices Builds instructional and leadership capacity simultaneously Builds and spreads district reputation as supportive of teachers' professional growth

Support for Ongoing Professional Development Pathway

The *support for ongoing professional development pathway* includes the full range of activity aimed at professional learning for teachers, administrators, and other staff. Although professional development is often equated with inservice workshops, a wide range of activities fall within this category, including individual coaching, institutes, professional development academies, intervisitation, and study groups. Collaboratively developing curriculum and other forms of collaborative work can also serve a professional development goal. Many individuals at different levels of the educational system contribute to these activities and can exercise leadership along this pathway, including coaches, staff developers, teacher leaders, and principals in the school (e.g., at the district level, administrators or other staff responsible for staff development, curriculum, assessment, and student learning needs are instrumental for this pathway). This pathway is especially open to leadership by individuals outside the formal educational system, such as professional associations and unions, institutions of higher education, and nonprofit professional development organizations.

Leadership Opportunities for Schools and Districts

School Leadership Opportunities

- Supporting schoolwide inquiry into questions of professional practice
- Making professional development a regular feature of the school structure and routine
- Modeling professional learning in all aspects of the school's work

District Leadership Opportunities

- Allocating fiscal, intellectual, and human resources to a focused professional development function
- Identifying sources of support for professional learning outside the school district
- Instilling a professional learning norm in the central office staff by modeling oneself as learner
- Working out district-union agreements that support powerful professional development

Connection with Other Pathways

Related Pathways	Linking Questions
Curriculum pathway	How does professional development increase the staff's command of the curriculum, pedagogy, and the underlying subject matter?
Assessment systems pathway	How can assessment data be used as prompts for professional learning?
Restructuring time, program, and facilities pathway	Does the schedule allow for a variety of professional development activities? Is meeting time allocated for professional development?
Support for ongoing professional development pathway	Does professional development include considerations for students with special learning needs and ways for all staff to address these needs?
Supervision and evaluation pathway	How can supervisors help to support, motivate, and define goals for further professional development?

Leadership Actions for Student, Professional, and System Learning

Student Learning	Professional Learning	System Learning
Increases likelihood that students will encounter a richer array of learning opportunities	Makes professional growth and development an expected, integral part of practice	Creates the mechanism for individuals to increase system capacity
Increases likelihood that staff will be able to understand what and how students are learning	Connects professional staff with key resources to support their own learning	Strategically focuses available resources on improving learning across levels
Creates greater opportunities for all students to learn, regardless of their needs	Increases staff's repertoire of pedagogical techniques and content knowledge	
	Sharpens staff's capacity for understanding what students are learning	

Supervision and Evaluation Pathway

The *supervision and evaluation pathway* includes activity to oversee and guide the work of professional personnel for formative, developmental, and summative purposes. For summative purposes, the supervisor is often an organizational superior such as a principal supervising teachers' work or a district administrator supervising principals' work. However, a peer, such as in collegial supervision models, or a third-party person, such as in a district-sponsored coach working with a school administrator or teacher, can also assume a supervisory role. A variety of activities can count as supervision including observation and commentary on the professional's work. In addition, for formative, developmental purposes, supervisors can recommend or require changes in the supervisee's position or status.

Leadership Opportunities for Schools and Districts

School Leadership Opportunities

- Creating structure and expectations for regular interaction between supervisees and supervisors
- Distributing leadership for instructional improvement through supervision
- Using supervision and evaluation to address issues for school-wide consideration

District Leadership Opportunities

- Modeling learning-focused instructional supervision and evaluation
- Providing a source of potential supervisors; creating flattened structures for improving instructional practice
- Developing districtwide criteria and rubrics for supervising and evaluating teachers and administrators

Connection with Other Pathways

Related Pathways	Linking Questions
Curriculum pathway	How well do the criteria for personnel evaluation reflect the subject-matter base, range of pedagogical approaches, and learning assumptions embedded in the curriculum?
Compensation and rewards pathway	Do supervisors publicly acknowledge, celebrate, or otherwise reward strong practice by their supervisees?

Support for ongoing professional development pathway	Does supervision and evaluation link to expectations for professional growth and development?
Accountability systems pathway	How can supervision and evaluation encourage norms of responsibility for students and other forms of internal professional accountability?
Support for noninstructional needs pathway	Do supervision and evaluation processes help professionals spot and attend to students' noninstructional needs?
Leadership development pathway	In what ways are supervisory or personnel evaluation assignments set up and used to develop skills for emerging leaders?

Leadership Actions for Student, Professional, and System Learning

Student Learning	Professional Learning	System Learning
Examines and verifies the connections between individual practice and student learning

Provides a safety net for ensuring equitable student learning opportunities | Identifies issues for individual professional improvement and establishes a bottom line for professional accountability

Provides opportunities for supervisors' learning about improving practice | Establishes the means for exercising quality control of teaching |

Compensation and Rewards Pathway

The *compensation and rewards pathway* includes monetary compensation and nonmonetary rewards for work performed, along with a range of incentives that acknowledge and encourage merit-based work. Thus, in addition to base pay and benefits, compensation packages may include bonuses for good performance, combat pay for work under adverse circumstances, and other forms of salary-based supplements. These are often determined by district-level leaders, central office administrators who interact with union staff members, and other personnel. School administrators have various ways to supplement the basic compensation package, sometimes with funding (e.g., for extra duties taken on) or with a range of more symbolic rewards. These rewards range from public acknowledgment of work done well to arranging assignments, facilities, materials, or other working conditions as a reward for performance.

Leadership Opportunities for Schools and Districts

School Leadership Opportunities

- Arranging stipends or other forms of compensation for staff who take on learning-focused leadership or support roles
- Publicly celebrating student and staff learning accomplishments
- Devoting significant building budget funds toward focused professional learning opportunities

District Leadership Opportunities

- Maximizing allocations of resources to directly support learning for students and professionals
- Experimenting with compensation or rewards for learning-focused leadership activities
- Working with union, state, and community members to increase overall compensation levels

Connection with Other Pathways

Related Pathways	Linking Questions
Accountability systems pathway	How are compensation and performance linked? How well does the system demonstrate payoff for investment in improvement?
Professional practice standards pathway	Are compensation systems and rewards reflective of explicit standards for good professional practice?
Recruitment and hiring pathway	How can compensation systems and rewards be used to attract qualified individuals to teaching and administrative roles?

Leadership development pathway	What financial incentives can be offered to encourage individuals to become school or district leaders?

Leadership Actions for Student, Professional, and System Learning

Student Learning	Professional Learning	System Learning
May help motivate good staff to persist in teaching	May motivate learning about teaching practice and leadership work	Represents system's investment in performance
Celebrates and values success in student learning (when rewards are tied to performance)	May support professional learning (when this function is explicitly linked to pay or additional support)	Offers reference point for performance measures as a return on investment
Supports progress toward professional learning goals	Promotes consistency between identified learning goals and fiscal policies	

Learner and Learner Support Pathways

Support for Special Learning Needs Pathway

Along the *support for special learning needs pathway*, educators address the unique needs of particular categories of learners, specifically those students with limited English proficiency and identified disabilities. This pathway also addresses students who are not well accommodated by regular school programs including gifted students and students who come from backgrounds shaped by poverty, cultural differences, and immigrant communities. Serving these students does not necessarily mean special or separate treatment, such as in tutoring, pullout programs, resource rooms, newcomer centers, gifted and talented tracks, or other conventional arrangements. Instead, various in-class and consultative arrangements can bring specialized help into the regular classroom for both these students and their teachers. These arrangements can also help other students develop healthy perceptions and relations with their targeted peers. Finally, support for special learning needs can be built into the overall structure and philosophy of the school or district (e.g., in inclusive or bilingual schooling arrangements). Aside from individuals with administrative responsibility, other staff members are in a position to exert learning-focused leadership along this pathway, including district-level staff members who are responsible for special learning support programs, professional development, and curriculum; and school-level staff members who have expertise in particular learning needs (e.g., itinerant ESL teachers, special educators).

Leadership Opportunities for Schools and Districts

School Leadership Opportunities

- Disaggregating and examining data with staff members about the progress of students with special learning needs
- Establishing norms of joint schoolwide responsibility for students with special learning needs
- Providing and funding ideas and expertise for serving students with special learning needs

District Leadership Opportunities

- Making services for students with special learning needs a visible high priority for districtwide improvement plans
- Adapting curriculum, staffing, and program structures for children with special learning needs
- Assigning high-quality staff members to students with special learning needs

Connection with Other Pathways

Related Pathways	Linking Questions
Family and parent engagement pathway	What connections are forged with the families of students with special learning needs? How are families helped to support these learners?

Assessment systems pathway	Are there appropriate ways of assessing what learners with special needs know and can do? How can assessment approaches be improved?
Planning and goal setting pathway	Are missions and improvement plans appropriately addressing students with special learning needs?
Support for noninstructional needs pathway	Are mechanisms in place to systematically consider and address the noninstructional needs of students with special learning needs?
Developing collegial connections pathway	How can regular, learning-focused communication between general and specialized staff be encouraged?

Leadership Actions for Student, Professional, and System Learning

Student Learning	Professional Learning	System Learning
Pushes toward more equitable student learning opportunities	Provides a focus for professional development	Develops a differentiated picture of system performance
Identifies specific learning needs and ways to address them	Helps professional staff work with learners' differences	Highlights and signals pockets of inequity

Support for Noninstructional Needs Pathway

Along the *support for noninstructional needs pathway* are nonaca-demic ways that leaders support students' readiness for schooling. Nutritional programs, mental health services, and family support are among the most obvious kinds of support along this pathway. Other supports on this pathway could include programs to prevent drug abuse, teen pregnancy, and other social deterrents. All of these activities build a foundation for academic learning while imparting other valuable benefits of schooling. The activities along this pathway can be quite varied, depending on the configuration of noninstructional needs in the school or district population. Counseling staff, health educators, psychologists, drug specialists, physical education staff, and nutritionists are likely to be well positioned to exercise leadership along this pathway, alongside staff with more generalized responsibility for the school or district.

Leadership Opportunities for Schools and Districts

School Leadership Opportunities

- Establishing school-based services that address the most critical noninstructional needs
- Engaging parents in efforts to address noninstructional needs
- Creating opportunities for dialogue and collaboration between instructional staff and noninstructional support personnel

District Leadership Opportunities

- Establishing priorities for noninstructional supports that show the greatest promise for improving learning opportunities
- Forging alliances with community service providers and seeking funds to support noninstructional needs
- Developing communication and other bridges between academic support and noninstructional support functions

Connection with Other Pathways

Related Pathways	Linking Questions
Recruitment and hiring pathway	Are schools and districts hiring staff members with expertise in addressing noninstructional needs?
Support for ongoing professional development pathway	Are staff members encouraged to learn, recognize, and meet noninstructional needs?
Planning and goal setting pathway	How explicitly does the school or district address noninstructional needs in its planning and mission statements?
Restructuring time, program, and facilities pathway	How well are noninstructional needs aligned with the academic program?

Leadership Actions for Student, Professional, and System Learning

Student Learning	Professional Learning	System Learning
Boosts students' readiness for learning

Brings on more varied resources for teaching and learning | Complements and enriches learning about classroom practice

Creates greater awareness and sensitivity to noninstructional needs among instructional staff | Offers a more robust understanding of academic performance patterns and associated student needs |

Student Placement and Assignment Pathway

The *student placement and assignment pathway* concerns grouping, clustering, or assigning students in particular classrooms, programs, schools, or tracks. Because instruction means factoring in the interactions between students as well as with their teachers, it matters a great deal who gets to learn with whom. Activities along this pathway include decision making by administrators and consulting with other staff members about the size and composition of class groups (e.g., Should groups be homogeneous or heterogeneous? Large or small?). These decisions can also address whether distinct tracks or programs will be created, what students to admit, and how families can exercise their choice. These decisions are intimately linked to how special learning needs are best served, the availability of staff resources, and other matters in the organization of schooling. Principals, assistant principals, and other staff members can also have an influence on student assignments and placement.

Leadership Opportunities for Schools and Districts
School Leadership Opportunities

- Convening conversations about assignment, placement, and tracking in the school, and the consequences of these decisions
- Focusing attention on creating high standards for all students with diverse learning needs
- Creating team structures and other assignment mechanisms that reduce the size of learning groups for part or all of the school day

District Leadership Opportunities

- Establishing assignment norms and policies that minimize segregating students with special needs
- Creating school assignment policies that balance parental or student choice with the goal of creating balanced student bodies
- Promoting diversity alongside an equitable, excellent learning agenda across all schools within the system

Connection with Other Pathways

Related Pathways	Linking Questions
Staffing and assignment pathway	Are teachers and students assigned to each other in ways that maximize their ability to develop a long-term relationship?
Restructuring time, program, and facilities pathway	What time and program structures are best to support students' learning?
Assessment systems pathway	Which multiple assessments best facilitate student placement?
Support for special learning needs pathway	For students with special needs, what placements will maximize their interaction with other students and provide them with the support they need?
Family and parent engagement pathway	How can parents and students participate in student assignment, placement, and program choices?

Leadership Actions for Student, Professional, and System Learning

Student Learning	Professional Learning	System Learning
Shapes how students can act as a learning resource to each other	Challenges staff assumptions about serving learning differences	Creates more optimal learning experiences for all
Optimizes group size and composition to support learning	Prompts new staff members to think about the student population they are teaching	Develops greater coherence between established learning goals for all students and organizational structure
Creates diverse learning communities inside classrooms		

Behavioral Support and Management Pathway

The *behavioral support and management pathway* concerns young people's social learning. Activities along this pathway set expectations for the students' behavior and help them acquire appropriate behavioral skills and maintain appropriate levels of order and safety in the school. Behavioral support and management is best thought of as a teaching function for which all members of the school community are responsible. This pathway is not just for principals, assistant principals, or special educators who manage disciplinary infractions or behavior disorders. There are many potential leaders along this pathway, particularly when behavioral support and management is connected to how students learn. While activity along this pathway is likely to be concentrated at the school level, system-level policies concerning expulsions, suspensions, or safety-related issues may also play a role.

Leadership Opportunities for Schools and Districts

School Leadership Opportunities

- Promoting norms of joint responsibility for student behavior
- Establishing and maintaining explicit standards for behavior schoolwide
- Recognizing and highlighting the connection between positive support for student behavior and learning
- Creating opportunities for staff to focus and share positive classroom management strategies

District Leadership Opportunities

- Convening districtwide conversations about student behavior problems as symptoms of deeper teaching/learning needs
- Allocating resources to building capacity for working with students with serious behavior disorders

- Maintaining a central focus on student learning needs when adjudicating suspensions, expulsions, or truancy cases

Connection with Other Pathways

Related Pathways	Linking Questions
Leadership development pathway	Are emerging leaders trained to view behavioral support and management as a teaching function?
Family and parent engagement pathway	Are parents involved in teaching their children how to manage their behavior?
Mentoring and induction support pathway	What supports are in place to help inexperienced staff members teach their students while encouraging and supporting appropriate behavior between classmates?
Curriculum pathway	Are measures in place to help teachers construct lessons and engage a class at large while dealing with a smaller subset of students with behavior problems?

Leadership Actions for Student, Professional, and System Learning

Student Learning	Professional Learning	System Learning
Connects social and academic learning Sets a tone for serious and purposeful learning	Helps staff connect their work on student behavior with the quality of learning opportunities Expands staff capacity to support social learning and develop effective classroom management strategies	Builds a learning focus into all conversations about student discipline and management

Family and Parent Engagement Pathway

The *family and parent engagement pathway* concerns communication, outreach, and parental involvement in school affairs. School leaders are in a position to inform parents about the school and its program through a variety of media, and also to welcome them as partners in supporting their children's learning. Home visits, attending community gatherings, and participating in parent education services may also connect schools more closely with students' families. Conversely, leaders may draw parents into the school as teaching aides or by encouraging them to participate with the PTA, onsite councils, task forces, or other school needs. These kinds of activities are largely governed by school leaders, but district leaders can also set the tone and stage for what schools do to reach the community (see *community engagement pathway* on page 241).

Leadership Opportunities for Schools and Districts

School Leadership Opportunities

- Developing regular, multiple communication routes to parents in terms that they can understand
- Inviting parents to play a variety of roles both in and out of the school to support the school's instructional program
- Focusing parent contacts and connections on the school's learning goals
- Developing means to encourage input from parents who are traditionally not heard within school-based parent groups

District Leadership Opportunities

- Explaining the nature and rationale for the chosen curriculum to parents
- Developing means to encourage input from parents who are traditionally not heard within school-based parent groups
- Using the district learning goals as the focus for convening parent forums

Connection with Other Pathways

Related Pathways	Linking Questions
Curriculum pathway	Does the curriculum connect to learners' home and community lives in multiple ways? Is it relevant for students?
Mentoring and induction support pathway	Are new staff members encouraged to regularly and positively connect with parents? Are they shown how to do this productively?
Leadership development pathway	Are emerging leaders given the chance to exercise leadership with parents and other community members?

| Student learning standards pathway | Do parents have a voice in the development of learning standards for students? |
| Community engagement pathway | How can the school or district offer services to the community at large? |

Leadership Actions for Student, Professional, and System Learning

Student Learning	Professional Learning	System Learning
Strengthens an additional layer of support for student learning Helps parents understand what students are learning and why	Combines professional and family considerations in improving staff practice Questions the relevance of learning to students' lives	Develops systemwide support for schooling practices Builds strategic partnerships with parents to support learning goals

Workplace and System Pathways

Planning and Goal Setting Pathway

The *planning and goal setting pathway* includes activity to create short- and long-range plans for improving learning and teaching in the school or district. Conceptually, these activities span a continuum from constructing broad mission statements and strategic directions to detailed planning to achieve specific objectives. Some leaders would view budgeting as an integral part of developing an annual work plan. At the school level, administrators and other school governance leaders (e.g., site councils, department heads, and teacher leaders) are most likely to exercise leadership along this pathway. Many administrators and staff at district level might be involved, as well as stakeholders from the community.

Leadership Opportunities for Schools and Districts
School Leadership Opportunities

- Engaging the school community in both short- and long-term planning for improving student and teacher learning

- Engaging external partners in developing school mission and plans
- Using inquiry into the school's functioning to target program improvement efforts and distribute leadership responsibility

District Leadership Opportunities

- Centering district strategic planning on student, professional, and system learning
- Making learning improvement an explicit consideration in annual budgetary planning
- Promoting and supporting meaningful school-level planning that is tied to learning improvement goals

Connection with Other Pathways

Related Pathways	Linking Questions
Student learning standards pathway	How are student learning standards connected to school and district planning?
Developing collegial connections pathway	How can staff members be encouraged to collaborate for planning and inquiry processes?
Information system development pathway	What information is needed to support school and district planning? How can staff be part of developing that information?
Accountability systems pathway	How does planning create accountability for staff members?

Leadership Actions for Student, Professional, and System Learning

Student Learning	Professional Learning	System Learning
Ties goals, plans, and evidence of student learning	Enhances the prospects of inter-staff dialogue and informal professional learning	Creates greater coherence among learning agendas
Connects classroom-level work to a broader learning agenda	Builds a system view of teachers and support staff	Establishes system norms for cyclical planning processes

Developing Collegial Connections Pathway

The *developing collegial connections pathway* includes activity that improves working relations among professional staff while also developing joint work related to improving learning and teaching. Team-building activities and basic mechanisms for improving communication among staff are part of this pathway. Other relevant activities on this pathway include creating team structures, developing norms for supporting collaboration, and assigning collaborative tasks. Activities along this pathway relate to Action Area 2 in the framework (building professional community). At the school level, department heads, team leaders, and site council members complement principals' efforts to strengthen collegial connections, while at the district level, unit heads and staff members multitask to complement superintendents' efforts.

Leadership Opportunities for Schools and Districts
School Leadership Opportunities

- Distributing leadership for different aspects of the school program and trusting others to carry this load adequately
- Helping staff members to view their work as part of an interconnected whole agenda

- Creating opportunities for school staff members to get to know each other
- Encouraging staff members to stimulate and engage in conversations across grade-level and subject-matter boundaries
- Creating team structures that encourage interaction

District Leadership Opportunities

- Promoting a learning focus in all areas of the district as a basis for joint work
- Visiting schools on a frequent basis, and using visits as an opportunity to learn and interact with staff members
- Modeling collegial connections among central office staff and throughout the district hierarchy
- Arranging and rewarding collaborative problem solving across the district

Connection with Other Pathways

Related Pathways	Linking Questions
Curriculum pathway	Are staff members encouraged or required to communicate with other staff members who are teaching the same content? Across content areas?
Restructuring time, program, and facilities pathway	Is time built into the schedule to encourage staff interaction?
Support for ongoing professional development pathway	What professional development activities foster connections among staff members who are unfamiliar with each other?
Staffing and assignment pathway	How can staff reassignment encourage new and productive connections among colleagues?

Leadership Actions for Student, Professional, and System Learning

Student Learning	Professional Learning	System Learning
Increases likelihood of equity in learning opportunities across classrooms	Enhances the prospects of inter-staff dialogue and informal professional learning	Increases the possibility for consistency in instruction
Models positive interactions for students	Builds trust among staff members	Builds trust in the system hierarchy
		Enhances promising teaching ideas; builds capacity

Leadership Development Pathway

The *leadership development pathway* includes activity aimed at identifying, selecting, and nurturing new leaders for learning-related roles in schools or districts. This pathway is geared toward individuals already working in the school or district. (The *recruiting and hiring pathway*, described on the next page, addresses efforts to attract and secure new leaders from outside the school or district.) This pathway can overlap with the *mentoring and induction pathway* or *ongoing professional development pathway*. However, the explicit goal of this pathway is to prepare people for specific leadership positions. Principals, assistant principals, superintendents, and assistant superintendents are positions that are most likely to be targeted on this pathway, given the increasing difficulty of filling these positions. This pathway also includes developing teacher leaders and individuals who are seeking to increase their leadership capacity in the school or district.

Leadership Opportunities for Schools and Districts

School Leadership Opportunities

- Creating and supporting teachers in leadership roles
- Creating school governance arrangements that maximize shared leadership
- Explicit planning for leadership transitions, with particular attention to sustaining change efforts

District Leadership Opportunities

- Partnering with external leadership development resources
- Constructing explicit leadership succession and leadership pipeline plans
- Developing the leadership capacity of the school board through study groups and other means

Connection with Other Pathways

Related Pathways	Linking Questions
Mentoring and induction support pathway	Can mentoring be used to nurture future leaders?
Professional practice standards pathway	Does the school or district have explicit leadership standards and are these standards used to guide developmental experiences?
Recruiting and hiring pathway	Are leadership recruitment efforts devoted to the areas where the school or district is least likely to grow its own?
Community engagement pathway	How can interactions with the community be used to give potential leaders exposure and practice articulating a learning improvement focus?

Leadership Actions for Student, Professional, and System Learning

Student Learning	Professional Learning	System Learning
Multiplies sources of support for student learning Focuses a wider array of leadership resources on student learning goals	Identifies promising participants who can step into learning-focused leadership roles Creates new arena for professional growth Builds a cadre of those who understand and operate within a system view	Builds system capacity for leadership Increases supply of individuals who can facilitate system learning

Restructuring Time, Program, and Facilities Pathway

The *restructuring time, program, and facilities pathway* addresses a range of decisions that arise in designing or redesigning the school and district. One focus on this pathway is establishing time for professional work. (Note the close relationship with the *student placement and assignment pathway*.) This pathway also concentrates on defining programmatic strands and groupings within the overall school or district program. (The *curriculum pathway* and the *student placement and assignment pathway* are intimately involved in this process.) Finally, this pathway helps leaders shape or alter the structure of the physical workplace. Depending on how decisions are made in the school or district, virtually any staff member may exercise leadership on this pathway.

Leadership Opportunities for Schools and Districts

School Leadership Opportunities

- Creating regular blocks of time for professional learning and collegial connections
- Focusing available professional meeting time on the learning agenda
- Creating blocks of student learning time to fit the needs of the curriculum and learners
- Constructing programs that focus on personalizing instruction

District Leadership Opportunities

- Creating opportunities or incentives for restructuring school programs to suit district goals and school-specific circumstances
- Avoiding "one size fits all" mandates related to time and program planning
- Partnering with the union to enable appropriate school-level restructuring
- Considering use and design of facilities in long-range planning

Connection with Other Pathways

Related Pathways	Linking Questions
Student placement and assignment pathway	How do assignments impact time and scheduling?
Curriculum pathway	Have the right kind of time blocks been created for the curriculum?
Support for ongoing professional development pathway	How can the school calendar be structured to ensure regular time for professional development?

Support for special learning needs pathway	Are programs and facilities set up with students with special learning needs in mind?

Leadership Actions for Student, Professional, and System Learning

Student Learning	Professional Learning	System Learning
Creates time for student learning Considers students' learning differences and special learning needs	Makes time and space for regular professional learning	Provides a basic resource for inquiry into system performance Aligns time, program, and facilities planning with the district's learning agenda

Staffing and Assignment Pathway

The *staffing and assignment pathway* concerns decisions about the kinds of professional staff who will work in the school or district. This pathway also focuses on the kind of work they will do and how they will be deployed within the school or district. Critical tasks on this pathway include defining position responsibilities, assigning teachers within their fields of expertise, and aligning these positions with collective bargaining agreements or personnel policies. Principals, department heads, district administrators, and state policymakers are in the best position to exercise leadership along this pathway.

Leadership Opportunities for Schools and Districts

School Leadership Opportunities

- Making the best use of available subject-matter experts in the school; limiting or eliminating out-of-field assignments
- Focusing high-quality teaching on students with greatest needs
- Minimizing reliance on specialized expertise in building the school's staff

District Leadership Opportunities

- Working with the union to set flexible yet rigorous expectations for defining position requirements
- Maximizing school-site discretion in deploying staff members
- Focusing expert leaders on schools facing the most difficult challenges

Connection with Other Pathways

Related Pathways	Linking Questions
Support for special learning needs pathway	Are students with special learning needs considered when schools assign staff members?
Mentoring and induction support pathway	How are potential mentors who have the strongest capacity to support learning improvement found and deployed?
Compensation and rewards pathway	Are there incentives and rewards for taking on difficult assignments?
Leadership development pathway	How can staff assignments increase opportunities for potential leaders to gain experience and support in learning-focused roles?

Leadership Actions for Student, Professional, and System Learning

Student Learning	Professional Learning	System Learning
Connects learners with individuals who can facilitate their learning Matches content experts with learners' needs	Creates potential for formal and informal professional learning relationships to develop Sets the stage for new professionals' learning	Positions staff members who can contribute to system learning at appropriate vantage points Builds capacity and expertise for dealing with challenging system learning needs

Recruitment and Hiring Pathway

The *recruitment and hiring pathway* focuses on attracting and securing new teaching or administrative staff for the school or district. Professionals' knowledge and commitment to their careers greatly affect the way they address learning improvement throughout the system. Therefore, it's important for principals, superintendents, personnel directors, and others to define the qualities for hiring the "right" people and ultimately selecting the best person for the position. Activities on this pathway include creating hiring policies and processes, advertising positions, and developing long-term relationships with feeder schools, institutions, or programs to recruit new staff members. These tasks become especially important in settings experiencing high turnover or rapid growth. As the hiring function involves multiple levels, decisions about distributing authority for hiring between the school and the district are critical in this pathway (e.g., are schools free to hire whomever they want?). Union leadership, exercised through collective bargaining, may also create conditions that affect recruitment and hiring.

Leadership Opportunities for Schools and Districts

School Leadership Opportunities

- Engaging school staff and community in defining criteria for new positions, recruiting, and hiring
- Making improving learning a central part of the school's effort to attract, screen, and secure new staff
- Attending to and recruiting promising interns, particularly in key subject areas

District Leadership Opportunities

- Maximizing the school's role in hiring and connecting hiring decisions to learning improvement goals
- Creating strategic partnerships with feeder schools, institutions, or programs
- Streamlining hiring processes to enable early hiring actions

Connection with Other Pathways

Related Pathways	Linking Questions
Community engagement pathway	Are leaders aware of sources for likely candidates for teaching and administrative positions? Are leaders cultivating relationships with these schools, institutions, or programs?
Leadership development pathway	Are learning-focused goals considered in recruitment and hiring?
Preparation and certification pathway	How can the preparation process be used to attract and secure sufficient numbers of well-qualified new staff members?
Curriculum pathway	Are new staff members sought for areas of the curriculum that show the greatest need?

Leadership Actions for Student, Professional, and System Learning

Student Learning	Professional Learning	System Learning
Establishes core knowledge and pedagogical skill that learners will experience in the classroom Increases the likelihood of offering students the best possible learning experiences	Seeks individuals who value professional learning Defines the mix of staff who participate as learners	Represents the future "institutional memory" of the school or district Brings new potential capacity to the school or district Establishes coherence between learning agendas and hiring priorities

Information System Development Pathway

The *information system development pathway* includes activity to gather, interpret, and distribute data that impacts the quality of learning and teaching. (Activities along the *assessment and accountability pathways* are closely linked to this pathway.) Activities on this pathway include installing information processing technology, developing reporting routines, and strengthening the staff's capacity to interpret and use information for learning improvement. (*Support for ongoing professional development pathway* is also linked here.) Various individuals have the potential to exercise leadership in creating information systems that inform learning improvement.

Leadership Opportunities for Schools and Districts

School Leadership Opportunities

- Motivating and guiding school-level inquiry into school performance, based on relevant information sources

- Setting expectations for information sharing across the school in relation to a learning improvement focus
- Creating school-specific measures of learning and teaching that matter to school staff
- Developing communication strategies that highlight learning goals and progress for parents and community members

District Leadership Opportunities

- Building a system that provides regular, timely information to schools about learning and teaching
- Modeling the use of information about learning and teaching in district decision making
- Making systematic information sharing about learning and its possible meanings part of interactions with the external constituencies

Connection with Other Pathways

Related Pathways	Linking Questions
Accountability systems pathway	Are incentives and consequences connected to data analysis and use, and is the data used in decision making appropriate for the purpose?
Assessment systems pathway	Are multiple forms of assessment built into the district's information system?
Support for ongoing professional development pathway	Is information available for professional development? Are staff members prepared to understand and work with this information?
Planning and goal setting pathway	Is the information aligned with teaching and learning goals? Is the information adjusted as plans and goals evolve?

Leadership Actions for Student, Professional, and System Learning

Student Learning	Professional Learning	System Learning
Represents what students are learning, internally and externally	Offers a focus for learning-focused professional development	Represents what the system is learning Creates one medium for system learning
Establishes a reference point for student accountability	Represents various facets of professional practice	Makes strategic planning processes transparent

Community Engagement Pathway

The *community engagement pathway*, a counterpart to the *family and parent engagement* pathway, concerns connections with the broader community. A wide variety of activities take place on this pathway, depending on the composition and political makeup of the community. Thus, superintendents and school board members may work through local media, participate on community boards, interact with municipal governments, form collaborative agreements with partner institutions, and seek funding or other resources to gain community support. Others at the school and district level are also likely to exercise learning-focused leadership along this pathway at the request of the superintendent or on their own initiative.

Leadership Opportunities for Schools and Districts

School Leadership Opportunities

- Identifying sites for community-based learning
- Drawing members of the community into teaching and instructional support roles

- Making sensitivity to community cultures a norm for school staff in planning and delivering instruction

District Leadership Opportunities

- Developing ways of listening carefully to community concerns about learning
- Educating key community groups about the district's learning improvement agenda
- Seeking out and engaging community-based leadership resources that are relevant to learning improvement

Connection with Other Pathways

Related Pathways	Linking Questions
Curriculum pathway	How can community members have input into the content of the curriculum?
Family and parent engagement pathway	How can community leaders garner feedback from traditionally underrepresented groups within the community?
Support for noninstructional needs pathway	How can community resources be mobilized to address noninstructional needs for students? (e.g., drug prevention, health awareness)
Planning and goal setting pathway	Are there ways to publicly shape learning improvement agendas and include significant input from community stakeholders?

Leadership Actions for Student, Professional, and System Learning

Student Learning	Professional Learning	System Learning
Encourages connection between student learning and the community	Offers another source of professional learning resources	Serves as a sounding board for evidence of system performance
Interprets student learning to key stakeholders	Presents an important focus for professional learning	Builds trust, credibility, and systemwide political support

Methodological Notes

The ideas presented in this book have many sources including research literature, examples of leadership in action, and educators' craft knowledge, in addition to our own ongoing research in a variety of sites across the nation. While we cast a wide net in the research literature, we concentrated on work related to instructional leadership, school reform and renewal, teacher learning and professional community, teacher leadership, organizational learning, policy-practice connections, and education in high-poverty, high-diversity settings. The sources appear in the footnotes and references.

From these sources, we developed an overall framework that includes reflective ideas and tools for educational leaders. To ground them in practice, we assembled examples that, with several exceptions, derive from actual cases that were reported in published research, suggested by scholars from ongoing current studies, or contributed by practitioners.

Constructing the Ideas for the Book

A working draft of this book was field tested across a five-month period from April to August 2002. It was refined through solicited critiques, interactive working sessions, and dialogue following presentations. More specifically, 25 reviewers, evenly divided between scholars and practicing educators at both school and district levels, scrutinized the draft from a variety of perspectives. Working sessions included a meeting with members of the National College of School Leadership from the United Kingdom, a session with the University of Washington Policymakers Exchange, a week-long institute for aspiring system-level educational leaders, and a similar gathering of school principals. In addition, we presented successive versions at national meetings of scholars and practitioners, including the American Education Research Association, the University Council on Educational Administration, the Wallace-Readers Digest Funds' Leaders Count Initiative, and the National Policy Board for Educational Administration.

In all, the development team received commentary and suggestions from more than 300 individuals. These included a broad spectrum of working educators and individuals outside of education, including scholars and practitioners from the United States and abroad, educators with different racial or ethnic backgrounds, educators working at the district level and in schools, and individual experts working in elementary and secondary schools. The majority were practicing school and district leaders.

Our initial efforts took form in several reports issued by the Center for the Study of Teaching & Policy at the University of Washington, including *Leading for Learning: Reflective Tools for School and District Leaders* (Knapp, Copland, & Talbert, 2003) and *Leading for Learning Sourcebook: Concepts and Examples* (Knapp, Copland, Ford et al., 2003). This book includes and expands on the material published in those two reports.

Following the publication of these reports, we continued to gather examples and elaborate the base of information for this book. In particular, we drew heavily from two sources. First, we drew from the experiences of practicing leaders who were participating in the Leadership for Learning (L4L) Ed.D. program. This program, sponsored by the Center for Educational Leadership at the University of Washington, offered a rich source of examples of strategic, learning-focused leadership in action. Second, unpublished data in ongoing research conducted by the Center for Research on the Context of Teaching at Stanford University, the Center for the Study of Teaching and Policy at the University of Washington, and the University of Washington Center for Educational Leadership gave us material for several of the extended cases in this book as well as a number of brief vignettes. Details about these sources appear below.

Research and Methods

The vignettes and quoted material in this book come from many places including published studies, ongoing research undertaken by us, the authors, or other scholars, and the working experience of a number of practicing educators whom we interviewed to prepare the original reports in this book. In developing this book, we substantially augmented the original set of examples by drawing on four unpublished data sources. The notes below explain the methods we employed to collect that data.

Ongoing research conducted by the Center for the Study of Teaching and Policy (CTP) at the University of Washington. One source of district- and school-level examples was CTP's Study of Policy Environments and the Quality of Teaching. This core study focuses on four states, California, New York, North Carolina, and Washington, and a large urban school district within each. Conducted between 1998 and 2002, this multiple-case, largely qualitative investigation examined connections between policy environments and teaching practice through fully nested state, district, school, and teacher samples. One line of analytic work examined the district policy context as a critical setting and as an opportunity for improving teaching, while a second line traced school-level responses to the district and state policy environments. We, the authors and our colleagues, conducted lengthy, semi-structured interviews with school and district leaders at the core study sites. These interviews provided the primary source information for the book and they supplemented the teacher interviews and documentary records. Except where a published source is noted, the examples used in this book that are referenced (Center for the Study of Teaching & Policy, 2003), are from unpublished, raw data files and case summaries that were never incorporated into any publicly available reports from this study. The authors wish to acknowledge the considerable contributions made by Chrysan Gallucci, Anneke Markholt, and Suzy Ort, who were responsible for much of the fieldwork and case summaries on which the vignettes and examples are based.

Follow-up research on continuing education programs offered by the University of Washington Center for Educational Leadership (UWCEL). A series of post-hoc interviews were conducted during spring 2004 with 22 practicing school leaders. These leaders spent two years in an inquiry-based continuing education program run by UWCEL that was aimed at helping principals and other leaders close achievement gaps in their schools. Interview data were used in conjunction with brief excerpts from unpublished written reports prepared by the participants as part of this inquiry sequence. These interviews were used to construct vignettes of learning-focused leadership in action that occur throughout the text, especially in Chapters 3–5. (These interviews were referenced as UWCEL, 2004 in the text.) Elsewhere, the work of several of these participants was used to construct lengthier examples, as in Chapter 6 (Isaacson Middle School vignette) and in Chapter 8 (Douglass Elementary School case).

Ongoing evaluation of the Bay Area School Reform Collaborative conducted by the Center for Research on the Context of Teaching (CRC) at Stanford University. Since the late 1990s, the CRC has conducted a longitudinal evaluation of the work of the Bay Area School Reform Collaborative (BASRC). Led by Milbrey McLaughlin and Joan Talbert, this project was originally funded by the Annenberg Challenge grants. One of us (Copland) worked on the evaluation project during his stint on the Stanford faculty (1999–2001) and focused particularly on leadership issues occurring in a subset of 16 BASRC schools (see Copland, 2003). Previously collected, unpublished data from this study, including material from interviews and observations in BASRC schools, are included as examples, vignettes, and short illustrations of leaders' efforts to focus on learning. (These are referenced as the Center for Research on the Context of Teaching, 2002, throughout the text.). In two instances, the CRC's BASRC data files and unpublished case summaries formed the basis for two of the extended examples (the Manchester High School Case in Chapter 8 and the Highland District Case in Chapter 9. We wish to acknowledge Dr. Joel Zarrow and Dr. Julie Marsh for their fieldwork and preparation of these case studies while they were graduate students at Stanford University.

Observation and reflective writing by participants in the University of Washington Leadership for Learning (L4L) Ed.D. Program, Cohorts 1 and 2. Finally, we drew on the experiences and craft knowledge of practicing school and district leaders who were participants in the L4L Ed.D. program. We used their feedback and interviews to construct several vignettes, and we quoted their reflections on using the framework in Chapter 10. These individuals wrote reflective papers following their participation in the L4L summer institute in summer 2004. They commented on the ways that their learning in the program related to their practice in their home institutions. The excerpts in this book capture instances of the framework in use by individuals who have been newly introduced to the idea of learning-focused leadership.

References

Alvarado, A. (2003, July). *Leading instructional improvement in schools and districts.* Presentation at the Summer Institute at the University of Washington Center for Educational Leadership, Seattle, WA.

American Federation of Teachers. (2000, October 17). Press release. Washington, DC: Author.

Argyris, C. (1991, May-June). Teaching smart people how to learn. *Harvard Business Review, 69*(3), 99–109.

Barkley, S., Bottoms, G., Feagin, C., & Clark, S. (1999). *Leadership matters: Building leadership capacity.* Atlanta, GA: Southern Regional Education Board.

Berends, M., Bodilly, S., & Kirby, S. (2002). *Facing the challenges of whole school reform: New American schools after a decade.* Santa Monica, CA: RAND.

Blase, J., & Blase, J. (1999). Principals' instructional leadership and teacher development: Teachers' perspectives. *Educational Administration Quarterly, 35*(3), 349–78.

Brandt, R. (1998). *Powerful learning.* Alexandria, VA: Association for Supervision and Curriculum Development.

Bransford, J., Brown, A., & Cocking, R. (1999). *How people learn: Brain, mind, experience, and school.* Washington, DC: National Academy Press.

Brophy, J., & Good, T. (1986). Teachers' behavior and student achievement. In M. Wittrock, (Ed.), *Handbook of research on teaching* (pp. 328–375) (3rd ed.). New York: Macmillan.

Burch, P. (2002). Constraints and opportunities in changing policy environments: Intermediary organizations' response to complex district contexts. In A. Hightower, M. Knapp, J. Marsh, & M. McLaughlin (Eds.), *School districts and instructional renewal* (pp. 111–126). New York: Teachers College Press.

Burns, J. M. (1978). *Leadership.* New York: Harper & Row.

Carpenter, T. P., Fennema, E., Peterson, P. L., Chiang, C. P., & Loef, M. (1989). Using knowledge of children's mathematics thinking in classroom teaching: An experimental study. *American Educational Research Journal, 26*(4).

Carter, G., & Cunningham, W. (1997). *The American school superintendent: Leading in an age of pressure.* San Francisco: Jossey-Bass.

Center for Educational Leadership. (2003). [Unpublished data, Program evaluation]. Seattle, WA: Center for Educational Leadership, University of Washington.

Center for Research on the Context of Teaching. (2002). [Evaluation of the Bay Area School Reform Collaborative]. Unpublished raw data. Stanford, CA: Center for Research on the Context of Teaching, Stanford University.

Center for the Study of Teaching and Policy. (2003). [Study of Policy Environments and the Quality of Teaching]. Unpublished raw data. Seattle, WA: Center for the Study of Teaching & Policy, University of Washington.

Clair, N., & Adger, C. (1999, October). Professional development for teachers in cultur-
ally diverse schools. *CAL Digest*. Retrieved December 2, 2005, from http://www.cal.
org/resources/digest/profdvpt.html

Clune, W. (1998). *Toward a theory of systemic reform: The case of nine statewide
systemic initiatives*. Madison, WI: Center for Educational Research, University of
Wisconsin, Madison.

Cohen, D., & Hill, H. (2001). Instructional policy and classroom performance: The
mathematics reform in California. *Teachers College Record, 102,* 9–26.

Cohen, D., Raudenbush, S., & Ball, D. (2001). Resources, instruction, and educational
research. In R. Boruch & F. Mosteller (Eds.), *Evidence matters: Randomized trials in
educational research* (pp. 80–119). Washington, DC: The Brookings Institution.

Copland, M. (2003, Summer). Instructional leadership in the context of district change:
The case of the Skyline school district. *Journal of Cases in Educational Leadership,*
special summer issue. Retrieved December 2, 2005, from http://www.ucea.org

Corbett, D., Wilson, B., & Williams, B. (2002). *Effort and excellence in urban classrooms:
Expecting and getting success with all students*. New York: Teachers College Press.

Cotton, K. (1996, May). School size, school climate, and student performance. Northwest Regional Educational Laboratory [Electronic version]. Retrieved June 29,
2006, from http://www.nwrel.org/scpd/sirs/10/c020.

Dana Center. (1999). *Hope for urban education: A study of nine high-performing high-
poverty urban elementary schools*. Washington, DC: U.S. Department of Education,
Office of the Under Secretary.

Darling-Hammond, L. (1996). The quiet revolution: Rethinking teacher development.
Educational Leadership, 53(6), 4–10.

Darling-Hammond, L. (1997). *The right to learn: A blueprint for creating schools that
work*. San Francisco: Jossey-Bass.

Deal, T., & Peterson, K. (1994). *The leadership paradox*. San Francisco: Jossey-Bass.

DeRosa, C. (2004). Unpublished paper, Center for Educational Leadership, University
of Washington, Seattle, WA.

Elmore, R. (2000). *Building a new structure for school leadership*. New York: The Albert
Shanker Institute.

Elmore, R. F., & Burney, D. (1999). Investing in teacher learning: Staff development
and instructional improvement. In L. Darling-Hammond & G. Sykes (Eds.), *Teaching as the learning profession: Handbook of policy and practice* (pp. 263–291). San
Francisco: Jossey-Bass.

Fuhrman, S. (1993). *Designing coherent education policy: Improving the system*. San
Francisco: Jossey-Bass.

Fullan, M. (1993). *Change forces: Probing the depths of educational reform*. London: The
Falmer Press.

Fullan, M. (2001). *Leading in a culture of change*. San Francisco: Jossey-Bass.

Fullan, M. (2005). *Systems thinkers in action: Moving beyond the standards plateau*.
Nottingham, UK: Department for Education and Skills Publications.

Gallucci, C. (2002). *Communities of practice and the mediation of teachers' response to
standards-based reform*. Unpublished doctoral dissertation, University of Washington, Seattle, WA.

Gallucci, C., Knapp, M. S., Markholt, A., & Ort, S. (2003). *Standards-based reform and
small schools of choice: How reform theories converge in three urban middle schools*.
Seattle, WA: Center for the Study of Teaching & Policy, University of Washington.

Gardner, J. (1990). *On leadership*. New York: Free Press.

Garvin, D. (1993, July-August). Building a learning organization. *Harvard Business
Review, 71*(4), 78–93.

Glickman, C. (2002). *Leadership for learning: How to help teachers succeed*. Alexandria,
VA: Association for Supervision and Curriculum Development.

Goldstein, J. (2003). *Teachers at the professional threshold: Distributing leadership responsibility for teacher evaluation.* Unpublished doctoral dissertation, Stanford School of Education, Stanford, CA.

Grossman, P., Thompson, C., & Valencia, S. (2002). Focusing the concerns of new teachers: The district as teacher educator. In A. Hightower, M. Knapp, J. Marsh, & M. McLaughlin (Eds.), *School districts and instructional renewal* (pp. 141–166). New York: Teachers College Press.

Grossman, P., Wineburg, S., & Woolworth, S. (2001). Toward a theory of teacher community. *Teachers College Record, 103*(6), 942–1012.

Hall, B. (2003, December). *Leading instructional improvement in Atlanta Public Schools.* Presentation at the District Leaders' Seminar, University of Washington Center for Educational Leadership, Seattle, WA.

Hallinger, P., & Heck, R. (1996). Reassessing the principal's role in school effectiveness: A review of empirical research, 1980–95. *Educational Administration Quarterly, 32*(1), 5–44.

Hallinger, P., & Heck, R. (1998). Exploring the principal's contribution to school effectiveness: 1980–1995. *School effectiveness and school improvement, 9*(2), 157–91.

Hallinger, P., & Murphy, J. (1982). The superintendent's role in promoting instructional leadership. *Administrator's Notebook, 30*(6), 1–4.

Hart, A. (1993). Reflection—An instructional strategy in educational administration. *Educational Administration Quarterly, 29*(3), 339–363.

Harwayne, S. (2003). *Going public.* New York: Heinemann Publishers.

Hawkins, D. (1974). I, thou, and it. In D. Hawkins (Ed.), *The informed vision: Essays on learning and human nature* (pp. 48–62). New York: Agathon Press.

Haycock, K. (1999). *Dispelling the myth: High-poverty schools exceeding expectations.* Washington, DC: The Education Trust.

Haycock, K. (2001). *Dispelling the myth revisited.* Washington, DC: The Education Trust.

Hess, F. (1999). *Spinning wheels: The politics of urban school reform.* Washington, DC: The Brookings Institution Press.

Hightower, A. (2001). *San Diego's big boom: District bureaucracy meets culture of learning.* Unpublished doctoral dissertation, Stanford University, Stanford, CA.

Hill, P., Campbell, C., & Harvey, J. (2000). *It takes a city.* Washington, DC: The Brookings Institution Press.

Hord, S. (1997). *Professional learning communities: Communities of continuous inquiry and improvement.* Austin, TX: Southwest Educational Laboratory.

Huberman, M. (1993). The model of the independent artisan in teachers' professional relations. In J. Little & M. McLaughlin (Eds.), *Teachers' work: Individuals, colleagues, & contexts* (pp. 11–50). New York: Teachers College Press.

Institute for Educational Leadership (2001). *Leadership for student learning: Restructuring school district leadership.* Washington, DC: Author.

Johnson, S. M. (1999). *Leading to change.* San Francisco: Jossey-Bass.

Jones, K. (2002). *Closing the mathematics achievement gap in Lakesend school district.* Unpublished dissertation, Renton, WA.

Knapp, M., & Associates. (1995). *Teaching for meaning in high-poverty classrooms.* New York: Teachers College Press.

Knapp, M. S., Copland, M. A., Ford, B., Markholt, A., McLaughlin, M. W., Milliken, M., et al. (2003). *Leading for learning sourcebook: Concepts and examples.* Seattle, WA: University of Washington/Center for the Study of Teaching and Policy.

Knapp, M., Copland, M., & Talbert, J. (2003). *Leading for learning: Reflective tools for school and district leaders.* Seattle, WA: Center for the Study of Teaching and Policy, University of Washington.

Kruse, S. D., Louis, K. S., & Bryk, A. (1995). An emerging framework for analyzing school-based professional community. In K. S. Louis, & S. D. Kruse (Eds.), *Professionalism and community: Perspectives on reforming urban schools* (pp. 23–44). Thousand Oaks, CA: Corwin Press.

Ladson-Billings, G. (1994). *The dreamkeepers: Successful teachers of African-American children.* San Francisco: Jossey-Bass.

Lairon, M., & Vidales, B. (2003, May-June). Leaders learning in context. *Leadership, 32*(5), 16–18, 36.

Lambert, L. (1998). *Building leadership capacity in schools.* Alexandria, VA: Association for Supervision and Curriculum Development.

Learning First Alliance. (2003). *Improving achievement, building instructional capacity: A study of instructional reform in five improving, high-poverty school districts.* Washington, DC: Learning First Alliance.

Leithwood, K. (1992). The move toward transformational leadership. *Educational Leadership, 49*(5), 8–12.

Leithwood, K. A., & Jantzi, D. (1990). Transformational leadership: How principals can help reform school cultures. *School Effectiveness and Improvement, 1*(4), 249–280.

Leithwood, K., & Duke, D. (1999). A century's quest to understand school leadership. In J. Murphy & K. Seashore-Louis (Eds.), *Handbook of research on educational administration,* (2nd ed.) (pp. 45-72). San Francisco: Jossey-Bass.

Leithwood, K., & Louis, K. (2002). *Organizational learning in schools.* Lisse, The Netherlands: Swets-Zeitlinger Publishers.

Levine, D., & Lezotte, L. (1990). *Unusually effective schools: A review and analysis of research and practice.* Madison, WI: Center for Effective Schools Research and Development, University of Wisconsin, Madison.

Lieberman, A., & Grolnick, M. (1999). Networks and reform in American education. In L. Darling-Hammond & G. Sykes (Eds.), *Teaching as the learning profession: Handbook of policy and practice* (pp. 292-312). San Francisco: Jossey-Bass.

Little, J. (1990). The persistence of privacy: Autonomy and initiative in teachers' professional relations. *Teachers College Record, 91,* 509–536.

Little, J. (1999). Organizing schools for teacher learning. In L. Darling-Hammond & G. Sykes (Eds.), *Teaching as the learning profession: Handbook of policy and practice* (pp. 233–262). San Francisco: Jossey-Bass.

Little, J., & McLaughlin, M. (1993). *Teachers' work: Individuals, colleagues, & contexts.* New York: Teachers College Press.

Lomotey, K. (1989). *African American principals: School leadership and success.* New York: Greenwood Press.

Lord, B. (1994). Teachers' professional development: Critical colleagueship and the role of professional communities. In N. Cobb (Ed.), *The future of education: Perspectives on national standards for America* (pp. 175–204). New York: The College Board.

Lortie, D. (1975). *Schoolteacher.* Chicago: University of Chicago Press.

Louis, K., & Kruse, S. (1995). *Professionalism and community: Perspectives on reforming urban schools.* Thousand Oaks, CA: Corwin Press.

Markholt, A. (2002). *Se hace camino al andar: Development of critical capacity in an urban elementary school.* Unpublished doctoral dissertation, University of Washington, Seattle, WA.

McDiarmid, G., David, J., Corcoran, T., Kannapel, P., & Coe, P. (1997). *Professional development under KERA: Meeting the challenge.* Lexington, KY: Partnership for Kentucky Schools.

McLaughlin, M., & Talbert, J. (2001). *Professional communities and the work of high school teaching.* Chicago: University of Chicago Press.

McLaughlin, M., & Talbert, J. (2002). Reforming districts. In A. Hightower, M. Knapp, J. Marsh, & M. McLaughlin (Eds.), *School districts and instructional renewal* (pp. 184–203). New York: Teachers College Press.

McREL. (2003). Professional learning community. In Mid-continent Research for Education and Learning series *Sustaining School Improvement* (p. 4).

Meier, D. (1995). *The power of their ideas: Lessons for America from a small school in Harlem.* Boston: Beacon Press.

Meier, D. (2002). *In school we trust: Creating communities of learning in an era of testing and standardization.* Boston: Beacon Press.

Meyer, M. (1978). *Environments and organizations.* San Francisco: Jossey-Bass.

Murphy, J. (1988). Methodological, measurement, and conceptual problems in the study of administrative instructional leadership. *Educational Evaluation & Policy Analysis, 10*(2), 117–139.

Murphy, J. (2004). *Leadership for literacy.* Thousand Oaks, CA: Corwin Press.

Murphy, J., & Hallinger, P. (1986). The superintendent as instructional leader: Findings from effective school districts. *The Journal of Educational Administration, 24*(2), 213–231.

Murphy, J., & Hallinger, P. (1988). Characteristics of instructionally effective school districts. *Journal of Educational Research, 8*(3), 175–181.

Nelson, B. (1998). Lenses on learning: Administrators' views on reform and the professional development of teachers. *Journal for Mathematics Teacher Education, 1,* 191–215.

Newmann, F., King, M., & Secada, W. (1996). Intellectual quality. In F. Newmann & Associates (Eds.) *Authentic achievement: Restructuring schools for intellectual quality* (pp. 161–178). San Francisco: Jossey-Bass.

Newmann, F., Marks, H., & Gamoran, A. (1996). Authentic pedagogy and student performance. *American Journal of Education, 104*(4), 280–312.

Newmann, F., Smith, B., Allensworth, E., & Bryk, A. (2001). *School instructional program coherence: Benefits and challenges.* Chicago: Consortium on Chicago School Research.

Ogawa, R., & Bossert, R. (1995). Leadership as an organizational quality. *Educational Administration Quarterly, 31*(2), 224–244.

Payne, C., & Kaba, M. (2001). So much reform, so little change. *Journal of Negro Education, 2,* 45–57.

Peterson, G. (1999). Demonstrated actions of instructional leaders: An examination of five California superintendents. *Educational Policy Analysis Archives, 7*(18), Retrieved December 2, 2005, from http://epaa.asu.edu/epaa/v7n18.html.

Pfeffer, J. (1998). *The human equation.* Boston: Harvard Business School Press.

Posnick-Goodwin, S. (2002, February). Home visits attempt to strengthen connection between parents and schools. *California Educator, 6*(5). Retrieved December 2, 2005, from http://www.cta.org/CaliforniaEducator/v6i5/MakingCase_1.

Quellmalz, E., Shields, P., & Knapp, M. (1995). *School based reform: Lessons from a national study, a guide for school reform teams.* Washington, DC: U.S. Department of Education.

Raywid, M. A. (1996, April). *Taking stock: The movement to create mini-schools, schools-within-schools, and separate small schools.* New York: ERIC Clearinghouse on Urban Education. Retrieved June 29, 2006, from http://iume.tc.columbia.edu/eric_archive/mono/UDS108.pdf.

Resnick, L. (1995). From aptitude to effort: A new foundation for our schools. *Daedalus, 124,* 55–62.

Resnick, L., & Glennan, T. (2002). Leadership for learning: A theory of action for urban school districts. In A. Hightower, M. Knapp, J. Marsh, & M. McLaughlin (Eds.), *School districts and instructional renewal* (pp. 165–172). New York: Teachers College Press.

Resnick, L., & Hall, M. (1998). Learning organizations for sustainable education reform. *Daedalus, 127,* 1–13.

Resnick, L., & Harwell, M. (2000, August). *Instructional variation and student achievement in a standards-based education district* (CSE Technical Report No. 522). Los Angeles, CA: University of California Center for Research on Evaluation, Standards, and Student Testing.

Scheurich, J. J. (1998). Highly successful and loving public elementary schools populated mainly by low-SES children of color: Core beliefs and cultural characteristics. *Urban Education, 33*(4), 451–491.

Scheurich, J. J., & Skrla, L. (2003). *Leadership for equity and excellence.* Thousand Oaks, CA: Corwin Press.

Senge, P. (1990). *The fifth discipline.* New York: Doubleday.

Sergiovanni, T. (1992). *Moral leadership.* San Francisco: Jossey-Bass.

Sergiovanni, T. (1999, September). Refocusing leadership to build community. *High School Magazine, 7*(1), 10–15.

Shepard, L. (1995). Using assessment to improve learning. *Educational Leadership, 54*(5), 38–43.

Shulman, L. (1986). Those who understand, teach: Knowledge growth in teaching. *Educational Researcher, 15,* 4–14.

Simon, H. (1999). Bounded rationality and organizational learning. In L. Sproull & M. Cohen (Eds.), *Organizational learning* (pp. 188–194). Thousand Oaks, CA: SAGE Publications.

Sirotnik, K., Kimball, K., & Copland, M. (2003, November). Leadership for learning: A self-sustaining, cohort-based, educational doctorate program in a public university. Paper presented at the annual meeting of the University Council of Education Administration, Portland, OR.

Sizemore, B. (1990). Madison elementary school: A turnaround case. In K. Lomotey (Ed.), *Going to school: The African-American experience* (pp. 202–234). Albany, NY: State University of New York Press.

Small Schools Project. (2004). [Unpublished data, research on small schools working with the Small Schools Collaborative]. Seattle, WA: Small Schools Collaborative, University of Washington.

Smith, W., & Andrews, R. (1989). *Instructional leadership: How principals make a difference.* Alexandria, VA: Association for Supervision and Curriculum Development.

Snipes, J., Doolittle, F., & Herlihy, C. (2002). *Foundations for success: Case studies of how urban school systems improve student achievement.* Washington, DC: Council of Great City Schools.

Snyder, J. (2002). New Haven unified school district: A teaching quality system for excellence and equity. In A. Hightower, M. Knapp, J. Marsh, & M. McLaughlin (Eds.), *School districts and instructional renewal* (pp. 94–110). New York: Teachers College Press.

Spillane, J. P. (2002). District policymaking and state standards: A cognitive perspective on implementation. In A. Hightower, M. Knapp, J. Marsh, & M. McLaughlin (Eds.), *School districts and instructional renewal* (pp. 143–159). New York: Teachers College Press.

Spillane, J., Halverson, R., & Diamond, J. (2001). Investigating school leadership practice: A distributed perspective. *Educational Researcher, 30*(3), 23–27.

Sproull, L., & Cohen. M. (1996). *Organizational learning.* Thousand Oaks, CA: SAGE Publications.

Stanford, J. (1999). *Victory in our schools.* New York: Bantam Dell Publishing Group.

Stein, M., Silver, E., & Smith, M. (1998). Mathematics reform and teacher development: A community of practice perspective. In J. Greeno & S. Goldman (Eds.), *Thinking practices in mathematics and science learning* (pp. 17–52). Hillsdale, NJ: Erlbaum.

Stokes, L. (2001). Lessons from an inquiring school: Forms of inquiry and conditions for teacher learning. In A. Lieberman & D. Wood (Eds.), *Teachers caught in the action* (pp. 141–158). New York: Teacher's College Press.

Szabo, M. (1996). Rethinking restructuring: Building habits of effective inquiry. In M. McLaughlin, & I. Oberman (Eds.), *Teacher learning: New policies, new practices* (pp. 73–91). New York: Teachers College Press.

Talbert, J., & McLaughlin, M. (1993). Understanding teaching in context. In D. Cohen, M. McLaughlin, & J. Talbert (Eds.), *Teaching for understanding: Issues for policy and practice* (pp. 167–206). San Francisco: Jossey-Bass.

Talbert, J., & McLaughlin, M. (1994). Teacher professionalism in local school context. *American Journal of Education, 102,* 123–153.

Usdan, M., & Cuban, L. (2003). Boston: The stars finally in alignment. In L. Cuban & M. Usdan (Eds.), *Powerful reforms with shallow roots* (pp. 38–53). New York: Teacher's College Press.

UWCEL (2004). [Unpublished data, research on the UW/CEL Experienced School Leaders Program, 2002-2004]. Seattle, WA: Center for Educational Leadership, University of Washington.

Wenger, E., McDermott, R., & Snyder, W. (2002). *Cultivating communities of practice.* Boston: Harvard Business School Press.

Westheimer, J. (1998). *Among school teachers: Community, autonomy, and ideology in teachers' work.* New York: Teachers College Press.

Wiggins, G. (1989, May). A true test. *Phi Delta Kappan, 70*(9), 703–713.

Index

Note: Page references for figures are indicated with an *f* after the page numbers; page references for footnotes are indicated with an *n* after the page numbers

accessibility of leaders, 187
accountability
    as core value, 32
    District M case, 163, 166–170
    Highland case, 155, 157–158
    influence over perception of, 39–40
    Manchester case, 135
    Parkside case, 126–127
achievement gaps. *See also* equitable learning
    and commitment to equity, 32
    Douglass case, 136–144
    external resources and, 57
administrative vs. instructional issues at meetings, 34, 35–36
aggregates vs. individuals, 1
alignment, 89, 91. *See also* coherence
alternative school structure. *See* Parkside Alternative Middle School case
Ames, Shelley, 146, 148–151, 176
assessment and measurement. *See also* data and analysis
    District M case, 167
    external pressures, 84–85
    Falls City case, 105, 109, 110, 112–113
    Highland case, 156–158
    influence over perception of, 39–40
    need for, 18
    Northern Valley case, 148
    Parkside case, 126–127
    portfolios systems, 84, 127
    rubrics, 84
    testing, influence over perception of, 39–40
    whole school assessments, 48
assignment. *See* staffing assignment and scheduling
assumptions, conversation about, 48–49
Austin, Sandy, 146*n*

autonomy and coherence, 96–98

behavioral support and management, 52, 115
beliefs. *See* values and beliefs
Bossert, R., 15
bullying and harassment, 74
business communities, 65, 66–67

California Standards for the Teaching Profession, 51
capacity building. *See* professional development
CEBE (Center for Evidence-Based Education), 181
Center for Educational Leadership, University of Washington, 181
Center for Evidence-Based Education (CEBE), 181
Center for Research on the Context of Teaching, 152*n*
Center for the Study of Teaching and Policy, 152*n*, 161*n*
centralized leadership, 86
central office. *See* district-level applications
CEO Cabinet, 65
certification programs, 180, 181
Chancellor of Schools (New York), 167
change, pace of, 95–96
Children and Family Center (Northern Valley), 149–150
civic groups, 65. *See also* communities, local
classroom observation. *See* observation in the classroom
coherence
    overview, 87–88
    District M case, 164, 165, 167
    in districts, 93–95
    essential tasks, 90–91

coherence (*continued*)
    Falls City case, 110
    Highland case, 157
    ideas underlying, 88–90, 90*f*
    leadership and, 98–99
    Manchester case, 129
    Northern Valley case, 152
    Parkside case, 123
    processes and challenges, 95–98
    in schools, 91–93
collaborative work. *See* teams and collaborative work
collegial connections
    Douglass case, 139
    Falls City case, 111
    Manchester case, 132
    Parkside case, 118, 121
colonias, 63–64
communication
    assumptions and, 48–49
    basic needs and, 52
    central office and school leaders, 93
    and focus on learning, 32–33
    with parents, community, and media, 36
    between teachers about student learning, 34
communities, local. *See also* external environments
    communicating learning to, 36
    Falls City case, 106, 107
    Highland case, 154–155
    Manchester case, 134
    Northern Valley case, 150–151
    proactive approach with, 66–67
    promoting learning agenda with, 65
    resources from, 57
    from school and district viewpoints, 60*f*, 61*f*
    underrepresented neighborhood groups, 63–64
    visiting community groups, 62–63
communities, professional. *See* professional communities
communities of practice, 53–54
community school districts, 117*n*
compensation and reward, 134
comprehensive planning, 71–72. *See also* strategic, distributed action
Comprehensive Test of Basic Skills (CTBS), 105, 112–113
consensus, 37, 89. *See also* coherence; resistances
content, learner engagement with, 13
content knowledge, 12–13
continuing education programs, 180, 181
conversations. *See* communication
core values. *See* values and beliefs
critique and strong relationships, 54–55

CTBS (Comprehensive Test of Basic Skills), 105, 112–113
cultures, professional. *See* professional communities
curriculum
    District M case, 167
    Douglass case, 137, 140, 142–143
    Falls City case, 110–111, 112
    learning-based strategies, 36
    Parkside case, 120, 121–123, 124–126
    resistance to changes in, 69
    school boards and, 64
curriculum specialists, 80

data and analysis. *See also* assessment and measurement
    district decision making and, 36–37
    ESL example, 30
    Highland case, 153–155, 156–158
    planning based on, 34
    procedures collection and analysis, 35
debates in the classroom, 10
decentralized leadership, 86
decision making, creating structures for, 47–48
deep subject-matter knowledge, 18
degree programs, 180, 181, 182–186
DeRosa, Corrine, 73–77
dilemmas faced by leaders, 1, 9–11
discipline, 52, 115
discretion and coherence, 96–98
district administrative meetings, 35–36, 51, 93–94
district-level applications
    overview, 145–146
    acting strategically and sharing leadership, 81–83
    coherence, 88, 93–95
    communication avenues, 93–94
    external environments and, 61*f*, 64–66
    focus on learning and, 35–37
    leadership, concept of, 15
    leadership changes and, 97–98
    Northern Valley case, 146–152, 176–177, 178
    professional learning communities, 49–51
    school boards, tensions with, 68–69
    structure of central office, 189–190
District M (pseudo) case
    overview, 161–163
    accountability assessment, 166–167
    collaborations, 165–166
    fiscal planning, 164–165
    improvement policy, creating, 163–164
    standards for professional learning, 167–168
    theories of action, combined, 168–170
Douglass Elementary School
    overview, 136

Douglass Elementary School (*continued*)
    clear focus, identifying, 137–138
    future work, 142–144
    literacy learning, 138–140
    progress assessment, 140–142
drawing in vs. reaching out, 67–68
drill-and-practice approach to instruction, 6

early childhood facilitator, 109
early release days, 50, 63
Easton, Denny, 174–177
ELL. *See* English Language Learners
English Language Learners (ELL) and English as a Second Language (ESL). *See also* literacy learning
    coherence and, 92
    data analysis example, 30
    Isaacson Middle School example, 73–77, 76*f*
    Mr. G. example and, 3–5
    for parents, 67–68
    regular education classes and, 75–77
    service delivery models, 74–75
entrepreneurial activity and coherence, 97
environments, external. *See* external environments
equitable learning, 16–17, 32
ESL. *See* English Language Learners (ELL) and English as a Second Language (ESL)
expenditures, control over, 164
external environments. *See also* communities, local
    overview, 56–58
    coherence and, 97–98, 99
    districts and, 61*f*, 64–66
    essential tasks for engaging, 59–62
    Falls City case, 106–107, 114
    Highland case, 154–155, 157, 159
    ideas and values underlying, 58–59
    learning agendas and, 23, 70
    Manchester case, 134
    Northern Valley case, 150–151
    Parkside case, 117–118, 126–127
    processes and challenges, 66–70
    schools and, 60*f*, 62–64
    summer institute and, 187
    types of, 58–59

faculty meetings, 34. *See also* meetings
faculty study groups, 71–72, 87–88
Falls City Elementary School case
    catalyst for change, 105–108
    leadership transition, 114–115
    mathematics instruction, 112–114
    professional community building, 108–112
Falls City Site Council, 106, 107
families. *See* communities, local; parents
family learning centers, 67–68
family model, 119

feedback in assessment programs, 40
focus on learning
    overview, 29–30
    coherence and, 98–99
    District M case, 162–163, 166, 167
    in districts, 35–37
    Douglass case, 137, 138
    essential tasks, 32–33
    Falls City case, 106, 108, 112
    Highland case, 157, 158, 160
    ideas and values underlying, 31–32
    Leading for Learning Framework and, 188–190, 192–194
    Manchester case, 130–131, 134
    Northern Valley case, 149–150
    Parkside case, 123
    payoff of, 41–42
    processes and challenges, 37–41
    professional community building and, 47
    in schools, 33–35
Fullan, Michael, 188
funding
    District M case, 164–165
    grants and learning priorities, 38
    Manchester case, 131
    Northern Valley case, 147
    private sector investments for improvement, 65

Gallucci, Chrysan, 116*n*, 161*n*
Gerstein, Deborah, 153–161
goals, 16–17, 34–35
grants, 38
groups. *See also* teams and collaborative work
    faculty study groups, 71–72, 87–88
    professional community building and, 46
    small groups and inquiry cycles, 48

harassment and bullying, 74
Harvard University, 127
Harwayne, Shelley, 91–92
hierarchical school role boundaries, 92
Highland School District case
    overview, 152–153
    achievement data and assessments, 156–158
    collaborative leadership, 155–156
    external collaborations, 159
    professional development, 160–161
    strategic planning and data analysis, 153–155
hiring. *See* recruitment and hiring
home visit pilot program, 36
human capacity as core value, 32
humanities instruction, 10–11, 121–122

imagining possibilities, 196–198
improvement agendas and external environments, 64, 65, 68–69
individuals vs. aggregates, 1
influence, key pathways of, 175–176, 178
information system development, 153–155
inquiry cycles, 48
inquiry processes, 32, 135
Institute for Learning, University of Pittsburgh, 51, 163, 165
instruction. See teaching and instruction
instructional leadership, 14–15
intelligence, effort-based views of, 32
interactional model, 11–13, 14f, 19–20, 20f
interaction with colleagues. See professional communities
interdisciplinary teacher teams and coherence, 92
International High School at LaGuardia Community College, 92
Iowa Test of Basic Skills (ITBS), 113
Isaacson Middle School, 73–77, 76f
isolation
        of ELL students, 74
        professional community building and, 45, 53, 55
        tendency toward, 6
ITBS (Iowa Test of Basic Skills), 113

Johnson, Mark, 146n
Jones, Michael, 146, 148–152, 176

knowledge, 12–13, 18, 33

LaGuardia Community College, 92
language learning. See English Language Learners (ELL) and English as a Second Language (ESL)
late arrival days, 50
leadership
        centralized vs. decentralized, 86
        context as bounding factor for, 104–105
        definitions and concept of, 13–16
        examining practices of, xi
        moral aspect of, 16
        political costs of, 39
        primary work of, 3
        sharing of (See strategic, distributed action)
        transitions in, 114–115
        visibility and accessibility, importance of, 187
leadership, types of
        grade-level and content leaders, 85–86
        instructional, 14–15
        transformational, 16
leadership councils, 133
leadership development
        District M case, 165

leadership development (continued)
        Highland case, 155–156, 159, 161
        Leading for Learning Framework as tool for, xi, 179–181
        Manchester case, 132–133
        Northern Valley case, 149
        Parkside case, 122, 124
        at University of Washington, 182–186
leadership team academy, 177
leadership teams, 49, 175, 177
Leading for Learning Framework
        conceptualization of, x–xii
        essence of, 23–25, 25f
        functions of, 192
        gains from, 186–191
        how to begin, 198–199
        imagining possibilities, 196–198
        planning and reflecting with, 174–179
        principles for effective use of, 192–194
        as tool for reflecting, planning, or teaching, 172–173, 188
        University of Washington program, 182–186
learning
        notions about, 13
        organizational, 21
        powerful and equitable, 16–17
learning acceleration programs, 57
learning agendas. See also professional learning agenda; student learning agenda; system learning agenda
        overview, 16–21
        connectivity among, 88, 89, 90f, 176–177 (See also coherence)
        district meetings and, 51
        interrelation of, 17f, 21–23, 22f
LeJeune, Renee, 117–127
leverage points, 175
literacy learning. See also English Language Learners (ELL) and English as a Second Language (ESL)
        data used for planning of, 34
        District M case, 162, 168–170
        Douglass case, 138–143
        Falls City case, 109–112
        Highland case, 160
        pace of change and, 96
        for parents, 63, 67–68
        Parkside case, 122
        subject focus on, 37–38
local communities. See communities, local
long-term change, 96

Manchester High School, 128–135
Manchester Leadership Council, 133
Manhattan New School, 91–92
marketeer role, 66
Markholt, Anneke, 161n, 196–198
Marsh, Julie, 152n
Maryland summer workshops, 180

mathematics instruction
> curriculum reform in, 69
> Douglass case, 143
> Falls City case, 112–114
> Mr. G. vignette, 3–6
> subject focus on, 37

McClellan, Dick, 107
measurement of achievement. *See* assessment and measurement
media, communicating learning to, 36
meetings
> with administrative council, 93–94
> administrative vs. instructional issues at, 34–36
> learning agendas and district meetings, 51
> presentations at, 123–124

mentoring, 111, 157
migrant families, 147
moral aspect of leadership, 16
multilayered improvement efforts, 81

National Association for the Education of Young Children, 167
National Council of Teachers of English, 167
National Council of Teachers of Mathematics (NCTM), 113
National Science Foundation, 38, 83
needs, basic, 52–53
neighborhood groups. *See* communities, local
nested learning communities, 51, 89–90
New Standards project, 167
new teachers, 82–83, 131
New York City Schools, 117*n*. *See also* District M (pseudo) case; Parkside Alternative Middle School case
New York District 2 and professional learning, 94
Northern Valley School District, 146–152, 176–177, 178

Oakville School District, 93–94
observation in the classroom
> and focus on learning, 33, 35
> focus on learning vs. teaching, 40–41
> professional community building and, 51

Ogawa, R., 15
openness to new ideas, 53–54
order, basic need for, 52–53
organizational environments, 60*f*, 61*f*
organizational learning, 21
Ort, Suzy, 161*n*
outreach vs. drawing in, 67–68

pace of reform, 95–96
Parental Educational Assistant Program, 107
parents
> classes for, 63, 67–68

parents (*continued*)
> communicating learning to, 36
> Falls City case, 107
> Northern Valley case, 150
> promoting learning agenda with, 65
> resistance from, 69
> visiting, 36, 62–63

Parkside Alternative Middle School case
> overview, 116–117
> accountability, 126–127
> collaborative curriculum development, 121–123
> professional community, growth of, 123–126
> reculturing, restructuring, and rebuilding the staff, 118–120
> roots of evolution of, 117–118

pathways to learning, 76*f*, 77–78, 79*f*, 190–191, appendix. *See also* strategic, distributed action
peer assistance and review policy, 82–83
performance evaluation, 34, 82–83
Perkins, Bob, 130–134
personnel directors, 95
planning, comprehensive, 71–72
planning, strategic. *See also* strategic, distributed action
> Highland case, 153–155
> Leading for Learning Framework as tool for, 172, 173, 174–179
> Northern Valley case, 149–150, 176–177

planning, visual, 178–179
planning and goal setting
> Falls City case, 106
> Highland case, 153–156
> Manchester case, 135
> Northern Valley case, 149–150, 151
> Parkside case, 121

policy environments, 59, 60*f*, 61*f*
political costs of leadership vision, 39
Poole, Kathleen, 136*n*
poor practice, confronting, 54–55
portfolios, 84, 127
possibilities, imagining, 196–198
powerful learning, 16–17
Powerful Partners coalition, 191
preparation and certification, 157
presentations at staff meetings, 123–124
Principles of Learning, 163
prioritization and focused learning, 37–38
proactive approach to external environments, 66–67
professional communities. *See also* teams and collaborative work
> overview, 43–45
> coherence and, 99
> District M case, 167
> in districts, 49–51
> Douglass case, 137–138

professional communities (*continued*)
    essential tasks for building, 46–47
    Falls City case, 106, 108–112
    Highland case, 155, 157
    ideas and values underlying, 45–46
    isolation, breaking, 55
    Manchester case, 131, 132–133
    open and closed, 53–54
    Parkside case, 118, 120
    processes and challenges, 52–55
    in schools, 47–49
    summer institute and, 189
professional development
    coherence and, 92, 93, 94–95
    consortium of, 97–98
    district leadership and, 50–51
    District M case, 162–166
    in district office, 190
    Douglass case, 137, 138–139, 141
    external experts and, 94–95
    Falls City case, 109, 110, 112
    Highland case, 158, 160–161
    Leading for Learning Framework as
        tool for, xi, 179–181
    Manchester case, 132
    Mr. G. example, 6
    Northern Valley case, 151
    opportunities to expand and share, 33
    systemic learning and, 22–23
    teachers' unions and, 50
    time reserved for, 50
    university partnerships, 83
    writing instruction and, 81
professional environments, 58–59
professional learning agenda
    overview, 19–20, 20*f*
    District M case, 163, 167–168
    Douglass case, 138–139
    Highland case, 161
    Northern Valley case, 151–152
    Parkside case, 118, 121–123
    pathways to learning and, 76*f*, 78, 79*f*
    for principals, 94
professional practice standards, 151
project-based curriculum, 122, 125

readiness skills, 109
reading recovery teachers, 111
reading skills. *See* literacy learning
recruitment and hiring
    Falls City case, 110
    Highland case, 157
    Manchester case, 131
    Parkside case, 119–120
    value consistency in, 49
reflection
    individual reflection with small group
        support, 48
    Leading for Learning Framework as
        tool for, 172–173, 174–179, 188

reflection (*continued*)
    structured, joint reflection, 49
reforms
    external pressures and, 66
    pace of, 95–96
    standards-based, 65
relationships
    and confronting poor practice, 54–55
    external, 62, 66
    professional community building
        and, 46
research projects, small group, 48
resistances
    coherence and, 95
    combined theories of action and, 169
    to community building, 53
    external, 62, 69
resources
    drawing in vs. reaching out, 67–68
    external, 57, 62
    strategic planning and resource al-
        location, 155
respect as basic need, 52–53
responsibility as core value, 32
restructuring
    District M case, 165
    Douglass case, 137
    Parkside case, 116, 118, 120, 121, 124
reward and compensation, 133–134
Rosario, Alicia, 162, 164–166, 169
rubrics, 84, 176

safety needs, 52–53
scheduling and staffing assignment, 50, 120
school boards, 64, 68, 95
school districts. *See* district-level applica-
    tions
School for Integrated Studies (Manchester),
    129–131
school-level applications
    overview, 101–103
    acting strategically and sharing lead-
        ership, 80–81
    coherence, 91–93
    district office, developing allies in, 63
    Douglass case, 136–144
    environments, external, 60*f*, 62–64
    Falls City case, 105–115
    focus on learning, 33–35
    leadership, concept of, 15
    Manchester case, 128–135
    Parkside case, 116–127
    professional learning communities,
        47–49
    strategic planning, 156
school-within-a-school programs, 129–131
science instruction, 38, 83
Seaview School District case, 174–176,
    177–178

second language learners. *See* English Language Learners (ELL) and English as a Second Language (ESL)

shared leadership. *See* strategic, distributed action

Skyline School District case, 183n, 184–185

small groups and inquiry cycles, 48

small school choice policy, 168–169

small schools movement, 116

Sparks, Lillian, 107, 114–115

Spears, Lorna, 105*n*

special learning needs. *See also* literacy learning
    assumptions about, 48–49
    Falls City case, 109, 111
    Highland case, 158
    Support for Special Learning Needs Pathway, 76*f*, 77

staffing assignment and scheduling, 50, 120

staff meeting presentations, 123–124. *See also* meetings

standards-based reforms, 65

standards for student learning. *See also* accountability
    in California, 51
    as core value, 32
    District M case, 162, 164, 165, 167, 169–170
    Falls City case, 109, 112–113
    Highland case, 157
    instruction, standards-based, 6
    Parkside case, 126–127

Stanford Achievement Test, 36

strategic, distributed action. *See also* planning, strategic
    overview, 71–72
    coherence and, 99
    defined, 72–73
    District M case, 162, 164, 165
    in districts, 81–83
    Douglass case, 138–139
    essential tasks, 78–80
    Falls City case, 110, 112, 114
    Highland case, 156
    ideas underlying, 72–78, 76*f*, 79*f*
    Manchester case, 129–130
    mobilizing effort along strategic pathways, 86
    Parkside case, 121–123
    processes and challenges, 84–85
    in schools, 80–81

student learning agenda
    overview, 18
    conversations about, 34
    District M case, 163
    Falls City case, 106, 113
    Highland case, 153, 157, 161
    interactional view of, 11–13, 14*f*
    Northern Valley case, 149–151
    Parkside case, 121, 123, 126

student learning agenda (*continued*)
    pathways to learning and, 76*f*, 78, 79*f*

summer institutes and workshops, 180–181, 183–191

supervision and evaluation, 131, 159

support, belief in, 32

system learning agenda
    overview, 21, 22*f*
    Falls City case, 113
    Highland case, 153, 157, 158
    Manchester case, 135
    Northern Valley case, 149, 151
    pathways to learning and, 76*f*, 78, 79*f*
    professional development and, 22–23

tasks, learner engagement with, 13

teachers' unions, 50, 69, 82–83

teaching and instruction. *See also* observation in the classroom
    drill-and-practice vs. standards-based approach, 6
    focus on learning and, 41
    improvement opportunities, 22
    Leading for Learning Framework as tool for, 172, 173

teams and collaborative work
    Douglass case, 139–140
    Parkside case, 119, 121–123, 124–125

testing. *See* assessment and measurement

theories of action
    coherence and, 92–93
    District M case, 168–169
    Douglass case, 138
    Northern Valley case, 147–148

theories of change, 188

theories of education, 188

Title I Distinguished School designation, 108

Title I programs
    Douglass case, 136, 140–141, 144
    Falls City case, 109, 110

transformational leadership, 16

trust, 46

unions, teachers', 50, 69, 82–83

university-based degree programs, 180, 181, 182–186

University of Pittsburgh Institute for Learning, 51, 163, 165

University of Washington, 181, 182–186

university partnerships, 83

values and beliefs
    assumptions about student learning, 48–49
    external environments and, 58–59
    and focus on learning, 31–32
    Leading for Learning Framework as tool for articulating, 179
    professional learning communities and, 45–46

values and beliefs (*continued*)
    recruitment consistent with, 49
visibility of leaders, 187
vision, 39, 89, 134
visual planning, 178–179

walk-throughs, 33, 94, 166. *See also* observation in the classroom
Washington, LaToya, 136–144

Washington Assessment of Student Learning (WASL), 113, 148
whole school assessments, 48
work cultures. *See* professional communities
workshop model, 124
writing instruction, 81

About the Authors

Michael A. Copland is currently assistant professor of Educational Leadership and Policy Studies in the College of Education at the University of Washington (UW). His previous roles include classroom teacher, assistant principal, and principal, all in middle schools in Washington state. Dr. Copland has extensive experience with the preparation and professional development of prospective and practicing school and district leaders. Currently, he is teaching and developing curriculum roles for the Danforth Educational Leadership program at UW, the Center for Educational Leadership at UW, and the UW Leadership for Learning Ed. D. program. Prior to his current duties, Dr. Copland was the director of the Prospective Principals Program at Stanford University. His research interests include issues related to the preparation and professional development of school and district leaders, learning-focused leadership in school and district reform, transformation of comprehensive high schools, and distributed leadership in the context of whole school reform. Dr. Copland's recent publications include pieces in *Phi Delta Kappan, Journal of School Leadership, Educational Evaluation and Policy Analysis,* and *Educational Administration Quarterly.*

Michael S. Knapp is currently a professor of Educational Leadership and Policy Studies and director of the Center for the Study of Teaching and Policy, in the College of Education at the University of Washington (UW). His work as a practitioner includes classroom teaching, work in a junior high school guidance department, curriculum development with the Education Development Center, teacher and administrator training both domestically and abroad, and administrative work in the central office of a multicampus community college district. In recent years, he has been heavily involved in the preparation of educational leaders who aspire to roles in districts, regional entities, and state agencies. As a scholar, Dr. Knapp's research focuses on educational leadership, the implementation of state and federal educational improvement policies, school reform, leadership preparation, and policy research methods, with particular emphasis on how policy and leadership connect to classroom and school improvement. His studies have often concentrated on the education of disenfranchised populations, mathematics and science education, and the professional development of educators. Dr. Knapp has written extensively about his research in five books, which are *Teaching for Meaning in High-Poverty Classrooms* (Teachers College Press, 1995), *Pathways to Partnership: University and Community as Learners in Interprofessional Education* (Rowman & Littlefield, 1998), *School Districts and Instructional Renewal* (Teachers College Press, 2002), *Investigating the Influence of Standards* (National Academy Press, 2002), and *Self-Reflective Renewal in Schools* (Greenwood Press, 2003).

Related ASCD Resources: School and District Leadership

At the time of publication, the following resources were available; for the most up-to-date information about ASCD resources, go to www.ascd.org. ASCD stock numbers are noted in parentheses.

Audio

Accountability for Learning: How Teachers and School Leaders Can Take Charge by Douglas B. Reeves (Audiotape #205061; CD #505085)

Balanced Leadership: What Research Shows About Leadership and Student Achievement by Tim Waters, Robert J. Marzano, and Brian McNulty (Audiotapes #204169; CDs #504303)

Can Powerful Leadership Questions Ignite Passion and Promise Results? by Mary Michailides and Larry Payne (CDs #505358)

Promises Kept: Sustaining Innovative School Leadership in a Turbulent Era by Steven Jay Gross (Audiotape #204151; CD #504285)

Networks

Visit the ASCD Web site (www.ascd.org) and click on "About ASCD." Go to the section on Networks for information about professional educators who have formed groups around topics such as "Performance Assessment for Leadership." Look in the Network Directory for current facilitators' addresses and phone numbers.

Online Courses

Visit the ASCD Web site (www.ascd.org) for the following professional development opportunities:
Contemporary School Leadership by Vera Blake (#PD04OC38)

What Works in Schools: An Introduction by John Brown (#PD04OC36)

Print Products

Accountability for Learning: How Teachers and School Leaders Can Take Charge by Douglas B. Reeves (#104004)

The Art of School Leadership by Thomas R. Hoerr (#105037)

Educational Leadership, April 2004: Leading in Tough Times (Entire Issue #104029)

Educational Leadership, May 2004: Schools as Learning Communities (Entire Issue #104030)

Leadership for Learning: How to Help Teachers Succeed by Carl D. Glickman (#101031)

Learning-Driven Schools: A Practical Guide for Teachers and Principals by Barry Beers (#106002)

The Learning Leader: How to Focus School Improvement for Better Results by Douglas B. Reeves (#105151)

School Leadership That Works: From Research to Results by Robert J. Marzano, Timothy Waters, and Brian A. McNulty (#105125)

What Works in Schools: Translating Research into Action by Robert J. Marzano (#102271)

Video and DVD

The How To Collection: School Leadership (Bundle of six 15-minute video programs on one 109-minute DVD #606140)

What Works in Schools (Three programs on DVD with a 140-page Facilitator's Guide #603047)

For more information, visit us on the World Wide Web (http://www.ascd.org), send an e-mail message to member@ascd.org, call the ASCD Service Center (1-800-933-ASCD or 703-578-9600, then press 2), send a fax to 703-575-5400, or write to Information Services, ASCD, 1703 N. Beauregard St., Alexandria, VA 22311-1714 USA.